Issues in Cultural Tourism Studies

The extensively revised second edition of *Issues in Cultural Tourism Studies* provides a new framework for analysing the complexity of cultural tourism and its increasing globalisation in existing as well as emergent destinations of the world. The book focuses in particular on the need for even more creative tourism strategies to differentiate destinations from each other using a blend of localised cultural products and innovative global attractions.

The book explores many of the most pertinent issues in heritage, arts, festivals, indigenous, ethnic and experiential cultural tourism in urban and rural environments alike. This includes policy and politics; impact management and sustainable development; interpretation and representation; marketing and branding; and regeneration and planning. As well as exploring the interrelationships between the cultural and tourism sectors, local people and tourists, the book provides suggestions for more effective and mutually beneficial collaboration. New edition features include:

- An increased number of topical case studies and contemporary photographs which serve to contextualise the issues discussed.
- A reorientation towards global rather than just European issues.
- Three brand-new chapters on the Geography of Cultural Tourism, the Politics of Global Cultural Tourism, and the Growth of Creative Tourism.
- An extensively revised chapter on Experiential Cultural Tourism.

At the interface between the global and the local, a people-centred approach to planning and development is advocated to ensure that benefits are maximised for local areas, a sense of place and identity are retained, and the tourist experience is enhanced to the full. The text is unique in that it provides a summary and a synthesis of all the major issues in global cultural tourism, which are presented in an accessible way using a diverse range of international case studies. This is a beneficial and valuable resource for all Tourism students.

Melanie K. Smith is Lecturer and Researcher in Tourism Management in the Institute for Environmental Studies at Corvinus University, Budapest. In addition to writing the first edition of this book *Issues in Cultural Tourism Studies* (2003), she has edited two further books on cultural tourism and contributed chapters to several others.

Issues in Cultural Tourism Studies

Second edition

Melanie K. Smith

Routledge
Taylor & Francis Group

LONDON AND NEW YORK

First published 2009
by Routledge
2 Park Square, Milton Park, Abingdon, Oxon, OX14 4RN

Simultaneously published in the USA and Canada
by Routledge
270 Madison Avenue, New York, NY 10016

Routledge is an imprint of the Taylor & Francis Group, an informa business

Typeset in Times New Roman and Franklin Gothic by
Keystroke, Tettenhall, Wolverhampton
Printed and bound in Great Britain by
TJ International Ltd, Padstow, Cornwall

British Library Cataloguing in Publication Data
A catalogue record for this book is available from the British Library

Library of Congress Cataloging in Publication Data
Smith, Melanie K.
Issues in cultural tourism / Melanie K. Smith. — 2nd ed.
p. cm.
Includes bibliographical references and index.
1. Heritage tourism. I. Title.
G156.5.H47S56 2009
338.4′791—dc22
2009012472

ISBN 13: 978–0–415–46711–7 (hbk)
ISBN 13: 978–0–415–46712–4 (pbk)
ISBN 13: 978–0–203–86985–7 (ebk)

ISBN 10: 0–415–46711–X (hbk)
ISBN 10: 0–415–46712–8 (pbk)
ISBN 10: 0–203–86985–0 (ebk)

I would like to dedicate this second edition to my family,
with special thanks to my dad and sister for the lovely photos.

 # Contents

Plates

 **Tables**

Boxes

Preface

The writing of this second edition has been an interesting experience, as the first edition was written nearer to the start of my academic career at a time when cultural tourism was also quite a new focus for academic research. Since that time, my ideas have moved on and cultural tourism has also become something of a growth sector, with many more academic books, articles and conferences dedicated to the subject. This has made my job both harder and easier! I am forced to question my original assumptions about cultural tourism, to update the content, but also to recognise that what were once innovative concepts are now well established. This means that I decided to exclude some old chapters and material (e.g. some of the work on World Heritage Sites, which are now the subject of whole books), and to replace them with newer ideas. For example, the inclusion of a whole chapter on Creative Tourism, and a partially new chapter on Experiential Cultural Tourism. Few could argue that the words 'creative' and 'experience' have become two of the biggest buzzwords of the 2000s.

Some of the first edition was arguably too Eurocentric, and therefore I have attempted to globalise the material, and to represent as many regions and countries of the world as I can. This led to the inclusion of two new chapters on the geography and politics of cultural tourism, which contextualise clearly many of the issues raised in the rest of the book. It is recognised that an entirely comprehensive publication is not possible, but this edition, I feel, comes closer than the first did with the inclusion of a broader range of case studies from all over the world. All the case studies have been changed. This allowed me to redress imbalances in the book and to provide coverage of some less well-known destinations, attractions and events.

Although the book still retains a rigorous theoretical framework, some of the theoretical ideas are less densely written and therefore more accessible. The theory has also been updated in the light of many of the new publications in the field of cultural tourism.

When I finished the first edition of this book, I was single and childless, whereas I am now married with a three-year-old son. I am also living in Budapest, Hungary, in contrast to London in the UK. This has changed my perspectives on travel and culture somewhat. Being a mother, I find I am often a frustrated cultural tourist rather than an actual one! Although my son enjoys running around art galleries, he is too young to tolerate a whole exhibition. Heritage sites appear to be a large playground to him, but he has little respect for conservation. This means I have to appreciate culture and the arts in bite-sized chunks, rather than having the leisure to spend whole days in museums or touring archaeological sites. Going out in the evenings to arts venues is a rare treat. On the other hand, a child provides an amazing way of bonding with different people of all cultures from around the world. Local people in a destination are much more likely to talk to a stranger with a child and to share the universal experience of being a parent. I also now understand and relate to a much wider range of tourists. Hopefully, my son will have the same enthusiasm for culture, heritage, museums and the arts as I do, thanks to parents like mine who believed that a lifelong appreciation should start young. In the meantime, I shall be policing his behaviour at heritage sites, encouraging him to respect silence in art galleries, and not to remove bits of collections from museums – in fact, much like any other cultural tourism manager!

Melanie Smith, Corvinus University, Budapest, March 2009

**Heritage appreciation
from an early age?**

(Source: László Puczkó)

Acknowledgements

I would like to thank Routledge and especially Andrew Mould for the commissioning of this second edition, and Michael P. Jones for his support and encouragement during the process.

Thanks to my husband, László, for his continuous support with my work and his helpful suggestions on what to include in this book.

Thank you to my dad, Melvyn Smith, and my sister, Georgina Smith, for supplying most of the photographs for this new edition, as well as to my mum, Kay Smith, and my brother, Ed Smith, for their shared love of travelling and all things cultural.

 # Introduction

Culture, like God and politics is everywhere.

(Adair 1982: 12)

Culture is still everywhere, and several years after the first edition of this book, there is still no consensus about what it really means! The first stage in any discussion of cultural tourism is therefore the troublesome task of defining culture, which is notoriously problematic as it has both global and local significance, and it can be deeply historic or highly contemporary. It can be represented as physical and material, tangible or intangible; as political and symbolic, or as the practices of everyday life. It is also articulated differently by the numerous stakeholders involved directly or indirectly in the processes of cultural tourism development.

Raymond Williams's (1958) notion of culture being about a whole way of life, as well as the arts and learning, is especially useful here. Williams viewed culture as being about the whole way of life of a distinct people or social group with distinctive signifying systems involving all forms of social activity, and artistic or intellectual activities. His are useful and comprehensive definitions, as they cover both the development of individual and group culture, conveying the importance of heritage and tradition, as well as contemporary culture and lifestyles. Culture is not just about the arts and the aesthetic judgements of a select minority who have been educated to appreciate certain cultural activities; it is also about the lives and interests of ordinary people. Anthropologists like Geertz (1973) also defined culture broadly recognising its holistic qualities, emphasising the totality of the human created world, incorporating material culture, cultivated landscapes, social institutions as well as knowledge and meaning. This means that culture is about the past and traditions (e.g. history and heritage), creative expression (e.g. works of art, performances) and also about people's ways of living, their customs and their habits. Many tourists are becoming just as interested in the culture of different peoples around the world as they are in historic sites, monuments, museums and galleries.

Although there is some consensus about what culture means in most tourism circles, the degree to which the term should be broadened to include all aspects of everyday life is debatable. Eagleton (2000: 32) states that '[i]t is hard to resist the conclusion that the word "culture" is both too broad and too narrow to be greatly useful.' It is indeed difficult to establish parameters around definitions of culture in the postmodern, global world where culture could quite reasonably be defined as almost any activity that relates to the lives and lifestyles of human beings. Eagleton questions the all-encompassing definitions of culture which relate to lifestyles and cultural preferences; for example, such concepts as 'football culture', 'café culture' or 'museums culture'. However, it is also limiting to confine discussions to narrow definitions of the arts and heritage, which are arguably elitist and represent and serve only a minority. As stated by Butcher (2001: 16):

> Culture, for those living in poorer countries, often corresponds more closely to the original meaning of the word – tending crops and animals – a way of life dictated by living on the margins of the global economy rather than a cultural lifestyle of choice.

Indeed, few indigenous and tribal peoples of the world sit around discussing the meaning of culture. Instead, they live and breathe it. It is handed down from generation to generation, and is deeply intrenched in their everyday practices.

The consideration of culture as everyday life and the way that this is articulated by local people is rarely given much consideration, and therefore cultural developments

Plate 0.1 Samburu people, Africa

(Source: Georgina Smith)

are often not well integrated into local areas and local residents can fail to engage with them fully, if at all. Of course, it is much harder to identify or define culture which is integrated into everyday life practices, as it is not explicitly articulated as it would be in a work of art or an exhibition, for example. There are much more subtle elements such as a sense of one's personal history and ancestry, a sense of community or identity, identification with certain practices, traditions or activities, even a feeling of being 'different' if one is from a minority culture or ethnic group. Questions therefore need to be asked of individuals or groups of residents in local areas for their own articulations of culture rather than using standardised definitions. (It might even be more appropriate not to use the word culture, but instead to refer to other indicators such as common activities, feelings of belonging, likes and dislikes, etc.) In reality, policy makers and practitioners may be largely unaware of intangible forms of culture such as the meanings attributed to landscapes or activities by local people. For this reason, it is important to consider multiple stakeholder articulations of culture when cultural tourism is being developed. Stakeholders often express themselves differently, even if they come from the same language group. Table 0.1 suggests the different ways in which culture might be perceived and expressed.

Table 0.1 Different perceptions of culture

Culture as . . .

Theoretical/political	*Social/aesthetic*	*Everyday life*
Culture is a tool	*Culture is an activity*	*Culture is a way of life*
Culture is educational	Culture is beautiful	Culture is about my family
Culture is experiential	Culture makes a place look nicer	Culture is who my friends are
Culture is therapeutic	Culture makes a place livelier	Culture is where I live
Culture is inspiring	Culture is relaxing	Culture is my nationality
Culture is transcendant	Culture is fun and exciting	Culture is my religion
Culture is conservation	Culture makes a change from	Culture is my language
Culture creates new	everyday life	Culture is my skin colour
opportunities for integration	Culture means the mixing of	Culture is what I eat and drink
Culture is an expression of diversity	different people	Culture is what I wear
Culture strengthens identities	Culture makes a place look special	Culture is what music I
Culture animates space	Culture makes a place look different	listen to
Culture creates a sense of	Culture means more tourists come	Culture is what I read
place and character	Culture means seeing and doing	Culture is where I shop
Culture creates uniqueness	new things	Culture is what I do on a
Culture enhances image	Culture makes people's lives better	daily basis
Culture is a catalyst for		Culture is where I go on a
regeneration		Saturday night
		Culture is where I take the
		family on day trips

The Theoretical/Political column is the vocabulary most likely to be used by academics or those making policies. The Social/Aesthetic column is the vocabulary most likely to be used by those working within the arts and culture and with local communities. The Everyday Life column is the vocabulary of everyday people and represents a more personal viewpoint. Cultural practitioners and community workers seem to be more attuned to the language of everyday life and people, and tend to focus on the lived experience of culture. Everyday people are more concerned with their individual and collective sense of culture and the daily practices that express it. However, those working outside the spheres of formal culture (e.g. the arts, heritage) or with local communities are unlikely to have a clear grasp of these different articulations. Many politicians and tourism practitioners fall under this category.

A summary does not do justice to the diversity of viewpoints, as there are variations even within one sector, not to mention conflicts between sectors. For example, culture is often viewed differently by those working within heritage, the arts, museums or tourism. This can lead to considerable frustration on all sides. Heritage managers may see culture as a valuable resource to be protected and conserved; arts managers may see culture as an inspiring phenomenon which enriches the lives of those who perform and observe it; museum curators may see culture as a collection of objects which is the subject of dedicated expert research, rather than a source of public interest; tourism managers, on the other hand, may see culture as a resource which should be made accessible to as many people as possible, and one which should be made entertaining and fun. This makes conflict inevitable, but communication and compromise are also imperative.

There are still conflicts within and between the cultural sectors and tourism, but many of these have become resolved in some way or greater collaboration has been encouraged or enforced by policy and funding decisions. This means that although the language and priorities of heritage, museums, arts and tourism can be very different, there has been an acknowledgement of the mutual benefits of joint working. The shift towards more experiential cultural tourism has come from an acceptance (albeit a reluctant one in some cases) of the need for 'edutainment' in the majority of cultural venues. There is too much competition from new media and technology for cultural attractions to be complacent in their offer; therefore more creative and experience-orientated products are essential. This is sometimes at odds with the perceived core function of the traditional cultural sectors, but it is an inherent part of cultural tourism development.

The politics of culture

This book focuses partly on the politics of cultural tourism, whose arguments are mainly derived from the fields of cultural studies and cultural politics, as well as tourism, heritage and museum studies. The work of the cultural theorist Raymond

Williams provides many of the definitions and perspectives on culture that are used within this book. His inclusive and democratic views of culture and cultural development are particularly fitting for a text that focuses predominantly on culture as a democratic and plural concept. Williams's work emphasises in particular the social and political ramifications of the class system, championing the culture of the masses. His work aimed to democratise cultural policy, challenging the perceived elitism of Arts Councils, and the past tendency to focus on so-called 'high' or 'elite' culture in cultural policy making. The concept of policy in cultural studies is not limited to the arts and public administration, but is also linked strongly to everyday politics, power struggles and empowerment. The concept of culture has become increasingly politicised, especially where it is defined as a way of life of a people or society. Sarup (1996: 140) states:

> Culture is not something fixed and frozen as the traditionalists would have us believe, but a process of constant struggle as cultures interact with each other and are affected by economic, political and social factors.

As a result of postmodern theory and more democratic policy making in many Western countries, distinctions between high and low culture are being broken down, and emphasis is being placed increasingly on popular or mass culture. This is equally true of the heritage and museum sectors where representation is becoming a key issue, and the histories of previously marginalised groups are being recognised. The rejection of so-called 'grand narratives' has meant that the discourses of the working classes, women and minority or ethnic groups are now being heard. Historicity is becoming a more valid concept than aesthetics rendering the social history and industrial heritage of the working classes as important as political history or the bourgeois heritage of royalty, for example. 'Inclusion', 'access' and 'democracy' are the new buzzwords, and the underlying concepts are important in defining the shape of the future, not just in terms of cultural development, but in terms of all the concomitant political and social struggles which surround it.

In the eighteenth and nineteenth centuries, the idea of culture was defined in opposition to nature as a range of social, political, ethical, religious, philosophical and technical values. A number of thinkers and philosophers such as Hegel deemed cultural forms that were close to nature as being inferior to those that were linked more closely to the human spirit. Hence, high culture was assumed superior to popular culture, and Western, predominantly Christian culture was considered superior to, for example, those of tribal peoples who lived closer to nature and often practised naturalistic rites. It was also believed by a number of key thinkers that the nation state was the true carrier of the culture or national spirit of a people (Castro-Gomez 2001).

Nineteenth-century cultural theorists who were part of the 'Culture and Civilisation' tradition, such as Matthew Arnold, emphasised the social and educational significance of Culture (with a capital 'C'), stating that '[c]ulture seeks to do away with classes; to make the best that has been thought and known in the world current everywhere' (1875: 44). Arnold argued that culture brings enlightenment or 'cultivation', which transcends social divisions, such as class, gender, race, religion and ethnicity. It is interesting, however, to note that Arnold refers to 'Culture' rather than 'cultures', implying an aesthetically narrow, rather than a plural or diverse concept of culture. His theories are now also deemed essentially Eurocentric and elitist, especially given his condemnation of popular culture for lacking aesthetic value (Jordan and Weedon 1995).

However, cultural debates have clearly moved on in recent years thanks partly to the development of postmodern theory which liberated culture from the 'grand narratives' of the past. Some postmodern theory favours a more participatory and democratic approach to cultural development including the breaking down of barriers between culture and society, art and life, high and low culture. It has been recognised that there is a need for democratic and pluralist participation in the institutions and practices of culture. Recent cultural theorists tend to adopt a plural concept of culture, and recognise the diversity and hybridity of different cultures. For example, Hannerz (1990: 237) claims that everyone participates in many 'cultures'. The word culture is created through the increasing interconnectedness of varied local cultures, as well as through the development of cultures without a clear anchorage in any one territory. These are all becoming subcultures, as it were, within the wider whole. However, in their work on world culture, Lechner and Boli (2005) suggest that 'objective' culture far outstrips 'subjective' culture, meaning that we can still talk of a 'world culture' which is dominant and pervasive. This is partly based on the imperialism of the past, coupled with the Americanisation of the present.

A theoretical framework for cultural tourism studies

The aim of this book is to provide an overview and an analysis of the key issues pertaining to cultural development within the context of tourism studies. Cultural tourism studies is a composite discipline, hence one that necessitates an in-depth analysis of many relevant and contemporary social, political and ethical issues. This book cannot be entirely comprehensive in its scope, nor can it cover all of the complex theoretical arguments that underpin cultural development. What it does do, however, is to provide something of a stimulus for debate, and to act as a springboard for further discussion and research. The text provides a synthesis of many key ideas drawn from a diverse range of fields, and serves to encourage a more interdisciplinary approach to the study of cultural tourism. The theoretical discussions have been applied to a range of contexts in different regions of the world.

A multidisciplinary approach to cultural tourism helps to makes sense of the complexity of the phenomenon. The use of history, geography, sociology, economics, anthropology, urban studies etc. is becoming more and more common in the study of tourism. The study of cultural tourism requires the addition of cultural studies, cultural politics, community studies, heritage studies and museology, among others. This book therefore draws on theories from a wide range of disciplines. Readers who find themselves wishing to explore any of the specific theoretical issues in more depth should avail themselves of some of the secondary data sources, which may provide a richer source of information. The theory in this book hence serves to provide a conceptual framework for the discussion of pertinent issues rather than being an end in itself. As stated by Milner (1994: 4), 'Culture has become a theoretical problem for us only because it is already socially problematic.'

Within the (post)modern world system, cultural tourism occupies a complex and shifting position. Wallerstein (1997) describes how the modern world system has entered a terminal crisis of disillusionment, uncertainty and turmoil, but one in which creativity can flourish. Part of this book therefore emphasises the growing interest in creative industries and creative tourism. Other recurrent themes within the text include globalisation, which is an inevitable subject within any book about tourism as it has become the quintessential global industry. Increasing mobility has led to a growth in travel, but also in immigration, and permanent or temporary migrant labour. These flows of people radically change the composition of societies and cultures, and can lead to the development of fusion or hybridised cultural forms. Issues also arise around the identity construction of immigrant or diasporic groups. The historical processes of imperialism and colonisation have shaped the nature of heritage, which becomes complex and multi-layered. Many indigenous peoples have been oppressed and marginalised, and even in countries which have been decolonised, the imperial legacy is still pervasive many decades later. Political, racial and social inequality is still a major issue for most countries of the world, despite some progress in Western developed countries. This means that the under-representation of minority cultures continues to be contentious.

Castro-Gomez (2001) distinguishes between traditional theory, which naturalises culture and focuses on concepts such as aesthetics and harmony, and critical theory which emphasises the socio-political or conflictive aspect of culture where culture is a site of contested meaning. It places culture in the context of political economy. This includes the historical backdrop of imperialism, Eurocentrism and now Americanisation, which have shaped the historiographies and political economies of many regions of the world. Following on from this is the theme of post-colonialism, which serves as a framework for the analysis of multiculturalism and identity construction. The socio-economic and geopolitical implications of the globalisation process are also discussed in some depth, especially insofar as they relate to commercialisation of culture and the impacts of tourism. Inherent in all of these themes are the broad, complex and often insidious axes of power, which serve to control all forms of social, economic and cultural development.

Within the field of cultural studies, identity construction and representation have become recurrent themes, with racial and ethnic issues gaining significance from the mid-1980s onwards. Central to these ongoing debates are postmodern theories of politics, power and ideology, which question hegemonic, Eurocentric and ethnocentric approaches to the representation of the culture of 'others'. Along with Stuart Hall, a number of other theorists such as Gilroy, Mercer, West and Said have focused on issues of ethnicity, challenging the perceived preoccupation with national identity. Hall writes of 'a politics of representation', and claims that there is a need for a stronger assertion of self-identity in order to eliminate stereotypes and combat misrepresentation. Mercer writes of African, Asian and Caribbean diasporas, and the emergence of hybridised identities. Hall also focuses on diasporic and plural identities, arguing that there has been a shift from nationalism to ethnicity in the formation of identity. Other post-colonial theorists such as Bhabha, Spivak and Sarup address similar issues. Bhabha's work on the concept of hybridisation (whereby two cultures retain their own distinctive characteristics, but form something new through a kind of fusion) is of particular interest. Spivak brings a feminist perspective to the post-colonial debate about identity construction and representation. She focuses on the concept of 'marginality' in her analysis of the 'epistemic violence' which governs history, imperialism and colonial discourse. As well as his critique of post-colonial studies, Sarup's work on the relationship between race, ethnicity and 'nation-ness' is also fascinating.

The work of Edward Said has been particularly influential in tourism and cultural studies, as it examines the relationship between the Occident and the Orient and the hegemonic nature of European culture and power. The high cultural humanism of European rule was informed by scholarship and rational enquiry, hence providing adequate justification for the subordination of Orientals, and the oppressive binarism of 'us' and 'them' or 'self' and 'Other'. Bhabha has argued that this binary opposition between power and powerlessness is oversimplified, leaving little room for negotiation or resistance. It is perhaps worth reading his critique of Said's *Orientalism*, where he suggests that there is a certain ambivalence in the power relationship between coloniser and colonised, and that their identities sometimes become elided.

However, there is little doubt that indigenous people were subordinated under colonial rule. By 1914 Europe controlled about 85 per cent of the Earth, functioning as a metropolitan centre ruling distant territories. Europeans appeared to believe that they had an obligation and a right to subjugate indigenous peoples, who were often depicted as barbaric, savage or primitive. Policies of assimilation or annihilation often had a devastating impact on native traditions, lifestyles and cultural practices. Sarup notes the impact that this had on indigenous identity:

> Imperialism . . . is an act of geographical violence through which virtually every space in the world is explored, charted and finally brought under control. For the natives, the history of their colonial servitude is inaugurated by this loss to an outsider of the local place, whose concrete geographical identity must thereafter be searched for and somehow restored.
>
> (Sarup 1996: 150)

Eurocentrism has been a major informing principle in our construction of world historiographies, and is based on the notion of European superiority in terms of technology, social thought and cultural forms. According to Dirlik (1999), Eurocentric thought embodies:

> the notion of a single, originary center, namely Europe, out of which everything superior emerges; the geopolitical division between the homogeneous West and a substantive, exotic East or, rather, Europe the center, and the rest of the world, the periphery.
>
> (Dirlik 1999: 13)

Dirlik suggests that any radical critique of Eurocentrism must take into consideration the contemporary questions of globalism and post-colonialism, both of which are recurrent themes within this book. Eurocentrism is, of course, only one centrism that has historically encompassed the globe, relocating whole societies and communities in space and time, and transforming their historical, social and cultural trajectories. Mowitt (2001) suggests that multiculturalism is effectively taking the place of Eurocentrism as being the focal core of humanities research.

However, some might argue that the new panoptic centre of world experience is America, especially if global capitalism is viewed as a phenomenon that has emanated largely from the USA. The history of America does not, of course, begin with the arrival of white settlers; however, it is often defined in terms of a narrative of white discovery and settlement. The discourse of indigenous groups and Black and Hispanic immigrants needs to be given equal weighting in any construction or affirmation of American identity. Nevertheless, the assertion of white supremacy, the assimilation, annihilation or denigration of indigenous and immigrant cultures appears to have been a common Euro-American trait.

In their post-September 11th analysis, Sardar and Wynn Davies (2002) suggest that the omnipresence of America is inescapable. The rest of the world is exposed to its politics, foreign policy, media and cultural products, while Americans are often less exposed to foreign influence than any other nation on Earth. The authors use the metaphor of the ubiquitous hamburger (frequently a symbol of much hated global consumerism) to describe the packaging and presentation of America to the world, implying that even if you take out the bits you don't like, the influence is still pervasive. America is described as a hyper-power, which has the potential to lay waste to indigenous cultures, echoing Ritzer's (1993) view that American culture has acquired 'obscene power' in the process of replicating itself in the rest of the world. However, they suggest that this process is not simply a form of cultural imperialism akin to that imposed by European empires. American products have become so desirable that the so-called 'victims' are complicit in the spread of American culture:

> There are no competing powers because there is only one power, only one source of law and order. In such a natural order, it makes little sense to talk of Empire and American imperialism; indeed, such rhetoric and analysis are dangerously obsolete.

> Empires require colonies in which unwilling folks are forced into becoming subject people; imperialism entails a dominating metropolis trying to capture the markets and impose its rule on a distant country. Today, the globe is much more like an extension of American society, where – mostly – all too willing individuals and communities embrace American cultures and values.
>
> (Sardar and Wynn Davies 2002: 65)

American culture is also highly attractive for many citizens of the world, and the USA always features as one of the Top Five tourism destinations in the world. In terms of the experience economy as discussed in Chapter 9, America is leading the way and showing the rest of the world how to develop unique and engaging attractions.

It is also misrepresentative to imply that America is an homogeneous nation; hence Sardar and Wynn Davies (2002) attempt to distinguish between America the political and economic entity, and the culturally diverse America of indigenous peoples and ethnic immigrants. However, despite living in a so-called democracy, the citizens themselves have relatively little political influence on their government's global decisions (but this is not, of course, unique to America). Nevertheless, the election of President Obama in 2008 may have a significant impact on the way in which American citizens feel about their country, and the way in which it is perceived elsewhere.

Many theorists have described tourism itself as a new form of imperialism, arguing that it has a similar impact on identity construction. As stated by Lanfant (1995: 4):

> Tourism, particularly 'cultural tourism', is often considered by international organisations as a pedagogic instrument allowing new identities to emerge – identities corresponding to the new plural-ethnic or plural-state configurations which are forming.

She questions the extent to which the forming of identities is motivated by ideology. Tourism has frequently been described as an imperialist or hegemonic power, and identity has become a product to be manufactured, packaged and marketed like another. However, Lanfant (1995: 5) suggests that it may be overly simplistic to describe tourism simply as a new form of imperialism, stating:

> The tourist system of action is not a monolithic force. It would be pointless to seize upon it as if it were a hegemonic and imperialist power perpetuating disguised neo-colonialism. This system is a network of agents: these tap a variety of motivations which are difficult to define and which in concrete situations often contradict each other.

Sarup (1996: 127) conceptualises tourism (at least travel to less developed countries) in terms of 'self' and 'other' and the notion of identity:

> Tourism is . . . a metaphor for the imposition of the Western gaze. There is enjoyment by the rich of the exotic difference of the Other and exploitation too. Travelling has also become an increasingly popular way of 'discovering one's identity'.

The philosophical basis of this argument may be derived from Existentialist theories of 'self' and 'other' whereby our sense of ourselves is partly defined by the 'other'. Edward Said clearly took this concept further within the context of colonial and post-colonial studies. Stuart Hall also explores such concepts in his work on the cultural politics of ethnicity. The concept of alterity (or 'othering') has indeed become central to the discipline of cultural politics and cultural studies, and subsequently cultural tourism studies (e.g. see the work of Hollinshead, MacCannell, Nash, Selwyn, to name but a few). Both dominant and marginal groups within a host society are subjected to the 'gaze' of the tourist (Urry 1990), often reducing them to inauthentic stereotypes. Their culture is somehow fossilised and romanticised under the tourist gaze. As stated by Kirschenblatt-Gimblett (1998: 54), the destination and its people can then become something of a museum or theme park:

> tourism more generally takes the spectator to the site, and as areas are canonized in a geography of attractions, whole territories become extended ethnographic theme parks. An ethnographic bell jar drops over the terrain. A neighbourhood, village, or region becomes for all intents and purposes a living museum in situ.

Without a strong sense of their own identity, host societies are likely to succumb to the temptations of commercialisation, and lose sight of their traditions. Although economic development and 'progress' should not be denied to such communities, care must be taken to ensure that the people themselves are in a position to make an informed decision about their destiny. The nature and scope of tourism development will, of course, be determined partly by the local natural and cultural resources available. Butcher (2001: 15) suggests that:

> how the host is viewed through the prism of culture, inevitably affects the prospects for and type of development on offer. Culture defined as function and difference effectively creates culture as a straightjacket for societies that may desire economic development. Culture becomes objectified; a romantic image cast in stone, rather than the creative subjectivity of the host. It can become a part of heritage, the past, preserved for the sensibilities of the tourist, rather than being made and remade in the context of social change.

Culture is of course dynamic rather than static; hence this fossilisation of culture is arguably a misrepresentation of ongoing indigenous traditions (as discussed in more detail in Chapter 5). However, the Western obsession with heritage has often reduced indigenous culture to the status of a dead or lifeless phenomenon. Heritage is, of course, a problematic and contentious concept, particularly in terms of interpretation and representation, and will be discussed in more detail in Chapter 4.

To a certain extent, it could be argued that the debates which are central to cultural politics, and the significance of race and ethnicity have been largely under-researched in the field of cultural tourism studies. Much of the research has tended to focus on post-colonial, developing countries, where tourism is sometimes viewed as a new form of imperialism, and the relationship between hosts and guests requires sensitive management. In countries where indigenous community culture and heritage form an integral part of the tourism product (e.g. Australia and New Zealand), much of the cultural tourism research has been focused on these communities, as discussed in more detail in Chapter 5. In post-imperial countries, it could be argued that the emphasis in cultural tourism research has often been placed on the significance of national and regional rather than ethnic minority cultures.

Overall, the book therefore focuses on some of the more unusual, dissonant or marginalised forms of cultural tourism. There are numerous books now documenting tourism and heritage management, the impacts of tourism on culture, etc. The politics of cultural tourism has also become more important in academic literature and research, but it still requires greater emphasis. New forms of cultural tourism, such as creative and experiential tourism, are also emerging (or, at least, are being repackaged). Practitioners need to be more and more alert to these quite rapidly changing trends,whether they be the implementation of more democratic cultural policies or the development of more creative, experiential attractions. All tourism is controversial and no one strategy can be applied to all contexts. Cultural tourism is especially complex, as every destination has its own specific culture(s) and traditions, and it is difficult for outsiders (whether they be academics, practitioners or tourists) to fully understand them. One of the joys of cultural tourism is the discovery of the world's rich diversity, but this is also its major challenge.

Structure of the book

Chapter 1 analyses the development of cultural tourism in recent years, including changing and broadening definitions. Cultural tourism is broken down into sub-sectors in order to analyse the key issues in heritage, arts, creative, urban, rural, indigenous and experiential cultural tourism. These are illustrated using a range of topical case studies. A typology is given of cultural tourists, including a discussion of their characteristics and motivations.

Chapter 2 focuses on the geography of cultural tourism, providing an overview of the main cultural resources and attractions in different regions and countries of the world. Although this chapter is not comprehensive, an attempt has been made to represent as many destinations as possible, especially those which have made cultural tourism a priority in their tourism development strategies. It is becoming more common for countries to diversify into cultural tourism in order to expand their attractions portfolio or to give themselves a unique selling point.

Chapter 3 looks at the politics of cultural tourism, starting with a discussion of globalisation and tourism as a perceived new form of imperialism. This is followed by an analysis of those countries which formerly had empires (often the major generating countries for tourism), those countries which were colonised (e.g. developing countries), those which were occupied (e.g. former socialist countries) and new nation states which have emerged post-conflict. Emphasis is also given to those countries which have indigenous peoples, those which have a particularly dissonant or dark past, and those whose tourism industry has been adversely affected by religious conflict.

Chapter 4 explores the relationship between cultural tourism development and issues of interpretation and representation, particularly within the heritage and museum sectors. The chapter reviews the relationship between history and heritage, including some of the problems of depicting an accurate picture of the past. The changing role of museums is also considered in depth, including a discussion of the need for a more inclusive approach to interpretation and representation of collections and exhibitions. There is also a discussion of dissonant or dark heritage.

Chapter 5 discusses the development of tourism which includes visits to indigenous or tribal villages or settlements. As well as discussing the impacts of cultural tourism on indigenous peoples, the chapter focuses on the need for more community-based cultural tourism initiatives. An overview is provided of the measures that need to be taken in order to support, encourage and empower indigenous people so that they can eventually own and manage their own tourism-related ventures and initiatives. The cultural representation of indigenous peoples is also discussed, as it is still not uncommon for ethnic and tribal groups to be exploited as the 'exotic Other' in exhibitions, postcards or tourist literature.

Chapter 6 deals with the relationship between cultural tourism, the arts and festivals, discussing how there has been an historical shift from mutual mistrust and incomprehension to a greater degree of collaboration between the sectors. The chapter also deals with some of the sensitive political issues within the arts relating to access, democracy and inclusion, and the need for the arts to become more accessible to wider audiences, and to promote lesser-known arts activities. This includes many of the ethnic and minority artistic endeavours, which have traditionally been ignored or underfunded. Emphasis is placed in particular on festivals, events and carnivals, which tend to be more inclusive and participatory, as well as being largely community based.

Chapter 7 examines the growth of creative tourism and how it relates to and differs from cultural tourism. This includes an extensive discussion of the growth of the cultural and creatives industries (or CCIs). Richards and Raymond (2000) analyse the importance of 'creative tourism' whereby visitors are more actively engaged in fulfilling their creative potential. This may include activities, such as painting, dancing, pottery, music, etc. It may involve direct interaction with a host community or attendance of a cultural event, or alternatively it can take place in a location with no direct cultural connections. Many forms of creative tourism are also centred around products which are part of the creative industries (e.g. architecture, fashion, design, film and media).

Chapter 8 looks at the phenomenon of urban regeneration and the role that cultural tourism can play in this process. This includes the development of cultural quarters within cities, the use of cultural 'flagships' as catalysts for further social and economic development, and the enhancement of external image through cultural tourism. Examples are taken from a range of locations, although regeneration was traditionally confined to de-industrialised, European or American cities which needed an alternative source of economic development to replace declining industries.

Chapter 9 examines the growth of the so-called 'experience economy' and the implications for cultural tourism. Tourism is clearly becoming more interactive and experiential. Pine and Gilmore's (1999) work on the 'experience economy' suggests the need for new approaches to both product and attractions development and marketing. Tyrell and Mai (2001) also emphasise the need for more innovative approaches to development, which satisfy the needs of 'money rich/time poor' consumers, who are highly individualistic and are increasingly seeking experiences rather than products. The chapter discusses the relationships between different types of 'new' tourists (e.g. the post-tourist, the new leisure tourist) and the ways in which cultural tourism products can be tailored to their needs and expectations.

Chapter 10 deals partly with the impacts of cultural tourism development in a range of contexts, placing emphasis on developing countries and traditional societies where the impacts of tourism are likely to be most significant. Economically, tourism might appear to be the best development option for the future growth of a country or region, but the social, cultural and environmental consequences of such a decision must be considered carefully. The discussion therefore focuses on the management of cultural tourism, identifying good practice from a range of different environments, using different products (e.g. cities, festivals, museums, heritage sites, cultural landscapes), demonstrating that with adequate planning and management, the benefits of cultural tourism can be maximised.

1 A framework for global cultural tourism studies

Today, cultural tourism seems to be omnipresent, and in the eyes of many it also seems to have become omnipotent.

(Richards 2007: 1)

Introduction

The aim of this chapter is to provide a framework for the rest of the book in terms of definitions, contexts and perspectives. Although cultural tourism has become a significant growth sector in recent years and has been the subject of increasingly numerous publications, there is still a need for a comprehensive book which brings together the main theoretical and practical issues. Cultural tourism is a global phenomenon which manifests itself somewhat differently in the various regions of the world. The aim of this chapter is to show that there are historical, geographical, political and social reasons for the diverse nature of cultural tourism, starting from the idea that culture can mean different things to different peoples. In addition, historical processes have created different legacies, social processes create different value systems, and not all political systems support culture in the same way.

Global tourism is growing, and consequently cultural tourism seems to be growing in equal proportion. Many have argued that almost all tourism trips can be considered cultural (e.g. Smith and Robinson 2006; Richards 2007), especially if culture is defined as the whole way of life of people (e.g. Williams 1958). However, most growth estimates are a consequence of this expansion of the definitions of cultural tourism, which can include shopping, sport and all manner of contemporary activities and lifestyle trends.

Defining cultural tourism

More and more people are travelling despite concerns about climate change, rising fuel costs and global terrorism. Since the first edition's publication in 2003, cultural tourism has continued to be a major growth industry, and its importance has been consistently recognised by a number of global organisations such as UNESCO and the WTO. However, definitions of cultural tourism are broadening and changing all the time.

Richards (1996) proposed two definitions of cultural tourism for his research for ATLAS (the Association for Tourism and Leisure Education), and this research is still ongoing. These are:

- Technical definition: 'All movements of persons to specific cultural attractions, such as museums, heritage sites, artistic performances and festivals outside their normal place of residence'.
- Conceptual definition: 'The movement of persons to cultural manifestations away from their normal place of residence, with the intention to gather new information and experiences to satisfy their cultural needs'.

However, these definitions do not take into consideration culture as a way of life of people, but Richards's later definition is more comprehensive, suggesting that cultural tourism covers:

> not just the consumption of the cultural products of the past, but also of contemporary culture or the 'way of life' of a people or region. Cultural tourism can therefore be seen as covering both 'heritage tourism' (related to artefacts of the past) and 'arts tourism' (related to contemporary cultural production).
>
> (Richards 2001a: 7)

Richards also argues that cultural tourism does not simply represent passive consumption, that is simply looking at historic sites, museum collections, paintings or theatre performances. Many tourists are increasingly becoming interested in 'creative tourism', which involves participation in cultural activities (e.g. painting, photography, crafts, dancing, cookery). Creative tourism is discussed in more detail in Chapter 7.

McKercher and Cros (2002) suggest that cultural tourism can be defined in a number of ways:

- As a form of special interest tourism where culture forms the basis of either attracting tourists or motivating people to travel.
- From a business perspective as involving the development and marketing of various tourists sites and attractions.
- From a motivational perspective whereby visitors travel as a result of their interest in cultural activities.
- As an experiential activity where engagement with culture can be unique and intense, and tourists are educated as well as entertained.

- From an operational perspective where tourists participate in a large array of activities or experiences (e.g. heritage, arts, festivals, local cultures).

However, for the purposes of this book and subsequent discussions, the following definition will be used:

> Cultural tourism: passive, active and interactive engagement with culture(s) and communities, whereby the visitor gains new experiences of an educational, creative and/or entertaining nature.

This definition reflects the shift towards more active and interactive forms of cultural tourism, such as creative or experiential tourism (discussed in Chapters 7 and 9). It also suggests that education and entertainment are not mutually exclusive, and that tourists are involved with multiple cultures and communities, sometimes simultaneously.

Cultural tourism is often cited as being a growth industry, and a sector of tourism which is becoming more diverse. It is therefore necessary to consider some sub-sectors or sub-segments of the product and the market. Hughes (1996) differentiates between 'Universal', 'Wide', 'Narrow' and 'Sectorized' cultural tourism. These definitions correspond broadly to perceiving culture as a whole way of life; to engaging with specific ethnic or indigenous groups; to experiencing the 'artistic and intellectual' activities of a society; and to visiting specific heritage attractions or arts venues.

Table 1.1 lists a fairly comprehensive typology of cultural tourism, including the following:

- Heritage sites (e.g. archaeological sites, whole towns, monuments, museums).
- Performing arts venues (e.g. theatres, concert halls, cultural centres).
- Visual arts (e.g. galleries, sculpture parks, photography museums, architecture).
- Festivals and special events (e.g. music festivals, sporting events, carnivals).
- Religious sites (e.g. cathedrals, temples, pilgrimage destinations, spiritual retreats).
- Rural environments (e.g. villages, farms, national parks, ecomuseums).
- Indigenous communities and traditions (e.g. tribal people, ethnic groups, minority cultures).
- Arts and crafts (e.g. textiles, pottery, painting, sculpture).
- Language (e.g. learning or practice).
- Gastronomy (e.g. wine tasting, food sampling, cookery courses).
- Industry and commerce (e.g. factory visits, mines, breweries and distilleries, canal trips).
- Modern popular culture (e.g. pop music, shopping, fashion, media, design, technology).
- Creative activities (e.g. painting, photography, dance).

It is relatively easy to fall into the trap of using terms such as 'heritage tourism', 'arts tourism', 'ethnic tourism' or 'indigenous tourism' almost interchangeably. However, in many ways, the arts and heritage are inextricably linked, and it is almost impossible

Table 1.1 A typology of cultural tourism attractions

Heritage tourism	Visits to castles, palaces, country houses
	Archaeological sites
	Monuments
	Architecture
	Museums
	Religious sites
Arts tourism	Visits to the theatre
	Concerts
	Galleries
	Festivals, carnivals, events
	Literary sites
Creative tourism	Photography
	Painting
	Pottery
	Dance
	Cookery
	Crafts
	Creative industries (e.g. film, TV, architecture, fashion, design)
Urban cultural tourism	Historic cities
	Regenerated industrial cities
	Waterfront developments
	Arts and heritage attractions
	Shopping
	Nightlife
Rural cultural tourism	Village tourism
	Agro or farm tourism
	Ecomuseums
	Cultural landscapes
	National parks
	Wine trails
Indigenous cultural tourism	Hilltribe, desert, jungle, rainforest or mountain trekking
	Tribal villages
	Visits to cultural centres
	Arts and crafts
	Cultural performances
	Festivals
Experiential cultural tourism	Theme parks
	Themed restaurants
	Shopping malls
	Pop concerts
	Sporting events
	Film and TV locations
	Celebrity-endorsed products

to distinguish between them, particularly in the context of indigenous communities where the distinction between past, present and future is not as clear-cut or linear as in Western societies. Many traditions within the arts form a distinctive component of the heritage of a people or a place. This is especially true of crafts production or festivals. Even in historic cities (e.g. in Italy), it is difficult to distinguish between the heritage and arts component of the cultural tourism product. Historic buildings host art exhibitions, theatre and opera take place in ancient amphitheatres, festivals and events are based in heritage streets. Boundaries are nebulous, and distinctions are not always possible or indeed useful.

It is argued in this book that cultural tourism is indeed broad in its remit, but that there is perhaps a need for differentiation within the cultural tourism sector. For the purposes of this book, and because of its diversity and complexity, cultural tourism can perhaps best be divided into a number of sub-sectors or typologies (while recognising some overlaps). These might include Heritage Tourism, Arts Tourism, Creative Tourism and Indigenous Tourism. The kinds of environments visited might be urban or rural, naturally occurring or man-made. Each of these areas tends to have its own specific issues, relating to both critical studies and practical management. Below is a summary of key issues for the main sub-sets of cultural tourism.

Heritage tourism

Heritage tourism is concerned largely with the interpretation and representation of the past. Hence it is a branch of cultural tourism that can be something of a political and ethical minefield. Heritage has become increasingly politicised as recognition has been granted to previously marginalised, minority and ethnic groups. The Western-dominated, Eurocentric approach to the study of history and its interpretation as heritage is no longer acceptable in the postmodern, global environment.

The study of history is always disjointed and distorted in some way. The quest for absolute truth and the depiction of 'reality' is ultimately a fruitless quest, as evidence is often hard to come by, and its interpretation is subjective and biased. The so-called 'grand narratives' of the past have often been refuted because of their patriarchal and ethnocentric bias. Instead, the social histories of the working classes, women, ethnic minorities and indigenous groups have gradually become the subject of considerable academic and public interest. The existence of plural histories is being increasingly recognised, although this in itself is problematic, since far more gaps tend to exist in the histories of marginal groups. This may be because such groups were often unable to record their own history or were disinherited, and their heritage displaced or destroyed. This is particularly true of ethnic groups and indigenous peoples.

There has been a growth of interest in such forms of history, and the heritage and museum industries are consequently responding to this development. It is still the case that ethnic and indigenous curators are in a minority, and education and training gaps can be identified. Much of the interpretation of ethnic and indigenous peoples is subsequently carried out by white Westerners, many of whom do not have the knowledge base or the empathy to take on this role effectively.

Tourism has sometimes led to increasing support for minority groups, as it has helped to raise their social and political profile internationally. However, interpretation of heritage is often sensitive and controversial. Some forms of heritage are 'dissonant' to certain groups, such as the heritage of atrocity (e.g. war, massacres, genocide). Care must be taken not to deprive groups for whom such collective events are sensitive of the right to interpret and represent this heritage to others. It may also not always be appropriate to develop tourism in such cases.

The 'globalisation' of heritage has manifested itself in the development of the World Heritage List. In recent years, UNESCO have been moving towards a more inclusive approach to the designation of sites, focusing on their historical and cultural rather than aesthetic value. This means that there is more representation of the intangible heritage of indigenous peoples, for example, or the industrial landscapes of the working classes. Although it could be argued that World Heritage Site inscription affords local communities few benefits in real terms, the initiative at least facilitates and helps fund conservation and encourages tourism development, which can sometimes bring great advantages.

Plate 1.1 Ancient Greek Corinth

(Source: Melvyn Smith)

In terms of the management of heritage, a number of issues have come to the fore in recent years, particularly in the 1990s when the concept of sustainability was at its height. Many of the debates relate to the dilemmas that confront heritage sites, for example, maintaining the sensitive balance between conservation, visitor management and community involvement. Others relate to the problems of funding and the extent to which the commercialisation of heritage and museums (e.g. through tourism and retail development) compromise their core function. There has also been a recognition of the importance of intangible heritage. The case study presented in Box 1.1 illustrates the need for a global concern for and protection of heritage.

Box 1.1

Case study of a cultural landscape: Bamiyan Valley, Afghanistan

Afghanistan, situated at an important junction on the ancient Silk Roads, has been the crossroads of cultures since time immemorial. Its unique cultural heritage reflects a history that is marked by the complex indigenous encounters between Achemenid Persia, Alexandrian Greece, Buddhism, Hinduism and Islam.

The cultural landscape and archaeological remains of the Bamiyan Valley represent the artistic and religious developments which from the first to the thirteenth centuries characterised ancient Bakhtria, integrating various cultural influences into the Gandhara school of Buddhist art. The area contains numerous Buddhist monastic ensembles and sanctuaries, as well as fortified edifices from the Islamic period. According to the World Heritage List, the justification for insciption were as follows:

Criterion (i): The Buddha statues and the cave art in Bamiyan Valley are an outstanding representation of the Gandharan school in Buddhist art in the Central Asian region.

Criterion (ii): The artistic and architectural remains of Bamiyan Valley, and an important Buddhist centre on the Silk Road, are an exceptional testimony to the interchange of Indian, Hellenistic, Roman, Sasanian influences as the basis for the development of a particular artistic expression in the Gandharan school. To this can be added the Islamic influence in a later period.

Criterion (iii): The Bamiyan Valley bears an exceptional testimony to a cultural tradition in the Central Asian region, which has disappeared.

Criterion (iv): The Bamiyan Valley is an outstanding example of a cultural landscape which illustrates a significant period in Buddhism.

Criterion (vi): The Bamiyan Valley is the most monumental expression of the western Buddhism. It was an important centre of pilgrimage over many centuries.

However, due to their symbolic values, the monuments have suffered at different times of their existence. Due to prolonged armed conflict and fanaticism, much of this outstanding cultural heritage has been destroyed, including the tragic destruction by the Taliban of the two standing Buddha statues, which shook the world in March 2001. In the following months most of the debris, together with the remains of the original sculpture, was taken away to be sold. In addition, the small statues in the collections of the Kabul Museum were smashed, including many stored for security reasons in the Ministry of Information and Culture.

Following the Government of Afghanistan's request to UNESCO to coordinate all international efforts in the field of culture, the International Coordination Committee for the Safeguarding of Afghanistan's Cultural Heritage was created under the auspices of UNESCO. The Committee's advice enables the Afghan authorities to develop a cultural policy framework for immediate and long-term heritage protection. The focus of this Campaign is the safeguarding of all aspects of Afghan cultural heritage, both tangible and intangible, including museums, monuments, archaeological sites, music, art, traditional crafts etc. The UN Secretary-General's dictum stated that 'Our challenge is to help the Afghans help themselves'.

(UNESCO 2003)

Arts tourism

Arts tourism has perhaps developed more slowly than heritage tourism. This is partly due to a traditional reluctance on the part of both sectors to embrace joint initiatives. The arts sector has often been reluctant to accept the value of tourism and the development or expansion of audiences through tourism. It is often felt that audiences composed largely of tourists would be less appreciative of the art form presented, or that the integrity or authenticity of the performance would be compromised in some way. Of course, there is some truth in this fear, especially as the arts have often struggled financially and been forced to adapt their programming to suit more mainstream audiences.

It could also be argued that the arts are more 'global' than heritage, which tends to be geographically specific and spatially bounded (except perhaps some museum collections). In contrast, the arts can be taken to the people, in the sense that theatre, dance, music and the visual arts travel well in the form of shows, performances and exhibitions. However, it is also true that many people, especially in urban areas, do not have to leave their home town to experience the arts, as the same ballet, opera, play or musical can often be seen there. They do not have to visit the place of origin of the art form to gain access to it.

Access has, of course, become a major issue in the arts, particularly in Western societies where the accumulation of 'cultural capital' or 'cultural competence' is often deemed necessary to understand or appreciate the arts. Attempts are now being made to increase access to the arts and to broaden the profile of audiences. In addition, the increasing cultural diversity and multiculturalism within post-colonial societies has led to the proliferation of new and hybridised art forms, many of which need to be better supported and to have their profile raised.

It is argued in this book that tourism can bring new, often uninitiated audiences to a wide range of arts events and performances, especially those of ethnic and other minority groups who may be struggling to gain recognition of, or funding for, their art form. There has been considerable pressure on the arts in recent years to adopt a more inclusive and democratic approach to their programming and funding, and to focus on issues relating to access. Tourism arguably creates a channel whereby new art forms can gain support (both financial and moral), and helps to broaden the audience for the arts. In many Western societies, where the arts have traditionally been criticised for elitism, this is perhaps a welcome development.

Chapter 6 focuses in particular on ethnic and minority art forms that reflect the culture, traditions and way of life of a particular group. This includes a discussion of the development of festivals and carnivals, which were traditionally community celebrations and now form part of the heritage as well as the ongoing culture of those communities. The development of cultural tourism can contribute to the flourishing of such events, especially as they tend to be part of the 'local colour' of a destination (see Box 1.2). Although tourism can sometimes play a role in compromising the authenticity of, or commercialising the event, it is generally regarded as a positive development because of its potentially inclusive and participatory nature.

Box 1.2

Case study of a multicultural arts festival

Most countries are multicultural, but few more so than Malaysia, where there is a fusion of three of Asia's oldest civilisations – a geo-cultural mix of Malay, Chinese and Indian heritage. In addition, there are the indigenous cultures of the Kadazans, Ibans and ethnic groups of Sabah and Sarawak as well as the colonial influence of the British, Portuguese, Dutch and Thais.

The annual Citrawarna or Colours of Malaysia festival takes place in July in the capital city of Kuala Lumpur. This spectacular event brings all the heritage and culture of Malaysians from all states into one place. The festival begins with a parade involving over 6000 performers dressed in a variety of traditional Malay costumes. It covers all varieties of performing arts, visual arts and crafts, involving all 13 states of Malaysia, plus the capital Kuala Lumpur, which present the best of their entertainment, art and food.

This festival is sometimes referred to as the festival of life and many Malaysians are very proud and look forward to celebrating this event every year. In addition, it was thought that it would help to attract foreign tourists if a special month was given to this celebration. The first celebration was showcased in 1999, and since then it has become a major tourism event bringing thousands of visitors from all over the world. It is the best time for visitors to see at a glance the entirety of Malaysian culture, including songs, dance, diverse cuisine, and revel in the culture and beauty of each ethnic group and the elements that make them truly unique. Each of Malaysia's distinctive communities – Malay, Chinese, Indian, Kadazan and Gawai – has its own unique lifestyle including traditions and architectures and also language.

> Malaysia is a nation proud of its culture and heritage. Tolerance, acceptance and appreciation of one another's cultures are traits that are intrinsic to Malaysians – so diverse, yet at the same time, unique. Underneath it all lies the same spirit – the spirit of being Malaysians, of being united and diverse. Despite the differences, they still live in peace and harmony.
>
> (Singh 2006)

Creative tourism

Creative tourism consists of active and interactive participation in cultural tourism activities, whereby tourists create something on an individual or collective basis. Holidays are increasingly being developed around artistic and creative practices, such as painting, pottery, photography or dance. In some cases, the activities will be undertaken by groups of tourists in isolation from local communities, but in others, the host–guest interaction will constitute a major part of the experience.

Richards (2001c) notes the development of the creative industries and the parallel development of a form of 'creative tourism'. He defines 'creative tourism' as tourism involving active participation by tourists in the creative process. This could include some of the more active forms of special interest tourism such as cookery, painting, photography, or arts and crafts holidays. Many people who do not have time for creative pursuits in their everyday lives are increasingly undertaking such activities on holiday. He suggests that creative tourism is being pursued particularly by those destinations which cannot compete on the basis of their cultural and heritage resources (e.g. de-industrialising cities or rural areas).

There has clearly been a growing emphasis on the importance of creative industries to the global economy. In a world of high technology, media and communications, it is inevitable that modes of cultural production are changing. The cultural industries (e.g. the arts, heritage and museums) are succumbing to the usage of new and interactive technologies and media to enhance their products. Even artists themselves are now increasingly using photography, video footage and new media to express their ideas. Within this context, it could certainly be argued that the boundaries between art and media, culture and commerce, and fiction and reality are being gradually eroded. The growth of the creative industries and the experiential forms of tourism which can be built around them means that a whole range of exciting new products are being developed (see Box 1.3).

Box 1.3

Case study of creative tourism in New Zealand

Creative Tourism New Zealand (CTNZ) was set up to promote a range of interactive workshops sampling the best New Zealand art and culture has to offer. CTNZ started in 2003 in the Nelson region and has now grown into a nationwide organisation. The workshop categories which are offered by the CTNZ are reflective of traditional New Zealand values: Art, Maori Culture, Taste and Nature. The workshops are designed to be fun, informal and hands-on. The participants spend time with the tutors and pick up new skills by creating their own handcrafted souvenirs. Many of the workshops are family friendly.

Maori culture workshops provide an authentic look at different aspects of Maori culture and are taught by local Maori tutors. Visitors learn about Maori traditions and beliefs and will leave with an insight into how Maori saw the world in the past and how they see the world today.

Taste workshops include winemaking, olive oil making, cheese making and cookery (e.g. seafood).

Art workshops are diverse, and offer visitors the chance to create their own bonecarving, clay or woodturning souvenir; to learn to make silver or green stone jewellery, a hand-forged knife, kiwiana paper art, felt from a selection of wool fleeces; or to explore the new medium of fused glass.

Visitors can enjoy the natural environment as well as the cultural elements by spending a day learning about the New Zealand bush in an interactive way or weaving a traditional flax basket. They can also gain inspiration from the New Zealand flora and fauna in order to create a unique painting or travel journal.

(Creative Tourism New Zealand 2009)

Urban cultural tourism

The development of urban cultural tourism, particularly in European cities, has become something of a mass phenomenon, and arguably a serious threat to the future sustainability of a number of historic towns. Whereas cultural tourism was traditionally thought to be a niche form of tourism, the proliferation of short-break holidays has fuelled its rapid, often uncontrolled expansion. It is interesting to note, for example, how quickly some of the emerging urban destinations in Eastern Europe such as Prague and Krakow have become overrun with cultural tourists (see Box 1.4). It should be noted, for example, that many historic towns and heritage cities are not only World Heritage Sites, but they have also been granted European Cultural Capital status at some time or other. Although this has afforded them additional protection and funding, it has also led to an increase in visitors due to their enhanced status.

However, this book's focus is not only on historic cities that have struggled to maintain the fine balance between conservation and visitor management. Emphasis

Plate 1.2 Historic centre of Krakow

(Source: Melvyn Smith)

is also placed on former industrial cities which have declined, and their attempts to use cultural tourism as a means of diversifying their economy and enhancing their image. Chapter 9 provides a detailed analysis of the concept of cultural regeneration and the role tourism plays within this process. Although such cities cannot compete easily with the world's most popular heritage destinations, they can often position themselves in the short-break market as 'alternative' destinations. Their focus is much more likely to be based on their contemporary cultural tourism product (e.g. popular culture, music, sport, shopping, nightlife), and there is now an identifiable market for destinations that incorporate such attractions. Such destinations are likely to attract more mainstream visitors than traditional cultural tourists, but many of these towns can also afford the visitor a glimpse of their former industrial heritage.

Clearly, the majority of cultural cities can offer visitors a wide range of heritage, arts and contemporary cultural attractions, as well as creative and experiential activities. 'World cities' such as London and New York are particularly cosmopolitan and multicultural; hence they can offer the tourist something of the world in microcosm. This includes access to many of the world's major cuisines, music, fashion, dance, sport and so on. Although it is recognised in this book that the globalisation process may be viewed as an unequal and oppressive force, it has also contributed positively to the diversification and hybridisation of cultural forms. Hence, the cultural consumer or cultural tourist can gain access to a broader range of new cultural experiences. It can also mean that traditionally local cultural activities or events become increasingly internationalised, or that global events are brought to a wider range of local audiences through technology, communications, media, travel or tourism. Either way, cross-cultural exchange on a world scale has perhaps never been quite so inclusive and participatory, particularly in the global city.

Box 1.4

Case study of a post-socialist city: Budapest

Central and Eastern European cities like Budapest find themselves in the position of trying to create new and unique experiences for visitors, while selecting which elements of the past to preserve and promote. In international tourism, the post-socialist period also meant the rediscovery of Budapest after 50 years. During 1867–1945, it was the second most important city within the Austro-Hungarian monarchy (after Vienna), but 50 years of socialism all but erased the former international centre from Europe's cultural and tourist map.

After 1989, Budapest, like many other post-socialist cities, found itself in the position of trying to create a (new) image for international tourism. Many tourists were unaware of what was there after 50 years of restricted access. In the competitive global tourist market, the socialist heritage attractions of Eastern European cities may originally have been seen as a valid differentiating factor; however, in recent years, this unique selling point has begun to wane as first time 'curiosity' visitor numbers are decreasing. The country is also changing rapidly, and the visible, intangible signs of the socialist system are fast disappearing. In fact, returning foreign tourists sometimes complain that Budapest is losing its 'exotic eastern' image and 'it's not like it used to be'. Therefore, the creation of socialist heritage-based attractions has seemed to be necessary for various reasons: in addition to preserving the memory of the period for Hungarian generations who are too young to remember, they also provide a unique opportunity for foreigners to get a glimpse of the country's past behind the iron curtain.

However, cultural tourism development also needs to recognise the multi-layered pre-socialist past of Budapest (e.g. the Austro-Hungarian, Turkish or Roman heritage), as well as newer and more modern developments. Budapest is also keen to be seen as a dynamic and cosmopolitan city.

(After Smith, Puczkó and Rátz 2007)

Rural cultural tourism

It is recognised in this book that there is an increasing need to focus on the future of rural areas and peripheral regions of the world. Many of the world's most economically and socially marginalised groups live in such areas, and it is necessary to consider how far tourism may be considered to be a positive development option.

Chapter 5 considers the situation of indigenous and tribal groups. In some cases, the encroachment of cultural tourism into the rural habitats of indigenous peoples has become a destructive or parasitical force; however, this clearly depends on the nature and scale of development. It also depends very much on the degree of fragility of the natural environment, and the attitudes and perceptions of local people towards tourism.

In some cases, tourism may be viewed as a positive force for change or growth within rural areas. Many communities are keen to develop tourism in order to counteract or compensate for the decline of traditional industries, particularly agriculture. The development of arts and crafts tourism, gastronomic tourism or ecomuseums can often help to diversify an economy and provide a supplementary or alternative source of income. It is also worth noting the development of 'creative' tourism in rural areas as discussed earlier in this chapter. Many tourists are partaking increasingly of 'special interest' holidays, which involve active participation in a cultural activity, such as painting, photography, pottery or cookery. Many of these activities tend to take place in rural areas where the landscape is beautiful (e.g. Tuscany or Provence), or in countries with a popular cuisine (e.g. Thailand or India). Many such tourists enjoy staying with families or on farms in order to enhance the authenticity and rusticity of their experience. Indeed, farm tourism or 'agrotourism' is becoming increasingly popular, especially in countries that are trying to diversify their tourism product; for example, Greece, Italy, Spain and Portugal. Traditionally, these countries have focused on the development of coastal tourism, but they are trying increasingly to diversify into other forms of tourism, such as rural or cultural tourism (see Box 1.5). In many cases, especially on Mediterranean islands, a combination of these forms of tourism is offered in the villages and small towns. This can sometimes be problematic in terms of sustainability, since it involves imposing tourism on traditional communities which may be unused, or even hostile to such developments.

Box 1.5

Case study of agro-tourism in Cyprus

'*Holidays in the Cyprus countryside guided by nature and tradition.*'

The Cyprus Tourism Organisation recognised the new trend of visitors wishing to experience a new, alternative way to holidaymaking, and subsequently set in motion a programme of restoration of traditional houses and enhancement of the traditional aspects of Cyprus villages. This took place within the framework of the philosophy of agrotourism. The need for a better and more organised co-ordination of agrotourism led to the establishment of the Cyprus Agrotourism Company, a body dealing exclusively with holidays in the Cyprus countryside. Today, agrotourism is an autonomous, vibrant part of Cyprus tourism hosted in traditional lodgings of historical value throughout Cyprus, ready to offer a new, alternative holiday option.

> Visitors can stay in one of the 50 or more restored lodgings, and experience the Cyprus countryside through nature trails, visits to historical monasteries and archaeological sites. They can also enjoy traditional villages with their unique character, distinctive architecture and simple, serene rhythms of everyday life.
>
> The visitor has the benefit of experiencing the rich traditions of village people, including their folk customs, daily activities, and the authentic tastes of traditional cuisine; all filtered through the sense of genuine hospitality.
>
> (Cyprus Agrotourism Company 2004)

Indigenous cultural tourism

Many of the most significant impacts of cultural tourism can clearly be felt in those destinations that are located in remote or fragile landscapes, or which are in developing countries, where the relationship between hosts and guests is an unequal one. Although it was assumed previously that cultural tourism was small-scale and more sensitive to local environments and cultures, its increase has led to its impacts becoming as major as any other form of tourism. Therefore, forms of tourism that originally attracted small numbers of tourists (e.g. ecotourism) have now become more and more mainstream. This might include jungle tours, hill trekking or wildlife tourism, all of which tend to involve contact with local or indigenous people, and often tribal groups. Clearly, the impacts of tourism are likely to be quite significant in such environments.

Chapter 5 focuses on the situation of indigenous and tribal people, including their socioeconomic conditions and political status, which have tended to be typical of that of any marginalised or oppressed groups. The colonial legacy in many countries has led to the displacement of indigenous people from their lands, the fragmentation of their culture, and the forced discontinuation of their traditions. This has often led to a certain degree of despondency or despair, especially among groups where whole families and communities have been uprooted and dispersed.

Apart from those relating to land rights, some of the most significant issues relate to the interpretation and representation of indigenous culture and heritage (see Box 1.6). As discussed in Chapter 5 this can become intensely political, and marginalised groups have a difficult task to make their voices heard, let alone gain the financial wherewithal to fund their own projects or enterprises. Cultural tourism is one way in which indigenous peoples can start to rebuild their communities and to renew their sense of pride in their culture and identity. The very fact that tourists are starting to take an interest in the culture, traditions and lifestyles of indigenous peoples has provided a means of strengthening their position. Although cultural tourism is no panacea, it can be viewed as a positive development option among communities which are favourably disposed towards tourism.

Clearly, a number of important issues need to be considered. Many of these relate to the well-documented phenomenon of community-based tourism, and identifying ways in which local communities can become empowered to develop and manage their own tourism ventures. An interim solution might be provided by joint ownership projects, but ultimately there is a need to increase political and financial support, as well as education and training programmes in order to further empower indigenous communities to manage their own tourism projects. Other issues relate to the interpretation of culture and heritage, which should always be carried out in consultation with indigenous peoples, or by indigenous peoples themselves. This could relate to the interpretation of a museum collection depicting the history of indigenous peoples, for example, or a cultural performance which needs to retain its authenticity. The development of cultural centres in some locations has helped to create a space in which indigenous peoples can represent and express themselves in the way which best befits their community.

Box 1.6

Case study of Saami tourism

The Saami people followed the melting of the inland ice and entered Lapland about 8000 years ago. Their origin area reaches from the peninsula of Kola to northern Norway, northern Sweden and northern Finland. This area is called Sápmi (the land of the Laplanders). Today only 10 per cent of Laplanders make their living by taking care of reindeers.

In recent years, there has been increased development of indigenous tourism as part of the tourism industry. Even the Saami of northern Sweden are now engaging in tourism, mainly because the restructuring of reindeer herding has forced them into taking up other occupations. However, tourism development has always been somewhat controversial. For example, a problem has arisen over the use of traditional Saami cultural symbols in the Finnish tourism industry. After a Saami Council meeting in Rovaniemi, Finland, the Nordic indigenous group passed a resolution calling for a ban on improper or demeaning use of their symbols. They also want the Finnish government to require permits for any tourist organisation to use a Saami icon.

In 2008 there were demonstrations in the streets of Rovaniemi, by Saami youths in which the Saami of Finland, Sweden, Norway and Russia took part. According to the demonstrators, the use of Lapland costumes was being used improperly by Lapland's tourism guides, advertising and tourist trinkets. The demonstrators hope to have access to establishing negotiations, over when, how and who can keep a Lapland suit and for replica dress sales to cease. They also state that tourism, with a lack of data, creates stereotypes and in turn is undermining the Saami identity. They said that the majority of Saami do not accept the government's position over the use of symbols in tourism and are making their statements based on a UN indigenous declaration on the protection of indigenous cultural heritage.

(Hauksson 2008)

Experiential cultural tourism

Chapter 9 focuses on the development of experiential tourism, a term which has been coined partly in response to the work of Pine and Gilmore (1999) on the experience economy. In many ways, as discussed earlier in this chapter, it is difficult to establish the boundaries or parameters around cultural tourism if it is defined as a whole way of life. However, calls for access, inclusion and democracy in heritage and the arts have somehow necessitated the broadening of the boundaries and the embracing of all forms of culture and cultural activities. Whereas in the past, 'Culture' (with a capital 'C') was largely regarded as the premise of an elite minority, the concept of multifarious 'cultures' has helped to diversify audiences and to increase access. Many of the most unifying forms of culture are those which are popular and enjoyed by the masses – for example, football and pop music.

In tourism terms, it needs to be recognised that the average tourist now wants to partake of a wide range of activities, which may or may not include traditional forms of heritage or arts tourism. More tourists are travelling than ever before; therefore the industry needs to cater for a broader range of interests and tastes. The majority of tourists are now actively seeking diverse experiences while on holiday, and are just as likely to want to go shopping or to engage in a creative experience as to visit a World Heritage Site. This is a welcome development for non-traditional destinations (e.g. industrial cities or rural areas), as they can now provide tourists with an alternative product and a broader range of activities.

Global developments in technology, media and communications have helped to break down the barriers not just between high and low culture, but also between reality and fiction. Many tourist attractions (e.g. theme parks, leisure complexes and shopping malls) constitute a kind of 'tourist bubble' suspended in time and space, isolated from any real context, and providing the tourist with an idealised environment and experience (see Box 1.7). Tourism has, of course, always been about the selling of dreams, the creation of fantasies and the perpetuation of myths. The development of simulations in cyber-space and the proliferation of TV travel shows has helped to bring new and potential travel experiences into the living rooms of the public the world over. This has clearly whetted the appetite for travel, and global tourism is consequently growing.

Box 1.7

Case study of Dubailand

Dubailand is currently the world's most ambitious leisure, tourism and entertainment destination with over 3 billion square feet of world-class theme parks and culture, well-being, sports, shopping, hospitality and entertainment facilities. The development was set to launch its first phase in December 2010, although global recession and a slow down in investment hindered progress. By 2010 it was intended that the visitor economy would be recognised as one of Dubai's and the region's major economic drivers, seen as adding significant value to the regional economy, and supporting the sustainable development of Dubai.

Dubailand's mission statement claimed that it would celebrate the cultural diversity of Dubai's nationals, residents and visitors, offering both nationally and internationally recognised attractions, including

- theme parks
- culture and arts
- science and planetariums
- sports and sports academies
- well-being and health
- shopping and retail
- resorts and hotels

Examples of attractions within culture and the arts include:

Falcon City of Wonders
The project will feature cultural facilities with structures based on famous sites and the architectural marvels of the world, such as the Pyramids, the Hanging Gardens of Babylon, the Eiffel Tower, the Taj Mahal and the Leaning Tower of Pisa. Spread over an area of 4 million square metres, it is shaped to represent the falcon, emblematic of the UAE's heritage. In addition to that the project will consist of a Pharaohs Theme Park with multiple white-knuckle rides and roller coasters.

Islamic Culture and Science World
The project provides state-of-the-art facilities for the promotion, understanding and research of space, natural and human sciences, as well as Islamic culture, arts and literature. It includes a multi-purpose stage, International Cultural and Scientific Centre, exhibition area, museum, labs and other relevant facilities.

Al Sahra Desert Resort
Al Sahra is a unique desert resort set in 40 million square feet of undulating sand dunes just 30 minutes from the heart of Dubai. Its star attraction, 'Jumana – Secret of the Desert', is a world-class extravaganza with spectacular light, laser, sound and pyrotechnics effects, staged in an imposing amphitheatre built in the style of an ancient Arabic settlement. Al Sahra Desert Resort offers restaurants, a traditional Souk with arts and crafts of the region, luxury tented lodges and a Caravanserai boutique hotel to ensure a memorable experience for visitors.

Current estimates suggest that over 40,000 visitors per day will visit Dubailand, attracting over 15 million visitors per year to the emirate. It would be difficult to see the Dubailand development not emulating and potentially surpassing the huge impact of the Disneyland and Disneyworld projects on the US tourism market in the 1970s and 1980s.

(Dubailand 2009)

Cultural tourists

According to some authors, culture can be *one* motivating factor for many so-called cultural tourists, but not necessarily the primary one. McKercher and Cros (2002) suggest five types of cultural tourists:

1 the *purposeful* cultural tourist, for whom culture is a primary motivator and who seeks a deep cultural experience;
2 the *sightseeing* cultural tourist, who travels for cultural reasons but seeks a shallower experience;
3 the *serendipitous* cultural tourist, who is not primarily motivated by culture, but who gets into a deep cultural experience by chance;
4 the *casual* cultural tourist, for whom culture is a weak motivating factor and who seeks a shallow experience;
5 the *incidental* cultural tourist, for whom culture is not a stated motive, but who does visit cultural attractions.

Richards (2001b) estimates that three-quarters of tourists in Europe visit a cultural attraction even if they do not consider themselves to be on a cultural holiday. Tour operators have consequently responded to this by developing packages which combine a number of activities, some of them cultural, but others based purely on entertainment, fun or relaxation. For example, Kuoni offers long-haul packages to Thailand, which combine beach stays on islands with city shopping and nightlife in Bangkok, and hilltribe trekking in Chiang Mai. The latter activity is particularly popular with cultural tourists seeking authentic contact with local people, as it generally involves homestays or visits.

ATLAS (2007) cultural tourism research has shown that almost 70 per cent of cultural tourists in Europe tend to have some form of higher education, and just under 30 per cent work in a profession related to culture. Only around 17 per cent are on all-inclusive packages. However, as definitions of cultural tourism become more and more inclusive, these profiles may change over time. Nevertheless, care must still be taken to differentiate between activities which are deemed cultural as opposed to recreational or leisure-based, especially for the purposes of research and data collection. As stated earlier, there is perhaps scope for more differentiation between typologies of cultural tourism.

Although it can be difficult to generalise about the profile and motivations of the average cultural tourist, the table of cultural tourist typologies suggests that there are significant differences between the interests, expectations and motivations of cultural tourists. The majority of cultural tourists will be keen to experience new and different places, and part of the pleasure of their experience will be derived from the process of travelling itself. Journeys are often not seen as a means to an end as they are in the case of package tourists, but as an exciting form of personal displacement, which affords new sights, sounds and smells. The use of local transport will be frequent, and many cultural tourists (especially backpackers) will often take great delight in being sandwiched between locals and their sacks of rice or grain, or their entourage of goats or chickens. Most cultural tourists are likely to be on some kind of quest for authenticity, either in terms of self-improvement or in terms of the sites, communities and activities that they engage with or in. They will want to engage fully with the destinations they visit and to interact with local inhabitants.

According to more traditional typologies of the tourist, cultural tourists might fall variously into the categories of 'explorer' or 'drifter' (Cohen 1972) or 'elite', 'off-beat' or 'unusual' (Smith 1989). Although 'unusual' tourists tend to prefer the tourist bubble to striking out alone, they nevertheless adapt reasonably well to local culture. Sharpley (1994) refers to five categories of tourist experience: recreational, diversionary, experiential, experimental and existential. The first two categories of visitors are mainly seeking relaxation and escapism, whereas the last three categories will wish to immerse themselves either partly or fully in local culture and society, and authentic experiences will be sought.

Motivations of cultural tourists

In his insightful analysis of the motivations that underpin our desire to travel, de Botton (2002) suggests that we may be forever clamouring to be where we are not, seeking escapism or 'getting away from it all'. Alternatively, he suggests, we may be drawn to exoticism like Flaubert, who was obsessed with travel to the Orient:

> In the more fugitive, trivial association of the word exotic, the charm of a foreign place arises from the simple idea of novelty and change . . . we may value foreign elements not only because they are new, but because they seem to accord more faithfully with our identity and commitments than anything our homeland could provide.
>
> (de Botton 2002: 78)

This craving for difference and exoticism is perhaps stronger in the case of cultural tourists who will actively seek out remote locations, unusual experiences or close and authentic contact with indigenous groups. Sarup (1996) suggests that travel allows us to enjoy and exploit simultaneously the exotic difference of 'the Other' while discovering our own identity. Wang (2000) suggests that many tourists are more likely to be in search of their own 'existentially' authentic selves rather than seeking 'objective' authenticity. Seaton (2002: 162) suggests: 'Tourism is at least as much a quest *to be* as a quest to see.' Of course, the notion of escapism through travel could apply as much to escapism from self as escapism from place or routine, but, as noted by de Botton (2002), one of the barriers to the enjoyment of travel is the fact that we cannot easily get away from ourselves and our persistent worries. However, many tourists still crave the enhancement rather than the avoidance of self, particularly cultural tourists. They subscribe to Nietzsche's view of travel that it should be a constant process of knowledge seeking and self-improvement. This would, of course, conform to the rationale behind the Grand Tour of the seventeenth and eighteenth centuries which was predominantly an educational and cultural experience. Many modern-day cultural package tours appear to emulate this philosophy.

Seaton (2002) describes the process of 'metempsychosis' whereby tourists engage in repetitive or ritualistic behaviour, often following in the footsteps of famous figures on their travels. Certainly, many forms of cultural tourism, such as literary, media or film tourism, could be described as metempsychotic, as could certain forms of heritage tourism; for example, those that include re-enactments, or tours with a mythical element to them. He also discusses the concept of 'metensomatosis', or the process of temporary role-playing whereby tourists adopt multiple personae: 'The tourist is . . . typically a multipersonae traveller, a polyphrenic *bricoleur* whose tourism enactments are based on representations of what others have been in the past' (Seaton 2002: 159). He argues that the act of role-playing with social peers in a new place is, in some cases, more significant and more common than interaction and engagement with local people.

De Botton (2002) suggests that most destinations fail to live up to our somewhat idealised or romanticised expectations, or are at least different from what we expected. Urry (2002: 13) also describes how '"reality" rarely provides the perfected pleasures encountered in daydreams, each purchase leads to disillusionment and to the longing for ever-new products. There is a dialectic of novelty and insatiability at the heart of contemporary consumerism.' So, many tourists keep travelling despite their disappointments, hoping that the next time might be better. However, other tourists are becoming weary of travel. Richards (2001a) suggests that people have effectively been overloaded with culture, and that many tourists are suffering from 'monument fatigue', wearied by the phenomenon of 'musterbation' (the apparent compulsion to visit 'must-see' sights!). The quest for new experiences, rather like the insatiable accumulation of material possessions in consumer societies, can be a wearisome and ultimately unfulfilling process.

De Botton (2002) notes that tourists often feel intimidated by guidebooks and fail to react spontaneously and subjectively to destinations and sights, but instead remain obedient to a prescribed route. Hence we fail to see the world clearly and to appreciate some of the smaller details of travel that could truly enhance our lives. Urry (2002) also notes: 'The contemporary tourist gaze is increasingly signposted. There are markers that identify the things and places worthy of our gaze.' Edensor (2001: 74) analyses this phenomenon in more depth, concluding that every potential space is effectively stage-managed and regulated: 'Thus there is a machinery of discursive, regulatory and practical norms which direct tourists' performances and often support their own understandings of how to behave.'

This means that cultural tourists may need to travel independently further afield to more and more remote locations, or increasingly exotic cultures to experience what they view as 'authenticity'. On the other hand, they may also choose to embrace some of the more creative and experiential forms of cultural tourism which do not necessarily require travel to specific locations. Many Japanese and American tourists have little holiday allowance, and are often forced to holiday at home or to fit in as many sites as possible on a world tour. The former option means that domestic attractions in Japan or the USA often emulate real countries or cities, even though they are entirely artificial (see case studies of Las Vegas and Huis Ten Bosch in Chapter 9). Although it is debatable how far tourism is 'cultural' if it is not based on 'real' and 'authentic' settings and people, the concepts of reality and authenticity are fairly contentious in the field of tourism (see further discussion in Chapter 9).

Conclusion

This chapter has shown that cultural tourism is constantly changing and diversifying. It is difficult to establish parameters around meanings of culture, especially as the boundaries between creativity, experience, business and technology become less clear. Thus it is not absolutely unthinkable that a cultural tourist might decide to visit a theme park as he or she is craving a spectacular experience, which is a vital part of contemporary tourism. However, that same cultural tourist may later be backpacking around a jungle visiting indigenous peoples in their natural habitat. There are clearly problems with labelling and fixing typologies, although tour operators still need to target specific segments. Cultural tourism, like most forms of tourism, is lifestyle and life-stage driven. The division of cultural tourism into numerous sub-sectors can be helpful and certainly helps to focus product development and marketing efforts; however, it is best not to adopt a rigid approach to cultural tourism studies, appreciating instead its dynamism and diversity.

2 The geography of cultural tourism

Fanfares for 'cultural diversity' have come just when most of it has gone.

May (1999: 84)

Introduction

This chapter analyses the geography of cultural tourism. This includes looking at the cultural resources of the main regions and countries of the world, including their built, natural, intangible and indigenous heritage. Every country has its own culture(s), and some may seem more global or traditional than others. Although we cannot generalise about whole regions, many countries within a region share similar characteristics and resources. This can include their natural landscape, architectural style(s), religion, traditions and customs. It is therefore sometimes difficult for them to differentiate themselves and to promote their uniqueness to visitors, whose cultural awareness may be relatively limited. This chapter is complemented by Chapter 3, which discusses the way in which different historical and political trajectories have shaped the development of culture. Some countries are blessed with beautiful scenery, whereas others have wonderful architecture, or rich folk cultures. Some countries have all of these, whereas others have very few. This means it can be difficult for some countries to develop widespread cultural tourism. This chapter provides an overview of these resources and attractions.

An overview of global cultural tourism distribution

It is well documented that certain countries of the world are more heavily visited than others, and that France and Spain frequently top the tourism charts. This has often been more to do with sun, sea and sand than cultural attractions, but increasingly visitors are attracted to not only built heritage attractions, but also the lives and lifestyles of people. For example, many visitors are exploring the villages of France, Spain, Italy and Greece. This may be combined with gastronomic tourism (e.g. food and wine tours), cookery courses or, more recently, creative tourism holidays. Historic cities have always been popular in European countries, and it is now just as likely that visitors would go to Barcelona or Seville as the Spanish Costas. The increase in budget airline travel has meant that many Europeans are taking long weekends in previously under-visited cities or towns, such as those in Eastern Europe, the Baltic states and Scandinavia. This has been boosted by developments in regeneration (see Chapter 8), whereby cities are transformed into exciting tourism destinations by cultural events and initatives.

Tourism in Europe has, however, been declining in recent years as visitors explore the rest of the world. World tours and round-the-world tickets have become cheaper and more popular with backpackers, gap-year students, even executives wishing to escape the 'rat race'. Despite the current world recession and fears of climate change, long-haul travel is still undertaken by increasing numbers of visitors. This means that destinations like Australia and New Zealand have more visitors from the other side of the world. South-east Asia has been growing exponentially in popularity, and countries like Thailand have started to become mass tourism destinations. In the future, China and India are likely to generate the largest numbers of tourists in the world (having a population of around one billion people each). The opening of China politically and the influence of mega-events like the Beijing Olympics in 2008 have done much to encourage incoming tourism, and China is now in the top five destinations in the world. India has also become an easier place to travel in terms of infrastructure, and many package tours are run to 'The Golden Triangle', for example (which includes Delhi, the Taj Mahal in Agra, and Jaipur).

The majority of World Heritage Sites were traditionally located in Western Europe. There was also a dominance of cultural heritage sites and generally those with 'aesthetic' appeal. However, the quest for World Heritage Site status appears to be growing, as both developed and developing nations compete for the acquisition of this much coveted global accolade. This is partly a result of a strategic shift in World Heritage emphasis over the past decade towards a less Eurocentric and more inclusive and democratic approach to designation. In 1994, the World Heritage Committee called for:

> rectification of the imbalances on the List between regions of the world, types of monument, and periods, and at the same time a move away from a purely architectural view of the cultural heritage of humanity towards one which was much more anthropological, multi-functional, and universal.
>
> (World Heritage Committee 1994: 4)

Some of the more developed countries were asked to slow down their rate of nomination so as to address the perceived imbalance and the apparent favouring of material over non-material cultures (Pocock 1997). The addition of the category of cultural landscape to the World Heritage List in 1996 has helped to take better account of non-material and indigenous cultures. Equally, more industrial landscapes have started to be included on the World Heritage List (see e.g. Smith 2000). As a result, the World Heritage List has become better distributed geographically throughout the world.

Europe

In the past few years in Europe there has been a noticeable shift in demand away from Mediterranean beach tourism in favour of city-based or rural tourism. It has generally been recognised that the tourism product can be greatly enhanced by the addition of a cultural element. In Europe, there appears to have been a definite trend towards short breaks and activity holidays. In addition, cultural entertainment is becoming an important part of business and conference tourism. The development of cheap air fares within Europe and the internet revolution have led to a proliferation in short-break urban tourism promotions. This includes many of the 'classic' historic cities (e.g. Venice, Bruges, Amsterdam), and also the cities in former Eastern Europe (e.g. Prague, Budapest and Krakow), Baltic states (e.g. Tallinn, Riga, Vilnius) and some previously under-visited Scandinavian destinations such as Copenhagen, Helsinki and Reykjavik.

Central and Eastern Europe

The potential for the diversification of the Central and Eastern European tourism product is considerable, and it is also essential if flows of tourists throughout the region are to be dispersed away from the heavily visited cultural cities. As the infrastructural capacity of new destinations is developed further, under-visited and lesser-known regions are likely to attract more and more tourists. Economically, this will be a boon for relatively deprived countries such as Romania or Albania, and visitors will be afforded an even greater range of exciting and unexpected cultural encounters. It is interesting to note that cultural or heritage tourism has been one of the first forms of tourism to be developed in this region, although hardly surprising given the curiosity of the outside world about life behind the Iron Curtain. Some destinations such as Bulgaria or former Yugoslavia were already developed predominantly as coastal destinations. Spa tourism was always a popular form of tourism in many Eastern European destinations, especially in the Czech Republic (e.g. Karlovy Vary) and Hungary (e.g. Héviz).

Cities such as Ljublijana in Slovenia and Zagreb in Croatia are becoming more popular. Dubvrovnik has always been Croatia's main cultural attraction, and remains so, despite heavy bombardment during the war. This is thanks to major reconstruction efforts. Despite being a small country, Slovenia is blessed with coast, mountains and lakes as well as cultural cities. Poland, the Czech Republic and Slovakia all have unique cultural and historic towns and villages. Different ethnic and folk cultures are also present in all of the countries, which are major assets for rural tourism development.

Southern Europe

Many of the coastal resorts of Southern Europe, particularly in Spain, Portugal and Italy, have experienced decline or degradation. These countries have hence been forced to consider appropriate ways of revitalising such resorts. The techniques used have been many and varied, ranging from the upgrading of the quality of the destination, the development of more environmentally friendly or sustainable forms of tourism, the targeting of new markets, or the diversification of the tourism product into rural tourism, business and conference tourism, sports tourism, and, of course, cultural tourism.

The Spanish government made a concerted effort to diversify the Spanish tourism product from the early 1990s onwards, including the Olympic Games in Barcelona, the Seville Expo and the European City of Culture initiative in Madrid. The Santiago de Compostela route was revitalised in 1993, and the Silver route, which follows the old Roman routes from north to south, was revived. A World Heritage Cities Project was also piloted to establish cultural routes in Avila, Carceres, Salamanca, Santiago de Compostela, Segovia and Toledo (Maiztegui-Onate and Areitio Bertolin 1996). More recently, Barcelona has become one of the most creative cities in Europe, and Bilbao has been regenerated thanks to the Guggenheim Museum (see Chapter 10 for a case study).

Portugal has tried similarly to diversify its product away from the heavy concentration of coastal tourism in the Algarve. Again, cultural events have been used mainly as catalysts for cultural tourism development and regeneration, starting with the European City of Culture event in Lisbon in 1994, the Lisbon Expo in 1998, the European City of Culture in Porto in 2001 and the European Football Championship in Lisbon in 2004. Sintra is promoted for its World Heritage Site status, and cities such as Evora and Coimbra are increasingly attracting cultural tourists. In addition, rural regions are promoting their culture; for example, the Douro region is being promoted for its gastronomy and wine tourism and the Alto Minho has developed crafts tourism (Fernandes and Sousa 1999). Portugal is also famous for its religious and pilgrimage tourism, especially Fatima.

Italy is clearly home to a wealth of cultural treasures, including numerous World Heritage Sites, world famous gastronomy, music and arts. The cultural cities of Italy are certainly over-visited, especially the 'big three': Rome, Florence and Venice. Italy's current challenge is perhaps to promote the regions better and to disperse flows of tourists away from the main tourist centres. Van der Borg and Costa (1996) note that much of Italy's heritage is to be found outside the traditional city destinations, but that there has not been much growth in the supply of heritage for tourism uses. The development of cultural tourism in southern Italy has been a much slower process, and one which is linked closely to political control. Religious tourism is quite strong in Italy, especially the Vatican City, but also in smaller towns. For example, there is a small town called San Giovanni Rotondo in the south of Italy, which receives 7–8 million visitors per year and where one in every two residents lives from tourism. Visitors come to see the body of a Cappucin monk called Father Pio, who died in 1958, but whose body has not decomposed. He also bore the marks of stigmata (Dobszay 2008).

Other Southern European destinations have managed cultural tourism development in different ways. Clearly, Greece's archaeological heritage is dispersed geographically throughout both the mainland and the islands; hence promotion of that heritage is used as part of the diversification process. There is also increasing interest in village tourism, gastronomic tourism and crafts tourism on many of the islands. Turkey has also capitalised on its rich archaeological heritage in order to diversify its predominantly beach-based product, particularly in the western part. Archaeological sites such as Ephesus and Pergamon attract huge numbers of visitors.

Although some of the southern French coastal destinations have been somewhat overdeveloped, especially in the Cote d'Azur and Languedoc–Roussillon regions, there has arguably not been the same level of degradation as in other Southern European coastal resorts. In addition, southern France affords the visitor a wealth of cultural experiences. For example, vistors can experience the wonderful Roman remains of Nimes, Arles, Avignon and Orange, or the artistic heritage of the Nice region with painters such as Picasso, Matisse, Chagall and Dufy, or the distinctive culture of the Basque region on the west coast.

European islands

The islands of Europe offer a rich diversity of landscapes and cultures. Protection of these islands has increasingly become of paramount importance, as their resources are more limited than those of mainland destinations, and the heritage, culture and identity of their people is arguably more fragile. Some islands, especially those in Greece, the Balearics and the Canary Islands, have quite developed tourism infrastructures, and crass overdevelopment has not been uncommon. As a result, many of these destinations are now trying to upgrade or diversify into other forms of tourism. For example, Mallorca has developed more environmentally friendly forms of tourism, and Cyprus has diversified into village and mountain tourism, including the promotion of gastronomy and traditional festivals. Crete is also increasingly promoting its archaeological heritage, village tourism and arts and crafts tourism in particular.

Sardinia has a number of protected heritage coastlines, and Sicily has been something of a hidden treasure for a number of years, although it receives a steady flow of visitors. It has a wealth of archaeological and architectural treasures just waiting to be discovered, and, like Sardinia, a unique culture, dialect and gastronomy. Azara and Crouch (2006) describe La Cavalcata Sarda, a festival in Sardinia which for many years was more popular with tourists than with local people. However, it has gradually been redeveloped as a way of rejuvenating many localised, folkloristic cultures which would otherwise have disappeared. Nevertheless, there has been some resistance to the development of Europe's islands, for example in Corsica, where residents actively campaigned against tourism (Richez 1996), and Mdina in Malta, where residents left the village because they felt like they were in a human zoo (Boissevain 1997).

Northern Europe

Clearly, many Northern European destinations have relied on cultural tourism as a way of developing their tourism industries. In the absence of a warm climate and good beaches, many such destinations rely on their cultural and heritage tourism to draw in visitors. Clearly business and conference tourism is also perceived as being a lucrative sector, and cultural activities and excursions are increasingly forming part of conference tourism products. City-break destinations such as Paris, Amsterdam and Bruges have been established for some years, and new destinations emerge all the time with the proliferation of cheap flights in Europe. Britain has variously promoted its heritage and contemporary culture in recent years, including literary, film and TV tourism, as well as more traditional castles and heritage sites.

Germany promotes its cultural cities such as Berlin and Munich. The Rhineland also attracts large numbers of tourists. Belgium is attempting to promote lesser-known cities such as Ghent and Antwerp, as well as the more established Brussels and Bruges. Similarly, tourists are recognising the cultural interest of cities like Rotterdam in the Netherlands which was European City of Culture in 2001. Towns like Delft with its famous pottery and Gouda with its cheese production have also been popular cultural destinations for some time.

Traditionally, Scandinavia and the Baltic states have perhaps been less visited than many other regions of Europe. Much of this has been to do with the perceived high cost of visiting the region, coupled with the cold climate and long, dark winters, particularly in the northern periphery. However, there has been a growth of interest in both the urban and rural areas of Scandinavia in recent years. This has been prompted partly by the growing affordability of air fares to cities such as Copenhagen, Helsinki, Reykjavik, Tallinn, Riga and Vilnius, as well as the development of cruises in the region which tend to incorporate visits to Stockholm and Oslo. Copenhagen was European City of Culture in 1996, Stockholm in 1998, Helsinki and Bergen in 2000, and Vilnius in 2009, which has helped to raise the profile of these destinations (see

Box 2.1). Some tourists have started to take an interest in specialist tours to the Arctic to see the Northern Lights, or in Christmas tourism to Santa's Grotto in Finland. Equally, the indigenous Saami people of northern Finland and Lapland are a source of interest for visitors. For example, Miettinen (1999) describes how there is a current move towards strengthening the status of Saami people through textile and crafts heritage tourism. However, it is probably true to say that outside the cities, Scandinavian tourism is perceived to be based more on a rural than a cultural product. Although much of Iceland's tourism is based around nature and the diverse geological landscape, including glaciers, fjords, geysers, waterfalls, hot springs and lakes, as well as horse riding, there is increasing interest in Icelandic culture, especially Viking heritage. Reykjavik has many interesting musuems, and arts and crafts tourism is also growing in popularity. Greenland (which is part of Denmark) has a culture which is mainly of Inuit origin. Hunting, fishing and dog-sledding are still common. The Faroe Islands are an autonomous province of Denmark, and can also offer limited opportunities in cultural tourism such as Viking history, but it is mainly a rural destination.

Box 2.1

Case study of cultural tourism in the Baltic States

The Baltic States have always been part of Europe, but were under Russian rule for 50 years until 1989. The three countries have many differences, but historically they share common invasions, common military occupations and common policies directed by foreign power. Many aspects of their recent heritage are therefore similar. However, the languages are different, with Estonian being closer to Finnish while Lithuanian and Latvian are Baltic languages. Estonian and Latvian cuture is closer to that of Germany and Scandinavia, whereas Lithuania's is closer to that of Poland and Central Europe (this is a result of past occupations).

Until the mid-2000s cultural tourism was mentioned in a series of national development plans and strategies, however mostly briefly. For example, Estonia's Tourism National Development Plan for 2002–5 pointed out that the cultural tourism resources of Estonia are historical heritage (city centres from the Middle Ages, fortifications and manor houses) and cultural heritage (music, dance and handicraft, folk festivals). Latvia tends to focus on its history, culture and traditions, such as castles, palaces and royalty, as well as museums and galleries, and cultural events such as music and ballet. Before the Eurovision Song Contest in 2003, Latvia also adopted the logo 'The Land that Sings'. Lithuania tends to promote rural and coastal tourism outside the capital. Indeed, rural and ecotourism, as well as spa and seaside tourism are still the most popular forms of tourism in this region, however cultural tourism is growing. For example, Vilnius was European Cultural Capital in 2009, and there was a focus on handicrafts, living history and contemporary arts and music. Estonia's Kumu Art Museum was European Museum of the Year in 2008, proving that good-quality cultural tourism attractions can be found in the Baltic States.

(adapted from UNESCO 2001)

Plate 2.1 Bergen, Norway

(Source: Melvyn Smith)

The Middle East and North Africa

Cultural tourism in the Middle East and North Africa is also growing. The United Arab Emirates, especially Dubai, have seen a surge in tourism because of the amazing beach, shopping, desert, luxury hotel combinations, but the most innovative developments include the 'simulated' attractions currently being built (see Chapter 7 for a description of a 'fashion island' at The World project in Dubai). Other UAE countries are also promoting tourism, but mainly of the 'experiential' kind rather than traditional cultural tourism (although Islamic and desert cultures may be of interest to visitors).

Ongoing instability and conflict has sometimes prohibited tourism development in the Middle East (e.g. Iraq, Israel). Strict Muslim countries like Saudi Arabia place many restrictions on visitors, especially non-Muslim visitors and women. However, because of the Hajj to Mecca it is one of the most visited countries in the world (up to 2 million visitors per year). There are concerns that Mecca is becoming a bit like the 'Las Vegas of the Middle East' and losing its spirituality because of the construction of commercialised developments around the pilgrimage sites. Billions of dollars are being pumped into shopping and entertainment complexes and the residential areas are some of the most expensive in the world. The average spend of pilgrimage tourists can be as much as $2000–3000 per trip, therefore it has become a lucrative form of tourism which is being dramatically expanded (HVG 2008).

On the other hand, countries like Jordan, Syria and Lebanon have really taken off in recent years, with many visitors fascinated by their built heritage, not to mention the local culture. Jordan is home to one of the most spectacular sights in the Middle East – Petra, the ancient city of the Nabateans, which is one of the world's most impressive ruins. The stunning desert scenery of Wadi Rum is also said to have enraptured Lawrence of Arabia. Lebanon has the city of Beirut, which was once known as the 'Paris of the Middle East'. Despite its history of conflict, it has been largely restored to its former glory. The old Phoenician ports of Sidon and Tyre in the south are popular with visitors, and Byblos is reputedly one of the oldest continuously inhabited towns in the world. There is also the Roman acropolis of Baalbek, Tripoli, and and the beautiful Qadisha Valley with Lebanon's famous Cedar trees, some of which are more than 1500 years old. Syria has been called the 'cradle of civilisations', and is rich in monuments from many cultures (e.g. the Amorites, the Kanaanites, the Phoenicians, the Arameans, the Nabateans, as well as Hittites, Persians, Greeks, Romans and the Islamic conquest of AD636). Emergent destinations like Yemen are also becoming better known outside the region. Yemen was at the crossroads of spice and incense routes, it is rich in historical sites, and is famous for its ancient 'skyscrapers' made from stone and mud.

Some of the best known and best loved World Heritage Sites in the world are in Egypt. These include the Pyramids in Giza, the Valley of the Kings and Queens, Abu Simbel, and the temples in Luxor and Karnak. However, Egypt has had its fair share of problems, not least the horrific terrorist attacks on tourists by Islamic Extremists throughout the 1990s. The massacre of 58 tourists at the temple of Hatshepsut in Luxor was perhaps the worst example of this. Stability and safety have been established since, however, and visitors are not easily deterred. North African cultural tourism in general has been increasing, as tourists discover the cultural cities and desert towns of Tunisia and Morocco. Marrakech has become one of the world's most exotic destinations in recent years.

Box 2.2

Case study of Bedouin tourism in the Sahara Desert in the Middle East and North Africa

The Bedouin are desert-dwelling, nomadic (or previously nomadic) pastoralists, who can be found throughout most of the desert belt extending from the Atlantic coast of the Sahara via the Western Desert, Sinai, and Negev to the Arabian Desert.

Many tour operators are now offering camel or jeep tours into the Sahara Desert in Tunisia or Morocco, which include at least one overnight stay with Bedouin people in their tents. Many provide opportunities for visitors to help out in the Bedouin camp, helping with the goats, collecting wood or fetching water from the well. In Israel, the Tourism Ministry has been developing Bedouin tourism as a part of the desert's tourist attractions. As a result, in the past few years, there has been a steady increase in the number of visitors to the Bedouin settlements and markets. They also supported two women-empowerment projects – 'The Desert's

Embroidery' and 'Negev Weaving'. Their dream is to build a tourist village which will be run by women and present the Bedouin women's heritage. 'Negev Weaving' currently employs over 150 women (Hatzeira 2007).

However, many Bedouin no longer live in the desert. Since the late 1990s, there has been a boom in Bedouin tourism in Egypt's northern Eastern Desert. Yet, as almost no rain fell between 1997 and 2005, the Bedouin were pushed into the tourist trade. Most have left the desert, and have clustered in a dozen tourist mahattas (stations) in the desert, where tourists visit for a few hours (Hobbs and Tsunemi 2007). Many Bedouin people have become dependent on tourism, and are therefore badly affected by recession or terrorism. For example, following the bombing of the Taba area of the Sinai in 2007, the Bedouin of the South Sinai, who now work in transportation, construction, hotels and handmade crafts, have been hard hit, with one employee quoted as saying 'No tourists, no work, no money, no life'.

(Hazlett and Carter 2007)

Africa

African cultural tourism has been growing significantly in recent years. However, this is only in certain parts of Africa due to infrastructural restrictions, civil strife, health risks and poverty in many countries. Apart from North Africa, South Africa is one of the fastest growing destinations in the world. Alongside the safari and wildlife tourism, South Africa is home to numerous indigenous cultures, there are many world-famous wine growing regions, and many visitors are still fascinated by the post-apartheid tourism and townships (see case study in Chapter 3). Gambia has a fairly well developed tourism industry, but it has not been without its problems in the past. The organisation Gambia Tourism Concern was therefore set up to help establish a more ethical and sustainable form of tourism. This was mainly in response to the number of all-inclusive resorts which had been developed, from which few benefits went to the local destinations and their inhabitants. Some tourists may visit Gambia or other parts of West Africa for drumming and dance holidays (e.g. Senegal). Ethiopia has some World Heritage Sites and, as Abyssinia, its culture and traditions date back over 3000 years. Africa is still mainly associated with safari and wildlife tourism, but countries like Kenya, Tanzania, Namibia, Botswana, Zambia and Zimbawe (when politically stable) offer forms of ecotourism which also have a cultural dimension (e.g. village stays or tours). Maasai tourism in Kenya and Tanzania is already quite well developed, if not always sustainable (see Chapter 5 for a case study). The island of Zanzibar has the World Heritage Site of Stonetown, and there are also spice tours and village tours. Some of the other African islands such as Madagascar promote ecotourism, and the Seychelles and Mauritius focus more on beach tourism, although they have interesting Creole cultures.

Box 2.3

Case study of cultural tourism in Mali

Mali is one of the poorest countries in the world. It is home to a number of World Heritage Sites and it offers many cultural and ceremonial events which could attract tourists. Due to Mali's historical significance as a trading route and its rich music, dance and handicraft traditions, it is recognised as an up-and-coming destination. The Malian government is making it a priority to develop tourism, especially ecotourism and cultural tourism. The country is home to festivals and events which attract local tourists as well.

According to Mahamadou Keita of the Office of Tourism in Mali, tourism was rising by 4 per cent a year and over 80,000 tourists from Europe, North America and Asia make their way to Dogon country. Dogon Land, a World Heritage Site, is the jewel of Malian tourism, the main attraction for about 90 per cent of the tourists who visit Mali. For the past thousand years they have hidden themselves away from the world by carving their villages out of a spectacular 200-km-long cliff. 'The magic of Dogon country is its inaccessibility, which has protected the authenticity of the culture and the people till now' (Mali tourism officer). Today Dogon country is wide open to anyone with the money and wherewithal to get there. But Keita admits that Dogon culture, which withstood centuries of pressure from Islamic conquerors, Mandingo empire-builders, Fulani slave-seekers and Christian missionaries, is now taking a battering from the most pervasive influence of all – tourism. He cites the example of the Sigui dance of the masks, which is performed in great secrecy only once every 60 years, following the cosmology of the star Syrius, from which the Dogon believe they originally came. 'The next authentic Sigui dance is scheduled for 2020. But these days you can see the Dogon performing an imitation Sigui every day for tourists . . . It's like something you'd see at an airport.'

Keita says tourism demystifies rituals and fetish carvings, eroding all their meaning. Local people receive few benefits from tourism, tourists are being exploited by unofficial guides, and many local people are trying to sell every last remnant of their culture.

Aly Gundo, a local guide, issues a plea to tourists not to try to penetrate these very last sanctuaries of Dogon culture.

(adapted from Baxter 2001)

The Americas

Timothy and Boyd (2006) note that there are more than 144 World Heritage Sites in the Americas, with Mexico, Brazil then the USA having the most cultural sites. The most acclaimed are Macchu Picchu in Peru and Chitzen Itza in Mexico; however, many other countries have at least one WHS or more. It is noteworthy that the region's cultural heritage consists of a combination of pre-colonial, colonial and post-colonial periods. This includes the ancient heritage of the Mayans, Aztecs and Incas.

Central America has quite well developed indigenous ecotourism programmes in countries like Ecuador, Costa Rica, Guatemala, Bolivia and Belize. Many visitors are attracted by the colourful handicrafts of the indigenous peoples, and there are many crafts networks which help to protect traditional methods of production. Ecotours in the Amazon rainforests are also common in countries like Brazil. Numerous tourists come to Peru for the Macchu Pichu trail and to learn more about the ancient Inca culture. Cancun in Mexico is a brash example of where tourism has destroyed most of the cultural character of the region, except in places like Tulum with its unusually located, remaining Mayan heritage sites. However, inland Mexico also has many traditional towns and villages.

Many visitors are attracted to the cosmopolitanism of cities like Buenos Aires, and tango dancing has become increasingly popular all over the world in recent years. The popularity of films like *Evita* with Madonna has boosted the profile of Argentina in recent years. Brazil is visited for its infamous beach culture, but also for its world-famous Carnival (see Chapter 6 for a case study). The Statue of Christ in Rio also brings religious pilgrims. Chile is better known for its beautiful landscapes, but people are also interested in its culture, especially that of the Gauchos (or Patagonian cowboys).

North American cultural tourism ranges quite considerably from the visiting of Disney theme parks and Hollywood in the USA, to visiting national parks and Native American Indian reservations. As well as Native American Indian culture, Inuit culture is important in Canada, especially close to the Arctic. Inuit communities are generally characterised by a 'mixed economy', but tend to rely largely on income from domestic production, such as hunting, fishing, trapping and gathering. However, little cash is generated from domestic production, and unemployment is high. Tourism development may offer a significant economic opportunity for such communities, but care must be taken to develop this sector in a way that befits best the social and cultural structure of Inuit community life. Previous community-based tourism development initiatives in the Canadian Arctic have tended to be largely unsuccessful and 'unsustainable' in the long term due to a lack of internal control and community consensus. However, in 1983 the Government of the Northwest Territories (GNWT) established a 'community-based' tourism strategy which aimed to develop an environmentally and culturally sustainable form of tourism that maximised economic benefits for residents as a source of income and employment (GNWT 1983). Alaska has a large number of native peoples (around 16 per cent of the population), and rural village tourism and ecotourism are in development (see Chapter 5 for a case study).

In the USA, each state has its own diverse culture, and some visitors are interested in the indigenous culture of Native American Indians, as well as the 'Wild West' and 'Cowboy' cultures. Cities like New York, San Francisco and Los Angeles are some of the most culturally diverse in the world. New York has an amazing concentration of visual and performing arts. San Francisco is also known for its gay friendliness, and therefore attracts high numbers of gay tourists. In Canada, there is a Creative Cities

Network, and many cities can offer a truly multicultural experience such as Toronto or Vancouver, and Montréal and Québec with their Anglo-French culture. The historic district of Québec City is a World Heritage Site, and Montréal hosts one of the largest jazz festivals in the world.

Box 2.4

Case study of multicultural tourism in New Orleans

New Orleans in the state of Louisiana is well known for its multicultural and multilingual heritage, architecture, cuisine and music, especially jazz. It also has an annual Mardi Gras and other celebrations and festivals. New Orleans' heritage is American, Creole and Creole French. It is a place where Africans, both slaves and free, as well as American Indians intermingled with European settlers. The French government encouraged this, and made New Orleans a very distinctive place, which is often referred to as the 'most unique' city in America.

The music heritage in New Orleans comes from the fact that it was originally the only place in the New World where slaves were allowed to own drums. A culture of music and dancing emerged, and by the late 1880s jazz had become a popular form of music. Many of the world's first great jazz musicians and orchestras were formed here.

The cuisine is hybridised as a result of the French, African and American influences. For example, Cajun food is a country-style food, found along the bayous of Louisiana, a combination of French and Southern cuisines, and Creole food is a distinctive cuisine, created in New Orleans with European and African roots. In fact, Slater (2004) notes that in the past, the main branding focus for the state of Louisiana was its food.

The celebration of Mardi Gras came to North America from Paris, where it had been celebrated since the Middle Ages. The first black Mardi Gras organisation, the Original Illinois Club, was launched in 1894. Two years later, Les Mysterieuses, Carnival's first female group, was founded. One of the most popular krewes (or group floats) to make its appearance in the twentieth century was Zulu. There are also American Indian krewes. In the 1980s there was a tremendous increase in tourism during the Carnival season. Mardi Gras became a year-round industry as more off-season conventions were able to enjoy a taste of Carnival when they were treated to mini-parades and balls held in the city's convention facilities

(The Official Tourism Site of the City of New Orleans 2009)

The Caribbean islands have traditionally been popular with visitors wishing to enjoy beach or nature tourism, with special packages including honeymoons or spa visits. However, all Caribbean islands have a different colonial history (e.g. British, French, Dutch, Spanish), and many visitors may be interested in this legacy which is often present in food, language and architecture. Caribbean culture is also much enjoyed for its relaxed pace of life and *joie de vivre*, which is fairly uncommon in more frenetic societies. Reggae music, drinking and dancing are part of the appeal of the Caribbean, as well as the warmth and hospitality of the people. The film *Pirates of the Caribbean* and its sequels have done much to boost tourism in the region. Cuba has a special appeal because of its Communist system, and many people are interested in the lifestyle of the people there. Although it is restricted, the faded grandeur of cities like Havana and Santiago with their vibrant salsa culture, cuban cigars and golden rum are enough to draw large numbers of visitors.

Hawaii has been visited for years by tourists from all over the world, but mostly from the USA. Unfortunately it has been through typical tourism cycles of saturation, decline and the commodification of indigenous Hawaiian culture. The ubiquitous sight of dancing Hula Hula girls was evidence of this. However, in recent years, there has been an attempt to renew local cultural pride in traditions and to reinstate some degree of 'authenticity'(Pacific Island Travel 2007).

Asia

Asia is clearly a rich and diverse region, and it is hard to generalise about the cultural resources there. Even within the countries of the former Soviet Union there is huge variation. Some of the newly formed countries are still struggling with infrastructural and attractions development. Gruner (2007) describes Tajikistan as having poor roads, unsafe taxis and street crime, and Turkmenistan as having a dull landscape, harsh winters and blazing hot summers. However, many of them – Georgia, for example – are developing tourism relatively successfully. Some intrepid tourists take the Trans-Siberian Express which runs from Moscow through the Ural Mountains to Vladivostok, a total of 6000 miles. Although the landscape is the main attraction, many tourists also stop off on the way to enjoy cultural activities. This can include visiting Moscow at the beginning or end, and branching off to Ulan Bator in Mongolia, as well as the 'Paris of Siberia', Irkutsk, or Kazan with its World Heritage Site Kremlin Fortress.

India is an incredibly diverse country, and many people spend months travelling around this 'subcontinent'. However, for the majority of tourists, a one- or two-week tour of the main palaces, forts and temples is rewarding enough, and India has numerous World Heritage Sites. The deserts of Rajastan are also visited by tourists who may wish to camel trek and encounter village cultures. Many visitors go to India because of its spiritual atmosphere and may spend a length of time in an ashram, meditation or yoga centre. The Ayurvedic healing tradition in Kerala, southern India, is also growing in popularity. The mountain regions of India can also offer opportunities to enjoy local culture, as can Nepal, Tibet and Bhutan.

Sri Lanka has been plagued by political problems and civil strife for many years, and in 2004 it was hit by a devastating tsunami. The combination of traditional Buddhist culture, temples, ancient city ruins, rock temples and colonial architecture make it a destination popular for cultural tourism as well as beach and wildlife tourism.

Plate 2.2 Temple complex in Nepal

(Source: Melvyn Smith)

The Maldives consists of over 1200 islands, and although they are best known for their stunning beaches, they can also offer cultural experiences. This might include visiting fishing villages or going out fishing with fishermen, visiting cultural centres and buying handicrafts. However, the Maldives generally keeps its tourists and its local people quite separate in order to avoid adverse impacts. This means that tourists can visit inhabited islands outside the tourist zone only by invitation.

South-east Asia has been one of the fastest growing regions of the world in recent years, and countries like Thailand, Vietnam and Laos are becoming increasingly popular. Buddhist culture is often attractive because of its beautiful temples, serene monks and meditation possiblities. Hilltribe trekking is becoming more popular: tourists are increasingly taken into the hilltribe country of northern Thailand in the region of Chiang Mai and Chiang Rai. Most of the trips involve a two- or three-day trek with a local guide through jungle areas and include overnight stays in tribal villages. The activities offered are mainly hiking, bamboo rafting and elephant riding. Cambodia attracts many tourists to Angkor Wat, but also to the genocide site 'The Killing Fields'. Burma, or Myanmar, is currently governed by an oppressive military regime, therefore tourism is limited and strictly controlled.

Malaysia is a very culturally diverse country with many ethnic groups, including Malay, Chinese and Indian cultures, the indigenous cultures of Sarawak and Sabah, as well as the colonial legacy of many European countries (see Box 1.2 for a case study of a multi-cultural festival and Box 3.4 for a case study of colonial tours in Malaysia). Tourism Malaysia promotes the country's spirituality in response to foreign interest in religious diversity, and tourists are invited to tour Islamic mosques, Christian churches, Indian and Chinese temples, Sikh gurdwaras and other spiritual sites around the country. The Iban are the largest ethnic group in Sarawak, Borneo, and their longhouses and villages are visited as part of river safari cruises. Some areas have been visited by tour groups since the 1960s. Tourists usually spend one or two nights in longhouse accommodation and are often invited to eat with the resident hosts. Activities include jungle walks, cultural performances (e.g. dances, music, songs), handicrafts shopping and witnessing special events and ceremonies. Singapore has a colonial heritage which is popular with visitors, in particular there is the world-famous Raffles Hotel.

Indonesia has popular destinations such as Bali. Despite the Bali bombings in 2002 and 2005, tourists continue to visit and enjoy not only the beaches, but the cultural attractions too. Toraja, Prambanan and Borobudur temples, Yogyakarta and Minangkabau are popular destinations for cultural tourism, as well as the many Hindu festivities.

The Philippines form an archipelago of 7107 islands which stretch from the south of China to the northern tip of Borneo. There are more than 100 ethnic groups as well as the multicultural mixture of Indo-Malay, Chinese, Spanish and American influences. They are best known for beach tourism (e.g. Boracay). However, the potential for cultural tourism is considerable, and the Philippines has one of the world's first 'eco-cultural destinations' in Bohol (Bohol Tourism 2009).

China is one of the biggest growth destinations in the world, and has more than 30 World Heritage Sites, numerous cultural cities, diverse ethnic groups and festivals. Taiwan is a quickly modernising country, but its traditional culture is still promoted. It has historic monuments and temples, numerous festivals and events, and world-class museums; for example, Taipei's National Palace Museum is ranked as one of the four best museums in the world, and is home to the largest collection of Chinese art in the world. The collection is so vast that it takes 12 years to display everything (the displays are rotated regularly). Japan has many World Heritage Sites, including ancient cities like Kyoto, sacred temples and pilgrimage sites, as well as war memorials such as that at Hiroshima. Many visitors are attracted by the famous cherry blossom ceremonies, Geisha culture and rituals, and the concept of Zen. Japan is also very rich in hot thermal and vulcanic waters and its onsens (ritual bathing establishments) are representative of tradition and heritage.

Mongolia is a destination which is increasing in popularity. Although much of the tourism is based on landscape and horse riding, many visitors stay in yurts with local people and learn more about their culture and lifestyle (see Box 2.5).

Plate 2.3 Naadam festival, Mongolia

(Source: Georgina Smith)

Box 2.5

Case study of the Naadam festival in Mongolia

The Naadam festival is the biggest and most joyful festival of the year for Mongolians. It takes place in July each year. The festival originated from the era of the Khunnu Empire and was originally organised as a competition to test the skills of Mongolian warriors of different tribes. Since 1921, Naadam has been held to commemorate Mongolia's revolution of independence. The 2006 National Naadam was introduced as the 85th anniversary of the revolution and the 800th celebration of Mongolian statehood. It runs for three days in all parts of the country and highlights the 'Three Manly Sports': wrestling, horse racing and archery, Mongolia's most popular sports. Women participate in all but the wrestling category. The word *Naadam* means game or competition in Mongolian. Competitions take place on the first two days and merry-making on the third.

The festivities start with a colourful parade of athletes, monks, marching soldiers, musicians playing military tunes, and Mongolians dressed in Genghis-style warrior uniforms. A fascinating and interesting event for all is where the nine White Flags of Genghis Khan are carried in a ceremonial parade from the State Parliament House to the Central Stadium. Wrestlers compete on the green field of the State Central Stadium – there is no time limit, and no weight category. There are six different categories of horse racing depending on the age of horses; the distance of the race ranges from 15 to 30 km. Archery, originating from time immemorial, is the oldest sport of the Mongols. Traditionally, this was only men's sport but nowadays both men and women compete in separate divisions.

Rushby (2008) notes that in Mongolia, the Naadam is like the Olympics, the Grand National and Christmas, all rolled into one. It is celebrated in every town, village and nomadic encampment. Missing it is unthinkable!

(Mongululs.net 2009)

Australia, New Zealand and the South Pacific

Although the cities of Australia and New Zealand offer a number of diverse cultural experiences, especially in Sydney and Wellington, the countries are perhaps better known for their amazing landscapes, including the coast. Australia has quite a distinctive bush or outback culture, and New Zealand has its unique geography of mountains, volcanoes and hot springs. However, the traditional heritage of the indigenous Aborigines in Australia and Maori in New Zealand is consistently used in the cultural tourism marketing of these two countries.

Maori have been involved in New Zealand's tourism industry for over 140 years, and much of this development has been in the Rotorua region in the North Island. Like many countries with a colonial past, the Maori and Pakeha (white settler) relationship has been somewhat fraught at times. Whereas many of the earliest tourism initiatives came from the Maori themselves (e.g. accommodation, guiding, transport), many were displaced by Pakeha in later years (Barnett 1997). The resurgence of interest in Maori culture over the past 20 years or so has led to the recognition of the importance for Maori control over tourism development, cultural production and the authentic representation of Maori culture. Since the 1990s, the Aotearoa Maori Tourism Federation has tried to represent Maori interests and to protect Maori culture. Maori are now owners and managers of an increasing number of tourism ventures (e.g. accommodation, attractions, transport, tours). Maori have been bathing in the geothermal muds and sulphurous waters of New Zealand for over 700 years for healing reasons, therefore they have also been involved in spa tourism development (e.g. the Polynesian Spa in Rotorua and Hell's Gate Wai Ora).

The situation of Aboriginal people in Australia has not been quite so politically advanced, and many social problems still exist among Aboriginal peoples. However, there is worldwide interest in Aboriginal culture, especially the arts (e.g. painting and crafts). A case study of Aboriginal arts tourism is given in Chapter 5.

The South Pacific islands are perhaps better known for their stunning beaches than for their culture; however, they are immensely rich in indigenous cultures and they also have a colonial legacy. Ecotourism is becoming more popular there, and includes tours led by local people, homestays and village tourism (see Box 2.6).

Box 2.6

Case study of cultural tourism on the islands of the South Pacific

Zeppel (2006) discusses numerous village ecotourism ventures in community-owned forests in the Solomon Islands, Fiji, Vanuatu, Papua New Guinea, Samoa and Micronesia. Most of these islands rely on foreign aid, agriculture, fishing, logging and tourism for income. On these islands and others (e.g. the Cook Islands, New Caledonia) tourism can account for up to 50 per cent of GDP. However, because of the remoteness of the islands, they tend to attract only one tenth of the number of visitors who go to the Caribbean.

Home-stay visits are becoming more popular as well as village-based tourism. Small-scale community ecotourism projects, such as village guest houses, ecolodges and rainforest walking tours have been developed in the Solomon Islands, Fiji, Vanuatu, Samoa and some other countries. Income is provided for villagers and communities are given an incentive to conserve their unique and sometimes fragile environment. Most village or tribal chiefs prefer tourism to be community-based rather than run by individuals or families.

Unfortunately, however, development is limited in some countries (e.g. Kiribati, Pohnpei and Niue) because of their remoteness, difficulties of access, low visitor numbers and lack of training, funding and marketing. Overall, development is largely dependent on donor assistance (e.g. from Australia, Japan, New Zealand) and support from conservation NGOs. Most community ecotourism projects in conservation areas therefore tend to focus on landscape, wildlife and scenery rather than indigenous cultural traditions. However, crafts, music, dance and other traditional cultural practices can be supported or revived through village ecotourism.

(adapted from Zeppel 2006)

Conclusion

This chapter has demonstrated the diversity of cultural tourism throughout the different regions and countries of the world. There are few countries which have no cultural tourism, although many combine it with eco- or nature tourism. Visitors may be drawn to certain locations because of their World Heritage Sites, or for their colourful indigenous cultures. Few areas of the world are completely inaccessible, although it is clearly more difficult for small, remote islands (e.g. those in the Pacific) to attract visitors. Although many tribal groups are keen to work in tourism, this can have adverse impacts when tourism is affected by terrorism or a natural disaster (e.g. the case of the Bedouins in the Sinai). This can leave local people without a livelihood. Visitors are becoming more attracted by the lives and lifestyles of people, so indigenous cultural tourism is growing quickly. As the World Heritage Site List starts to include more intangible sites in less developed countries (see also Chapter 4), the distribution of heritage tourists is also likely to change. This does not mean that the classic cultural cities, towns and monuments of Europe will become neglected, because these are also still visited in large numbers, even over-visited. Tourists will, however, be able to choose from an even more vast array of cultural destinations, activities and experiences, which can greatly enrich their lives and, it is hoped, the lives of their hosts.

3 The politics of global cultural tourism

> We can talk of the globalising of the tourist gaze, as multiple gazes have become core to global cultures sweeping up almost everywhere in their awesome wake.
>
> (Urry 2002: 161)

Introduction

This chapter focuses on the globalisation of cultural tourism, recognising that different regions and countries of the world have developed in different ways as a result of their complex histories and political trajectories. Although it is difficult to generalise, this chapter attempts to provide an overview of those countries which have had a similar history (e.g. post-colonial countries, countries with aboriginal or indigenous peoples, former socialist countries, newly emergent nation states), and to consider typical patterns of cultural tourism development in those countries. It also briefly analyses those countries which have been involved in religious conflicts and the impacts this has on tourism. The framework for the chapter begins with a discussion of globalisation, including the extent to which tourism can be described as a new form of imperialism.

Globalisation and tourism

Socio-analytic cultural theories in recent decades have tended to focus on globalisation, clearly not a new phenomenon, but one which has arguably increased in intensity in the wake of new media, technology, communications and transport developments. The world is apparently becoming a smaller place because of instantaneous transactions and communications, increased and faster travel, and technological innovations. English is becoming the global language, and culture is becoming more and more dominated by American or Western European models.

Barber (1992, 1995) suggests that there is a parallel but conflictual process occurring in the world. He states that just as the planet is falling apart because of cultural conflicts, it is also coming together (often reluctantly) as a result of the process of globalisation. This is a process which he terms 'Jihad' versus 'McWorld'. The former represents a revival of protectionism whereby nation states, regions, tribes and other groups assert their cultural autonomy and identity, often willing to fight to the death for them. On the other hand, McWorld is a uniform, integrated world of fast food, fast music, fast computers and other globalised, standardised products. He cites examples of countries like Yugoslavia, which were exploding into fragments just as they were applying to join the EU. The Soviet Union disappeared almost overnight, only to be replaced by many new nations demanding independence and autonomy. While India tries to maintain its status as the world's most integrated democracy, powerful new fundamentalist parties like the Hindu nationalist Bharatiya Janata Party, along with nationalist assassins, are threatening this unity. Interestingly, Barber (1992) describes how 'McWorld does manage to look pretty seductive in a world obsessed with Jihad. It delivers peace, prosperity, and relative unity – if at the cost of independence, community, and identity.'

However, the globalisation process is clearly an uneven and unequal one; as stated by Li (2000), globalisation is not truly global. The global economy tends to be led by a limited number of predominantly Western nations and corporations, who control and standardise economic and cultural production. There are therefore concerns that globalisation benefits only certain communities of the world and marginalises others, and it can have a significant impact on regional and local cultures, traditions and languages. Despite the apparent democratisation of culture, the world of global politics, media, communication and technology is a polarised one in which only a minority can truly participate. The majority of developing countries are afforded few opportunities to play their part in the global economy, except perhaps through tourism. Even then, this is likely to be only in terms of hosting rather than generating tourism. The contrast is particularly stark in some of the world's poorest destinations. For example, in the remote villages of Rajasthan in the middle of the Thar desert in India, foreign trekkers are able to purchase Coke and Fanta from the coolbox-carrying villagers, many of whom have barely enough water to survive and have to travel several kilometres a day in order to collect this precious commodity. The same is true of the isolated jungle areas in northern Thailand, where the global brand is omnipresent, yet local villagers are only just subsistent. The globalisation of tourism has partially exacerbated the relationships of inequality and subservience that are so commonplace in host–guest encounters. It is not simply enough for local people to accept their role as servants, guides or companions to a range of ever-changing tourists. They are also confronted increasingly by the luxurious global products of Western indulgence which remain far from their reach, rather like the thirsty Tantalus in his elusive pool of water. The juxtaposition of local poverty and global wealth may appear to be an inherent part of tourism, but it need not remain that way.

As the world becomes increasingly globalised, some might argue that culture is becoming more standardised or homogeneous. However, despite the well-documented negative impacts, post-war decolonisation, mass immigration and the growth of international tourism have all contributed to an enrichment of the world's cultures, leading to a profusion of cultural diversity, and the creation of new, cosmopolitan cultural forms. Globalisation is clearly a complex and apparently contradictory phenomenon, which helps to create new spaces of commonality, but also new spaces of difference. It may be viewed as a creative process which leads to the hybridisation of different cultural forms, but it can also be considered in terms of the homogenisation or standardisation of culture. Cultural hybridisation is arguably the exciting and liberating face of globalisation, whereby new cultural forms are created through the fusion of diverse elements. This is particularly evident in Western food, fashion and music, for example, where ethnic influences are becoming more and more pervasive.

Culture can be incredibly mobile and universally available, but it can also be quite localised. Meethan (2001: 135) states that 'The idea of cultures as being both mobile and place bound is . . . fundamental to the whole notion of cultural globalisation.' People may be able to do virtual tours of the world's museums, enjoy culture via travel shows from their armchair, or buy indigenous art on the internet. However, there are many activities which cannot easily be experienced except in the 'home' of that culture, or which are not easily 'mediatised'. Although people enjoy simulated experiences and displaced creative activities, for cultural tourists there is no substitute for a (perceived) authentic and interactive experience within a unique cultural environment.

However, almost everywhere and everything is now becoming accessible to tourists. Urry provides a detailed discussion of the globalisation of the gaze, and he outlines the many gazes that have been adopted by tourists throughout the history of tourism and in recent times: 'There has been a massive shift from a more or less single tourist gaze in the 19th Century to the proliferation of countless discourses, forms and embodiments of tourist gazes now' (2002: 160). Graham *et al.* (2000: 238) describe how (cultural) tourism development has been instrumental in 'globalising' heritage:

> It can be argued that the inexorable growth of foreign tourism, and the importance of culture, heritage and art to that industry, is the most powerful expression of the existence of a common global heritage as the property of all peoples. Every international tourist is asserting the existence of a world heritage and the right of a global accessibility to it.

Managing global attractions: World Heritage Sites

As a result of the perceived fragility of the world's heritage, a number of global measures have been taken to protect such sites and attractions from the ravages of 'mass cultural tourism'. The most significant of these is the establishment of the World Heritage List. In 1972, UNESCO adopted the World Heritage Convention in order to protect cultural and natural heritage worldwide, and to provide organised international support for the protection of World Heritage Sites. The member states, which contribute funding to UNESCO, ratify this document, which is then managed by the World Heritage Committee. The Convention protects heritage sites of 'outstanding universal value'. Politically, World Heritage status necessarily transcends national boundaries. As stated by Graham *et al.* (2000: 97):

> Internationally, UNESCO, particularly through the medium of World Heritage Sites, pits the ideas of universal heritage values (themselves at times the subject of intractable dissonances) against the self-interest of the various host states, chiefly concerned with national-scale priorities.

The 'globalisation' of heritage could be perceived as being a source of dissonance (Graham *et al.* 2000), especially in terms of local ownership (collective or otherwise) and interpretation. Tunbridge and Ashworth (1996) have argued that all heritage is dissonant, and that the designation of sites is often used by nation states as a means of engaging in national aggrandisement, as well as being an assertion of Eurocentricity on the part of international agencies. They emphasise the discordance between heritage identity and local developments. Clearly, the development from a local monument, park or town to an internationally recognised symbol can be problematic. The subtle social, cultural and political implications of the transformation of sites into global tourist attractions and, by implication, visual signifiers or branding tools, requires further analysis, especially in terms of local dissonance. Evans (2001: 226) emphasises the need to reconcile national and local needs as part of global heritage tourism management. The focus on world and symbolic heritage sites in the cities of both developed and developing countries requires that a balance be struck between local and national imperatives – qualities of life, economic and physical access, minimising gentrification effects and the imposition of 'staged authenticity' in terms of the heritage that is conserved (see Box 3.1).

Box 3.1

Case study of World Heritage Sites in China: global/local and East/West challenges

World Heritage Sites in some of the emergent cultural tourism destinations of the world present particular challenges. China is a good case in point, as many of the WHSs were initially not visited very much at all, then subsequently by domestic visitors as the country opened up. However, since the mid-1980s international visitors have been coming in ever increasing numbers, and it becomes a new challenge providing the right form of interpretation to inform both domestic and international visitors simultaneously. One of the main issues is that Chinese and Western visitors may have very different cultural expectations and perceptions of the site. Western visitors may need far more cultural information; for example, there is a need for new interpretation and signage which does not rely on visitors' (often non-existent) knowledge of Chinese culture. They may also miss colour symbolism, or references to mythology and spirituality if they are not informed of their significance.

Li and Sofield (2006) note that this is all true at the site of Huangshan, where the differing philosophies of Chinese and Western agencies are very much in evidence in the management of the site. Such a landscape has considerable cultural and spiritual significance for the Chinese, whereas Westerners may see it as merely a natural landscape (this can include those agencies inscribing and managing the site, as well as international visitors). The Chinese have more anthropocentrically oriented values, which see no problems with creating facilities and services for visitors within the WHS boundaries. Western agencies, on the other hand, have difficulties accepting the intrusion of man-made structures on landscape. Adding to existing heritage (e.g. using the ancient art of calligraphy) may be seen as acceptable, as it is a continuous cultural process, whereas Westerners tend to separate past and present.

Tourism: a new form of global imperialism?

Tourism has clearly become a global force dominated mainly by Western developed nations whose globe-trotting citizens have left few places unexplored. Only the remotest locations of the world are 'safe' from tourism, but even then, other global forces look set to encroach on such environments if tourism does not get there first. Tourism, and especially cultural tourism, has become a force to be reckoned with, irrevocably transforming destinations, traditions and lifestyles. For this reason, cultural tourism has become increasingly politicised as governments weigh up the advantages and disadvantages of this potentially lucrative industry, often viewing it as their sole economic option if they wish to compete in the global arena. The environmental and socio-cultural consequences of such decisions are often overlooked; hence it falls to the communities themselves to protect their own interests, usually with inadequate political support.

The debate about whether tourism is like a new form of imperialism has been prominent since the 1970s (see e.g. Turner and Ash 1975; Nash 1977). There is justifiable concern that tourism is, and will remain for the foreseeable future, dominated by Western developed nations, rendering host nations dependent and subservient to its needs. Tourism still flows predominantly from the developed to the developing world. The majority of the world's population, particularly in some of the poorest nations, will never have the chance to venture outside their country, nor perhaps even their home town or village. Hence local people are stationary in both a physical and material sense, and they are often condemned to a life of serving mobile, free-spending Western tourists. The psychological effects of such an unequal relationship are arguably as significant as the socio-economic problems they engender.

Many of the theories relating to the discussion about tourism as a new form of imperialism have their origins in economic development theory. Economists have focused traditionally on core–periphery theory and the growth–dependency relationships between host nations and their Western 'benefactors'. Dependency is viewed as a process whereby the indigenous economy of a developing country becomes reorientated towards serving the needs of exogenous markets (Hall 1994). Mowforth and Munt (1998) describe how Western capitalist countries have grown as a result of expropriating surpluses from developing countries, which are largely dependent on export-orientated industries (e.g. bananas and coffee). The notion of core–periphery relationships is used within dependency theory to highlight this unequal, often exploitative relationship. Nash (1989) describes imperialism as the expansion of a society's interest abroad. Metropolitan centres or cores (usually former imperial nations) exercise their power over peripheral nations or regions of the world. This debate is particularly pertinent to former colonies such as the Caribbean where tourism appears to be reasserting itself as a new form of colonialism. Burns (1999: 157) describes how for dependency theorists development and underdevelopment are two sides of the same coin: surpluses from the exploited countries generated first through mercantilism and later through colonialism, had the combined effect of developing the metropolitan countries and under-developing the peripheral countries.

Mathieson and Wall (1992) suggest that three economic conditions substantiate the claim that tourism is a new form of imperialism or colonialism. These are:

1 Developing countries grow to depend on tourism as a means of securing revenue.
2 A large proportion of expenditures and profits flow back to foreign investors and high leakages occur.
3 Non-locals are employed in professional and managerial positions.

Hall (1994) suggests that the extent to which tourism will be viewed as a form of imperialism or economic dependency is determined by the nature of the relationship between the metropolitan centre and the periphery. If it is a hegemonic relationship, its influence will be pervasive in both social and cultural spheres. For example, local people may be unquestioning in their subservience to tourists, since it is viewed as being an inherent, often inherited part of their social and cultural norms.

However, in many ways, it is too simplistic to talk about tourism paralleling the processes of imperialism. As stated by Lanfant (1995: 5):

> the tourist system of action is not a monolithic force. It would be pointless to seize upon it as if it were a hegemonic and imperialistic power perpetuating disguised neo-colonialism. The system is a network of agents: these tap a variety of motivations which are difficult to define and which in concrete situations often contradict each other.

Glocalisation and tourism

Richards (2005) describes how the processes of globalisation and localisation are providing new platforms from which to view tourism, as well as new conceptual viewpoints for tourists and locals. He notes that in the face of globalisation, the local is remarkably persistent. The interface between the global and the local need not necessarily be negative. The word 'glocalisation' has become common parlance in recent years. It might best be described as the relationship between global and local processes, which are increasingly viewed as two sides to the same coin rather than being diametrically opposed (e.g. Robertson 1992). Glocalisation represents the intersection of political, economics and socio-cultural concerns, with its emphasis on the local and community impacts of global structures and processes. Ritzer (2004: 73) defines glocalisation as 'the interpretation of the global and the local resulting in unique outcomes in different geographic areas'. Glocalisation can thus represent the consequences (both tangible and intangible) of globalisation; for example, the creation of heterogeneous or hybridised cultures, communities and identities. In the context of global tourism, international visitors are brought into contact with local environments and their communities, thus influencing cross-cultural exchange. Tourism can also sometimes help to strengthen the importance of retaining place identities and local character.

Nevertheless, glocalisation could also be viewed somewhat negatively. For example, Bauman (1998) suggests that the term glocalisation is best thought of as a restratification of society based on the free mobility of some and the place-bound existence of others. Tourist flows, for example, are mainly uni-directional (e.g. West to East, or developed to less developed countries). For this reason, tourism has sometimes been described as a new form of imperialism, which causes acculturation and radical social change rather than hybridisation (the inevitable consequence of sustained foreign influence over time). Similarly, global economic and business developments are often deemed 'imperialistic', even where they have a local orientation.

However, Ritzer (2004) suggests that this dominance of capitalist nations and organisations might be termed 'grobalisation' rather than 'glocalisation'. He argues, like Robertson (1994), that the key characteristics of glocalisation are sensitivity to differences, the embracing of cosmopolitanism, and respect for the autonomy and creativity of individuals and groups. The notion that the local is largely passive in the face of globalisation is therefore a misrepresentation. Friedman (1999) sees 'healthy glocalisation' as a process by which local communities incorporate aspects of foreign cultures that enrich them, but reject others that would negatively affect their traditions or identity.

Overall, therefore, glocalisation could be seen as a positive interpretation of the local impacts of globalisation, that is a process by which communities represent and assert their unique cultures globally, often through new media (Smith 2005a).

History and politics: the shaping of cultural tourism

The world can be divided into a number of regions which share similar characteristics and resources. Individual countries and regions still have their cultural specificities, but sometimes historical processes and political oppression have limited the extent to which nation states could express their cultures. This is especially true of those countries which were frequently colonised or which lived under restrictive political regimes. However, there are also cases of countries and regions which are in the midst of constant political conflict, which may only occasionally affect tourism. For example, the struggles of the Catalonians in Spain to be autonomous, or the Basque region, where bombings have sometimes threatened tourism. Corsicans have physically resisted tourism development in the past as part of their battle for independence from France. In these cases, political conflict is not part of the attraction of the destination, nor is it a major hindrance to development. In other cases, politics may have a more significant impact on tourism.

Tourism and political regimes

Cultural tourism is growing in Cuba because of the world's passion for salsa and Cuban music. This is coupled with a fascination for a political regime which is likely to die with Castro, resulting in an inevitable 'Americanisation' of Cuba. The novelty has been intensified now that there are few 'bastions' of Communism left since the dissolution of Central and Eastern Europe in 1989. One of the other very few remaining Communist countries is North Korea, where tourism is highly controlled by the government. As a result, it is not a frequently visited destination – only a small number of Western tourists visit North Korea each year, along with larger numbers of Chinese and other Asians. Tourists must go on guided tours and have their tour guides with them at all times. Photography is strictly controlled as is interaction with the local population. Visitors are not allowed to travel outside designated tour areas without their Korean guides

Burma, also known as Myanmar, is ruled by a military junta which uses its power to oppress and terrorise the people. Some tourists choose to visit Myanmar despite the pleas of the democratically elected leader, Aung San Suu Kyi (who has been imprisoned and restricted since the late 1980s), not to support the Junta by visiting. Tourism Concern has been regularly campaigning to stop Lonely Planet guidebooks encouraging visitation to Myanmar. Those who do visit are taken only to selected places and are unable to travel freely.

Many visitors were fascinated by South Africa in the early post-apartheid era, as they were curious (and mostly horrified) by the legacy of the political system. Richards (2007) and Ramchander (2007) suggest that although tourists may not be attracted to township life in South Africa, they are somehow nostalgic about passing history (see Box 3.2).

Box 3.2

Case study of township tourism in South Africa

Townships were established in South Africa under the apartheid regime away from central business districts as a means of segregating black labour. During this time, such townships were regarded as 'no-go' areas due to perceived high levels of crime and violence. 'White' and 'black' areas were strictly segregated. However, since the end of apartheid and the first democratic elections in 1994 township tourism has been growing rapidly, with many cultural tourists curious to see how post-apartheid life has developed. Ramchander (2007: 41) describes township tourism as 'traveling for the purpose of observing the cultural expression and lifestyles of black South Africans and offers firsthand experience of the practices of another culture'. Tourists usually visit in a minibus in small groups (up to 15), and are often surprised by the vibrancy that greets them contrary to expectations of poverty and crime. Tourists can choose to stay in bed-and-breakfast accommodation, but this is less common than a shorter excursion. They are usually taken to eat in carefully selected places (e.g. 'safe' shebeens or taverns), drink and dance in certain bars, buy souvenirs from arts and crafts centres, and can visit traditional healers.

Township tourism can provide employment and entrepreneurial opportunities to many black South Africans who were previously excluded from the tourism industry. Ramchander (2007) describes how Soweto has become the best known township as it was the centre of the anti-apartheid movement and symbolises political freedom to people around the world. Tourists can visit sites which are directly connected to the struggles and hold many memories. Most cultural tourists want to see 'real' people and experience authentic culture, but township residents see tourism as a mixed blessing. It can create economic benefits and cross-cultural exchange, including white and black interaction, but it also can cause friction, commercialisation, demonstration effect (i.e. where local residents copy the behaviour of tourists) and inflated prices. Tours can become like a kind of 'drive through safari' or a human zoo.

> However, if township tourism is managed well, it can create new careers in tourism, especially for young people. Many previously disempowered women have been able to become involved in hospitality or arts-and-crafts production. Nevertheless, tour operators need to include local residents and funds and grants for entrepreneurship should be provided by governments. Consultation of residents is essential and gaining their consent is imperative.
>
> (Briedenhann and Ramchander 2006; Ramchander 2007)

After the fall of Communism, many Central and East European (CEE) countries were keen to join the EU and the euro system as soon as possible. It was thought that this would partly enhance their image and attract tourists. However, Javrova (2005) states that European integration has been difficult for many accession countries, who are still defining their own identities before they can embark on European projects relating to common policy. Despite EU accession, there is more of a desire to promote national diversity than to sell a common Central European heritage. Almost half a century in an ideological 'bloc' left CEE countries with suppressed national and regional identities. Political freedom was not permitted and cultural expression was often censored. However, for the newly independent CEE countries of the 1990s, there was a clear desire to re-assert individuality and difference. Tourism can play an important role in this assertion of identity. Graham *et al.* (2000) describe how many Central and Eastern European countries have rediscovered their national heritage from the pre-Communist era, and are even harking back to their formal imperial greatness (e.g. Hungary):

> the wider recent experiences of Central and Eastern Europe serve to perpetuate compelling evidence of the enduring significance of nationalism as the primary mode of identity and national heritage as a principal means of delineating and representing that identity.
>
> (Graham *et al.* 2000: 69)

However, most CEE countries and Baltic states are still capitalising on their Communist past, partly because of visitor interest, and partly for educational or memorial reasons (see Box 3.3). Rátz (2006: 255) describes for example how the House of Terror in Budapest reflects 'the ghosts of the country's unsettled past', and serves as a memorial for the victims of the Communist regime as well as a warning for future generations.

Box 3.3

Case study of Stalin World, Lithuania

Grūtas Park is an open-air museum that collects and showcases relics, bronze busts and memorabilia of Lithuania's tragic Soviet past. Located some 40 minutes outside the capital city of Vilnius, Stalin World draws large numbers of tourists with its Soviet statues and communist souvenirs. The park opened in April 2001 and spans 50 acres. Next to the sculptures, monuments and paintings is a merry-go-round, a restaurant and a small zoo.

The attraction mainly commemorates Stalin's murderous regime. Visitors learn that, during the Nazi and Soviet occupations, Lithuania saw the murder and expulsion of hundreds of thousands of Jews and more than 500,000 Lithuanians, many of whom were either deported, exiled, jailed or shot. There are gigantic statues of Lenin, Marx and Stalin, a museum of communist propaganda and a train carriage which was used to deport Lithuanians to remote parts of Siberia. Some 28 million people passed through Gulag camps.

Park founder and owner Viliumas Malinauskas, a Lithuanian millionaire, opened this private park to teach new generations about the horrors of the past. The aim of Grütas Park is to remind people what life was like living under a dictatorship, so history will never be repeated. He states: 'People can come here and joke about these grim statues. This means that Lithuania is no longer afraid of communism.' He also points out to critics that 63 per cent of Lithuanians were in favour of the park being built. The park receives about 200,000 visitors annually – a number Malinauskas said was increasing by 20,000 per year – and employs 80 people. Groups of schoolchildren visit the park, and it is also popular with families. 'It isn't profitable,' says Malinauskas, 'but it isn't losing money either.'

Dimon (2008) questions whether the park really commemorates or just commodifies. Some have bitterly criticised it as an affront to the those deported or killed during the Soviet occupation, which started during the Second World War. At one time there were plans to have visitors herded into a reception centre by guides dressed as Red Army soldiers! As a family day out, critics say, it represents an unpalatable cross between Disneyland and the Gulag.

(Dapkus 2006)

Post-colonial countries

The flows of Western tourists often go in the direction of former colonies, perhaps because of a nostalgia for a former, more 'glorious' era in a country's history, or simply as a result of the familiarity of language, architecture, cuisine and other legacies. Therefore the British enjoy trips to India, the Spanish visit South America, the French go to Vietnam, etc. Post-imperial European societies have struggled to come to terms with the decline of their empires and their global dominance. Craik (1994) notes that ex-colonies have increased in popularity, and the 'detritus' of post-colonialism has been transformed into tourist sites. Hall and Tucker (2004) suggest that many post-colonial islands are described as 'paradise', which merely reinforces Western ideas of a romantic other, and erotic or sexual imagery may also be used of local 'exotic' people. The majority of authors in Hall and Tucker (2004) show how colonial thinking and discourse are far from over in contemporary tourism, especially as many Europeans may be nostalgic about imperialism, and may idealise it. As a result, they are attracted by their own myths and fantasies about colonial landscapes, buildings and people. Wels (2004: 77) describes how many Europeans have a romanticised view of how the African landscape should look, for example, with 'huts and women with buckets on their head'. Local people, on the other hand, may be quite happy to remove the colonial legacy and start afresh. For example, Fisher (2004) cites the case of Levuka in Fiji, where many non-European local residents believe that old colonial buildings should be knocked down and replaced by functional ones. Very few consider them to be representative of Fijian history. They also believe that the place where buildings were located would somehow retain their spirit or 'mana' regardless of whether the buildings were still there.

Henderson (2004) writes of colonial history in Malaysia, which is quite diverse, with architecture reflecting the Portuguese, Dutch, French and British legacies. She notes that the post-colonial government's job was further complicated by the diverse ethnic communities in Malaysia (Chinese, Indian and Malay, among others), as well as different religions. Many of the tangible edifices of colonial rule have been conserved, but the function of buildings has often changed. The case study in Box 3.4 shows the continuing appeal of colonial tours in Malaysia.

Box 3.4

Case study of colonial tours of Malaysia

Day 1 UK–Kuala Lumpur

Day 2 Kuala Lumpur
Kuala Lumpur boasts an exciting mix of tradition and modernism where colonial-style buildings rub shoulders with new skyscrapers and colourful markets bustle next to air-conditioned shopping malls.

Day 3 Kuala Lumpur
Enjoy a free day to explore Malaysia's cosmopolitan capital. Visit Merdeka Square, the site where Malaysia's independence was declared 51 years ago, and see the Moorish-styled Sultan Abdul Building, now home to the High and Supreme Courts. Take time to visit Kuala Lumpur's historic railway station, built in 1911 to a British design, before viewing the delightful Masjid Jamek (Friday Mosque). Built in 1907 by a British architect, the pink and cream domes and minarets of this mosque are set among palm trees in a tranquil setting on the site where the city's first founders set foot on the confluence of the Klang and Gombak Rivers.

Day 4 Malacca
Experience a taste of Malaysia's colonial past today as your included tour takes you south from Kuala Lumpur to the busy port town of Malacca. Ruled by the Portuguese, the Dutch and then the British, Malacca is a fusion of cultures easily identified by its unique architecture. The Porta de Santiago, a Portuguese archway, still stands today, as does the Stadthuys, one of Asia's oldest Dutch buildings. This full-day tour offers a real insight into this fascinating town. Return to Kuala Lumpur this evening.

Day 5 Kuala Lumpur–Cameron Highlands

Travel north for three and a half hours to Malaysia's charming Cameron Highlands. Named after the man who mapped them, William Cameron, this famous but remote hill resort lies over 6,000 feet above sea level and was used by the British during their colonial rule.

Day 6 Cameron Highlands

Established in the 19th century and developed in the 20th, the Cameron Highlands were used as an escape from the heat and an ideal place to cultivate tea, rubber and vegetables. Perhaps, in true colonial tradition, visit a tea plantation house for some tea and scones or view one of the region's many butterfly gardens. Take a walk around one of the area's picturesque lakes or waterfalls, explore the verdant forests or simply enjoy what made the Cameron Highlands attractive to begin with – a cool climate and breathtaking scenery.

Day 7 Cameron Highlands–Penang

Journey north to one of Malaysia's most well known resorts. Widely known as the 'Pearl of the Orient', the tropical island of Penang is rich in natural beauty and cultural heritage. Transfer across one of Asia's longest bridges, which links Penang to the mainland, and enjoy the facilities of your beach resort hotel.

Days 8–10 Penang

You have three days at leisure to do as much or as little as you wish in Malaysia's oldest British settlement, a destination steeped in colonial history. Ensure you visit Penang's historic capital, Georgetown. Journey to the Temple of the Reclining Buddha, Snake Temple and Fort Cornwallis, one of the first European structures built on the island. To escape the hustle and bustle, visit Penang Hill, Penang's highest mountain lying over 800 metres above sea level, or simply relax on one of the many golden sand beaches.

Day 11 Penang–Kuala Lumpur–UK

(Connections 2009)

'New' nation states

Sarup (1996) describes how nation states are essentially defined according to a political arrangement of boundaries, as well as a somewhat enforced assertion of common heritage or uniform characteristics. The discourse of the nation state will refer to land, to territory, to myths, to culture. The inherent human need to belong to such a homogeneous entity may help to fuel nationalist ideologies, which require either the integration or assimilation of extraneous (e.g. immigrant) cultures. However, identities are not static, and they will change according to the strength of different social forces. Hence national identities that are suppressed under political regimes (e.g. Nazism or Communism) may eventually reassert themselves in new and different ways (see Box 3.5).

Box 3.5

New countries of the world since 1990

Fifteen new countries became independent with the dissolution of the USSR in 1991. Most of these countries declared independence a few months preceding the fall of the Soviet Union in late 1991:

1   Armenia
2   Azerbaijan
3   Belarus
4   Estonia
5   Georgia
6   Kazakhstan
7   Kyrgyzstan
8   Latvia
9   Lithuania
10 Moldova
11 Russia
12 Tajikistan
13 Turkmenistan
14 Ukraine
15 Uzbekistan

Former Yugoslavia

Yugoslavia dissolved in the early 1990s into five independent countries:

1   **Bosnia and Herzegovina**, 29 February 1992
2   **Croatia**, 25 June 1991
3   **Macedonia** (officially the Former Yugoslav Republic of Macedonia) declared independence on 8 September 1991 but was not recognised by the United Nations until 1993 and the US and Russia in February 1994
4   **Serbia and Montenegro** (also known as the Federal Republic of Yugoslavia), 17 April 1992 (see below for separate Serbia and Montenegro entries)
5   **Slovenia**, 25 June 1991

Other new countries

Twelve other countries became independent through a variety of causes:

- March 1990 – **Namibia** became independent of South Africa.
- May 1990 – **North and South Yemen** merged to form a unified Yemen.
- October 1990 – **East Germany and West Germany** merged to form a unified Germany after the fall of the Iron Curtain.
- September 1991 – **The Marshall Islands** was part of the Trust Territory of Pacific Islands (administered by the US) and gained independence as a former colony.
- September 1991 – **Micronesia**, previously known as the Caroline Islands, became independent from the US.
- January 1993 – **The Czech Republic and Slovakia** became independent nations when Czechoslovakia dissolved.

- May 1993 – **Eritrea** was a part of Ethiopia but seceded and gained independence.
- October 1994 – **Palau** was part of the Trust Territory of Pacific Islands (administered by the US) and gained independence as a former colony.
- May 2002 – **East Timor** (Timor-Leste) declared independence from Portugal in 1975 but did not became independent from Indonesia until 2002.
- June 2006 – **Montenegro** was part of Serbia and Montenegro (also known as Yugoslavia) but gained independence after a referendum.
- June 2006 – **Serbia** became its own entity after Montenegro split.
- February 2008 – **Kosovo** unilaterally declared independence from Serbia.

(Rosenberg 2008)

Clearly not all of these new countries can become popular with tourists, and some took considerable time to convince tourists that they were safe (e.g. former Yugoslavian countries after the war). Some of the countries are still politically unstable and this is not conducive to tourism development. Many of the countries do not have an established image which is sufficiently known by tourists, precisely because of their new country status. However, Croatia and Slovenia are now two of the most popular tourism destinations in Europe. The Czech Republic, especially Prague, has a very positive image and high levels of visitation, and Bratislava is an up and coming urban break destination in Slovakia. Montenegro was considered by the WTTC (2004) as the fastest growing travel and tourism economy in the world. Moldova can offer some interesting forms of heritage and village tourism. Some of the countries offer other forms of tourism rather than cultural tourism (e.g. Palau is one of the diving paradises of the world and the same is true of Micronesia; and Namibia largely offers wildlife tourism).

Countries with indigenous and tribal peoples

Many parts of the world have indigenous communities who are sometimes known as 'first nations' (e.g. in Canada), who have been there for thousands of years and preceeded all colonising inhabitants. Examples include Australia, New Zealand, the USA, Central and South America, Africa, as well as many islands in the Caribbean and South Pacific. The rapid and extensive spread of the various European powers from the early eighteenth century onwards had a profound impact upon many of the indigenous cultures with whom they came into contact. The exploratory and colonial ventures in the Americas, Africa, Asia and the Pacific often resulted in territorial and cultural conflict, and the intentional or unintentional displacement and devastation of the indigenous populations (see Chapter 5).

However, it has ironically become somewhat controversial to talk about the identity of colonising nations who were somehow complicit in oppressing native peoples (see Box 3.6). Therefore, in countries like Australia, there are now some concerns about what national (non-indigenous) identity even is.

> There are many Australians who say that Australia has no national identity, and does not need one. In fact, in the 1970s Whitlam Minister Al Grassy declared that even something as simple as identifying one's ancestors as Australian on a census form was a sign of racial supremacist attitudes . . . While the rest of the world wallows in fear of cultural loss as a result of globalisation, Australians are assimilating foreign ideas and becoming stronger in the process.
>
> (Convict Creations 2009)

Box 3.6

Case study of Camp Oven Festival in Australia: the discovery of an identity

Chappel and Loades (2006) discuss the significance of the Camp Oven Festival in Millmerran in southern Queensland in Australia. The camp oven was used by shepherds in the early days of European settlement in Australia to cook food. Over the years it has become a part of Australia's heritage and is a symbol of Australia's much-envied outdoor living. The festival includes cookery competitions and demonstrations.

The Camp Oven Festival also asserts a particular image of 'Australianness' which developed in the nineteenth century. The early European settlers were transplanted from Britain and sometimes retained a British connection. The later image of Australians was that they were pastoral labourers and bushworkers who endured many hardships to help develop the economy. Although there were some conflicts with Aboriginal people (the original inhabitants), these were mainly about competition for land, water and sheep.

After the Second World War large numbers of non-English-speaking migrants from continental Europe were brought over to help populate the country. This resulted in considerable diversification of cultural practices. By the 1960s, non-White migrants were also encouraged from Asia.

Conflicts arose in the early 1990s about the identities of non-indigenous Australians and Aborigines. Although cultural diversity was celebrated, there were also concerns about Europeans' role in the dispossession of Aborigines and an official apology was issued by the government. However, the later governments of Prime Ministers Howard and Hanson (late 1990s) started to express the 'grievances' of the old White Australia and the shared 'Legend' of Anglo-Australia. Camp Oven goers tend to be less culturally diverse, and want to hear the story of the 'real Aussie'. This desire for a common heritage and identity could be perceived as xenophobic or racist as it coincides with a time when Aborigines were majorly dispossessed, but is is an important and arguably legitimate quest for many White, non-indigenous Australians.

(adapted from Chappel and Loades 2006)

Other 'new' nations composed of migrants, but with indigenous populations also have problems asserting their cultural identity. For example, some people say (and not only in jest) that the USA has 'no culture' aside from that of the Native American Indians or African Americans. Despite the globalisation of American 'culture', this is somehow not seen to be a 'real' or a 'good' culture. As stated by Mazza (2004): 'The Europeans claim we have no culture, yet they can't help but copy it.' She states that the USA has a culture and history – just a much shorter one than in Europe. Apart from Hollywood and Disney (postmodern, experiential, creative culture as discussed in Chapters 7 and 9), there is also Cowboy culture, whose music and dancing has been exported all over the world, as well as the rich diversity of so many nationalities living within one country. This is especially true of big cities like New York and San Francisco.

Countries with dissonant or dark heritage

The Dark Tourism Forum describes 'Dark Tourism' as 'the act of travel and visitation to sites, attractions and exhibitions which has real or recreated death, suffering or the seemingly macabre as a main theme' (Stone 2005). All countries have their dark pasts, of course, and it is difficult to single out countries which have focused especially on this aspect of tourism. However, there are certain historic events which are seen as having impacted on the consciousness (and conscience) of the whole world, for example, the Nazi Holocaust or the Killing Fields in Cambodia. The world stood still as the Twin Towers in New York were attacked by terrorists, and Ground Zero is now an international dark tourism attraction. Some countries have a relatively recent history of atrocity and are still in the process of grieving, making it difficult to develop a tourism industry which does not acknowledge this tragic history. Rwanda is an example of this (see Box 3.7).

Box 3.7

Case study of genocide tourism in Rwanda

The Rwandan travel industry hinges on two main attractions: eco-tourism and genocide tourism. Rwanda is home to around two-thirds of the 700 mountain gorillas left in the world, and, for several decades now, the country has been at the forefront of gorilla conservation. However, while in Rwanda, macabre, but necessary tourist attractions are the genocide memorials. There are many of these scattered all over the country, noticeable by the purple ribbons or paint, the colour of mourning and remembrance.

The first, and essential, site is the Kigali Memorial Centre. This site houses mass graves, but also an incredible museum and research centre. Inside the history of the Rwandan genocide is laid out in clear, multi-lingual displays. One of the rooms is filled with thousands of photos of people. These are all victims of the genocide. In many cases, families gave up their only surviving photographs of loved ones, so they could be remembered here. Another room has a collection of bones and skulls taken from victims. A third room has clothing and personal effects taken from victims and massacre sites. Upstairs in the centre is another series of rooms, dedicated to other genocides of the twentieth century. The Armenian genocide, the Holocaust, the Balkans, and more. The last display is also upstairs. It is about children who died in the genocide; a lost generation. Located an hour and half matatu ride away from Kigali are the Ntarama and Nyamata memorials. These are particularly tragic as these memorials are former churches where people flocked to, hoping to find protection within the house of God. There are stories of priests who died next to their flock, offering protection and solace until the end. Devastatingly, there are also the stories of priests who welcomed people into their places or worship and then handed them over to the Interahamwe, civilian militia death squads who were responsible for most of the killings. Nyamata is another church, now a memorial. Here, as many as 10,000 people were killed. There was a sacrifice here, of thousands of innocents, their only crime being the wrong word in their identification card – Tutsi. The latter became victims of the Hutu extremist civilian militia who did most of the killing.

(Travelpod 2007)

Some countries openly accept their role in the perpetration of atrocities: German schoolchildren, for example, regularly tour concentration camps so that they acknowledge their nation's past. Some other nations 'whitewash' their history books and refuse to publicly accept their role in committing atrocities. Even historians sometimes go to the extreme of trying to prove that historical events did not occur, the most notable case being that of David Irving, a British historian who denied the existence of the Holocaust and ended up being arrested in Austria in 2005 for his revisionist writings, Holocaust denial and anti-Semitic expressions.

The politics of religious tourism

Religious tourism is not easy to define, therefore the terms 'religious', 'spiritual' or 'pilgrimage' tourism may be used interchangeably. The majority of religious sites attract cultural tourists who may or may not have a religious affiliation. Religious tourists of one particular faith are likely to travel together in a group, and may not welcome non-religious tourists or tourists from other faiths.

Barber's (1992) use of the word 'Jihad' for the assertion of culture and identity makes us think of the rise in terrorism which has affected tourism the world over. Few can forget the image of the aeroplane hitting the Twin Towers in New York, and many tourists were deterred from travelling by the seemingly random bombings in Bali and elsewhere. However, religious conflicts are ongoing all over the world. Some countries even prefer to protect their religion from tourists: for example, Saudi Arabia does not allow non-Muslims to visit Mecca, or Christian churches to be built there, and does not allow Jewish visitors or workers.

Egypt has had its fair share of problems because of religious fundamentalism and objections to the government's liberal attitude towards tourism and tourists. This resulted in ongoing terrorist attacks on tourists by Islamic extremists throughout the 1990s. The massacre of 58 tourists at the temple of Hatshepsut in Luxor was perhaps the worst example of this. As a consequence, tourism declined dramatically, and for some time Egypt's main sites were guarded by tourist police and escorts who accompany tour groups. Certain transport routes were restricted, including the cruise from Cairo to Aswan and back, and the only way to reach Abu Simbel was at one time by aeroplane, as the road from Aswan was closed to tourists for security reasons.

Jerusalem is a city where three religions share a common heritage, but the reality is somewhat more complex. The Holy City, as it is also known, is one of the world's major religious centres for Jews, Christians and Muslims, with many prominent sites and places of worship located in the heart of the city. However, it is very difficult to mix religious groups without some conflicts arising. One of the most recent conflicts has been around a Museum of Tolerance which was planned by Israel in 2006, but which was to be built upon an ancient Muslim cemetery. Another includes a Basilica which is shared by Roman Catholics, Greek Orthodox and Armenian, Syrian, Ethiopian and Coptic Christians. The site has to be segregated carefully, otherwise physical fights between these different religious groups break out on a regular basis (Izsák 2008).

Sri Lanka is a country which has been troubled by conflict, much of it stemming from religion. Sri Lanka is a multi-faith state composed of 69 per cent Buddhists, 15 per cent Hindus, 8 per cent Christians and 8 per cent Muslims (Religious Tolerance 2003). The ruling majority Sinhalese community (who are mostly Buddhist) and the Tamils (who are mostly Hindu) have been locked in civil war for over 20 years. Despite several attempts at truces, the violence has prohibited tourism in many parts of Sri Lanka.

Since the signing of the Good Friday Agreement of 1998, Northern Ireland has transformed itself from the land of 'Troubles' to a relatively successful tourist destination. Before that, sectarian violence between Protestants and Catholics made it an unsafe place to visit. However, visitors now are keen to take tours which show them the history of Belfast's religious divide: for example, a Black Taxi Tour takes visitors to see some of the many wall murals painted during the Troubles as well as the 'Peace Wall' that still divides Catholic and Protestant neighbourhoods.

There is an interesting religious memorial site in Siauliai in Lithuania, where there are 100,000 crosses or more. The site has existed for centuries, and was thought originally to be a memorial to soldiers whose burial places were unknown. Local people have been bringing crosses to this location since the fourteenth century. However, the Russians, who occupied Lithuania during the eighteenth century, removed the crosses, which nevertheless started to build up once more. After the Second World War when Russia occupied Lithuania again, they tried to destroy the

Plate 3.1 Giant Buddha in Hikkaduwa, Sri Lanka

(Source Georgina Smith)

area, but without success, and by 1990 there were 60,000 new crosses. The site therefore became more than just a memorial and pilgrimage site, it became a political protest against Russian occupation and the surpression of religion. In 1993 it was even blessed by Pope John Paul II. It is visited by many Lithuanian and Polish tourists; however, it is managed by volunteers, and there is currently no official organisation responsible for it (Németh 2008a).

Not particularly political but definitely controversial is the Creationist Museum in Petersburgh, Kentucky in the USA. This museum cost $27 million to build, and has used the skills of one of the former directors of Universal Studios and Disneyland to create multi-media, interactive exhibitions which focus on the creation story from the Bible. Certain historical discrepancies are overlooked, such as dinosaurs roaming the earth at the same time as Adam and Eve (dinosaurs draw big crowds!), but, more significantly, in this relatively conservative part of America, the main point of the museum is to disprove evolution theory using every means possible (Nagy 2009).

Conclusion

This chapter has demonstrated the political complexity of cultural tourism in some areas of the world where history has created dissonant legacies, or forced a reassertion of national or cultural identity. Tourists may sometimes be 'caught in the crossfire' of irresolvable conflicts, or forced to face disgruntled locals who have a sense of history repeating itself (e.g. in neocolonial countries). However, tourists are inevitably drawn to areas of political interest, for example, those which have been part of oppressive regimes or which have had a dark past. They are often nostalgic about imperialism, and create fantasies around the destinations, which fail to reflect the reality of life for local inhabitants. New or recently liberated countries may have a novelty factor for many years. Overall, it seems that political problems are not a deterrent but quite the opposite for most tourists. They remind us that despite the process of globalisation, many destinations are unique precisely because of local historical and cultural processes.

4 Heritage, tourism and museums

> Heritage and tourism are collaborative industries, heritage converting locations into destinations and tourism making them economically viable as exhibits of themselves. Locations become museums of themselves within a tourism industry.
>
> (Kirschenblatt-Gimblett 1998: 151)

Introduction

This chapter examines the complex relationship between heritage and cultural tourism, including some of the debates concerning the commodification of history and the 'heritagisation' of the past. There are also many controversial and sensitive issues relating to the ownership, interpretation and representation of heritage, which are discussed in some detail. These are clearly subject areas which have been debated fairly extensively within heritage literature and museum studies, but this chapter focuses mainly on 'populist' heritage and the heritage of groups that have traditionally been marginalised in historical narratives. The postmodern emphasis on the pluralisation of history and the shift from so-called 'grand narratives' has led to increased interest in, and concern for, the culture and heritage of ethnic, regional and indigenous minorities. There is clearly a need to consider the extent to which such groups are sufficiently empowered to represent themselves and their culture, as well as discussing issues relating to access, democracy and the accumulation of cultural capital.

What is heritage?

The following list suggests examples of the types of heritage sites that have become cultural tourism attractions in recent years:

- Built heritage attractions (e.g. historic townscapes, architecture, archaeological sites, monuments, historic buildings).
- Natural heritage attractions (e.g. national parks, cultural landscapes, coastlines, caves, geological features).
- Cultural heritage attractions (e.g. arts, crafts, festivals, traditional events, folk history museums).
- Industrial heritage attractions (e.g. mines, factories, mills).
- Religious sites and attractions (e.g. cathedrals, abbeys, mosques, shrines, pilgrimage routes, cities and festivals).
- Military heritage attractions (e.g. castles, battlefields, concentration camps, military museums).
- Literary or artistic heritage attractions (e.g. houses, gardens or landscapes associated with artists and writers).

It is important to consider a few of the debates surrounding the relationship between history and heritage before discussing some of the more politically sensitive issues relating to heritage interpretation and the representation of heritage for tourists. The debates about the transformation of history into heritage are generally contentious, and consensus has rarely been reached among scholars and academics within the heritage field. However, Lumley (1994: 68) is positive about the impact of such debates on the development of the heritage and museums sectors: 'There are many who work in museums and other cultural institutions associated with heritage for whom a less narrow and insular conception of the national past has undoubted attractions.'

In terms of definitions, heritage has been associated traditionally with that which is inherited or handed on from one generation to the next. Graham *et al.* (2000) differentiate between the terms 'past', 'history' and 'heritage'. The past is concerned with all that has ever happened, whereas history is the attempts of successive presents to explain selected aspects of the past. Heritage is defined as 'a view from the present, either backward to a past or forward to a future' (p. 2). Essentially, heritage is the contemporary use of the past, including both its interpretation and representation. For example, Herbert (1995a: 215) states that 'History must not be compartmentalized as something which belongs in the past, it is part of a continuity and is intrinsic to our modern heritage', and Gruffudd (1995: 50) suggests that 'Historical narratives reveal contemporary anxieties, and contemporary desires are fulfilled in the presentation of the past.' Clearly the actions of the present help to shape the preservation, conservation and management of heritage in the future. However, it should be noted that for many traditional (e.g. tribal) societies, the differentiation between past, present and future is not made. Culture and heritage are seen as continuous and dynamic rather than 'dead'.

Hewison (1987) is notoriously damning of the heritage industry, perceiving heritage to be static, fossilising the past, or, worse still, distorting historical facts for the purposes of entertainment. Walsh (1992: 103) is similarly critical of the 'heritagisation' of the past, stating: 'Heritage sites are constructed as "time capsules" severed from history . . . they represent a form of historical bricolage, a melting pot for historical memories.' He also argues that '[h]istory as heritage dulls our ability to appreciate the development of people and places through time' (ibid.: 113). This implies that heritage is a false representation of the past, which captures a moment or moments in history, and isolates them from any historical context.

However, many writers have been relatively positive about the development of heritage, arguing that heritage is a means of linking past and present, and enlivening history. Lowenthal (1998) claims that heritage is not 'bad history', it is simply a celebration of the past rather than an inquiry into it. He argues that we do not need a fixed past, but one that fuses with the present: 'History explores and explains pasts grown ever more opaque over time; heritage clarifies pasts so as to infuse them with present purposes' (p. xv). Kirschenblatt-Gimblett (1998: 7) is even more positive, implying that heritage brings history back to life:

> While it looks old, heritage is actually something new. Heritage is a mode of cultural production in the present that has recourse to the past. Heritage thus defined depends on display to give dying economies and dead sites a second life as exhibitions of themselves.

The postmodern pluralisation of history and its interpretation and representation have led to a growing appreciation of industrial, agricultural and popular folk heritage. Edwards and Llurdes (1996: 343) refer to the 'aesthetics of deindustrialisation' in their discussion of industrial heritage sites in Britain and Spain, and quote Hoyau (1988: 29–30): 'Once the notion of "heritage" has been cut free from its attachment to beauty, anything can be part of it, from miners' cottages or public washouses [*sic*] to the halls of Versailles, so long as it is historical evidence.' The idea here is that 'historicity' or historical value takes priority over the aesthetics of the site. However, industrial heritage tourism also serves an important regenerative purpose, and more industrial landscapes have started to be included on the World Heritage List (see Box 4.1).

Box 4.1

Case study of Wieliczka salt mines

The Salt Mines of Wieliczka were on the first World Heritage List ever, which was publicized in 1978. The evolution of the mining processes since the Middle Ages is shown here, with the conservation of the old galleries and the exhibition of tools used. First references to the mining of salt in Wieliczka were made in 1044. Salt was the most important economic commodity in Poland during the Middle Ages. The mining of salt quickly became a government monopoly. Technological progress turned the Wieliczka Salt Mine into a modern business enterprise in the 16th century. Machinery was used to improve productivity, and the search for new salt deposits took the miners lower and lower underground. The production of salt here ceased only in 1992 due to heavy flooding.

The Wieliczka Salt Mine is an important attraction in the Krakow area. It has a long history of tourism: already in the 15th century visitors were taken underground. Prominent Europeans like

Copernicus, Goethe and Chopin also visited. The site nowadays attracts thousands of visitors every day in summer, and group tours are conducted in several languages. The underground tour takes visitors on a walk of 2 km. It passes through 20 caves, many of them adorned with sculptures the miners made. It is quite clean and spacious, unlike in a coal mine for example. The walls are dark grey everywhere; you can only see they are made of crystals when you hold a light to it. The gangways are held upright by complex wooden structures.

The highlight of the tour is the Underground Cathedral. Everything in it is made of salt: the wall decorations (The Last Supper and other biblical scenes), the altar, the religious statues, floor and ceiling. Even the chandeliers are made from salt crystals. This masterpiece was created by three miners in their spare time, taking 68 years of work.

(World Heritage Site 2009)

As well as the World Heritage Site List, there was also an attempt to create a list of the new Seven Wonders of the World, as many of the old ones no longer exist. In 2007 the public were able to vote online for the sites they thought should be included. The cultural sites voted for were:

- Chichen Itza (Mexico)
- The Colosseum (Italy)
- Machu Picchu (Peru)
- The Statue of Christ (Brazil)
- The Great Wall of China
- Petra (Jordan)
- The Taj Mahal (India)

By 2011, the seven natural Wonders of the World will also have been voted for, with Federico Major, the former director of UNESCO as the main judge (see www.new7wonders.com).

In addition, the concept of intangible heritage is becoming more significant, and UNESCO (among other heritage bodies) has recognised this fact. McKercher and Cros (2002) note that Japan was the first country to recognise the value of intangible cultural heritage, and is one of the few countries to legislate for its protection. However, UNESCO has now developed a Convention which helps to protect intangible cultural heritage in addition to the existing World Heritage Site List, including language, stories, art styles, music, dance, religious beliefs – in other words, those aspects of culture not directly embodied in material things (UNESCO 2009). This decision was partly based on anxiety about the cultural effects of globalisation, the disappearance of unique traditions and languages, and the increasing recognition of the importance of intangible heritage for many non-Western cultures.

According to the 2003 Convention for the Safeguarding of the Intangible Cultural Heritage (UNESCO 2009), 'the intangible cultural heritage (ICH) – or living heritage – is the mainspring of the world's cultural diversity and its maintenance a guarantee for continuing creativity'. The Convention states that the ICH is manifested, among others, in the following domains:

- Oral traditions and expressions including language as a vehicle of the intangible cultural heritage;
- Performing arts (such as traditional music, dance and theatre);
- Social practices, rituals and festive events;
- Knowledge and practices concerning nature and the universe;
- Traditional craftsmanship.

The 2003 Convention defines ICH as the practices, representations, expressions, as well as the knowledge and skills, that communities, groups and, in some cases, individuals recognise as part of their cultural heritage. The definition also indicates that the ICH to be safeguarded by this Convention:

- is transmitted from generation to generation;
- is constantly recreated by communities and groups, in response to their environment, their interaction with nature, and their history;
- provides communities and groups with a sense of identity and continuity;
- promotes respect for cultural diversity and human creativity;
- is compatible with international human rights instruments;
- complies with the requirements of mutual respect among communities, and of sustainable development.

The Convention describes how ICH is traditional and living at the same time, and how it is mainly recreated orally. The skills are often shared and performed by communities. The human body and mind are the main instruments for enactment or embodiment. One of the main aims of the Convention is to protect these traditions from disappearing, especially among cultures where young people may need some encouragement to continue them (see Box 4.2).

Box 4.2

Examples from the representative list of the Intangible Cultural Heritage of Humanity

Bhutan
The Mask Dance of the Drums from Drametse

Cambodia
Sbek Thom, Khmer Shadow Theatre
The Royal Ballet of Cambodia

Colombia
The Carnival of Barranquilla

Costa Rica
Oxherding and Oxcart Traditions in Costa Rica

France
Processional Giants and Dragons in Belgium and France (Belgium – France)

Georgia
Georgian Polyphonic Singing

India
Ramlila – the Traditional Performance of the Ramayana
The Tradition of Vedic Chanting

Japan
Ningyo Johruri Bunraku Puppet Theatre

Lithuania
Cross-crafting and its Symbolism
The Baltic Song and Dance Celebrations (Estonia – Latvia – Lithuania)

Madagascar
The Woodcrafting Knowledge of the Zafimaniry

Malawi
The Vimbuza Healing Dance

Mongolia
Urtiin Duu – Traditional Folk Long Song (China – Mongolia)

Peru
Taquile and its Textile Art
The Oral Heritage and Cultural Manifestations of the Zápara People (Ecuador – Peru)

Togo
The Oral Heritage of Gelede (Benin – Nigeria – Togo)

Turkey
The Arts of the Meddah, Public Storytellers

Uganda
Barkcloth Making in Uganda

Vanuatu
Vanuatu Sand Drawings

Viet Nam
Nha Nhac, Vietnamese Court Music
The Space of Gong Culture

(UNESCO 2009)

Brown (2003) describes how the protection of intangible heritage can be complicated by the fact that indigenous people are often secretive about their traditions (see also Box 4.3). Many indigenous groups fear that their cultural heritage will be appropriated by powerful outsiders, and are therefore reluctant to release information. For example, various Native American and Australian Aboriginal groups have demanded that publicly accessible records of their beliefs are removed from the public domain. Some Indian tribes discourage outsiders from learning the local language. Such actions go against the UNESCO philosophy of trying to save heritage by publicising it! Brown (2003) also states:

> Living cultures cannot be reduced to diagrams on a printed page or data on a CD. They are unlikely to benefit greatly from the ministrations of technocrats who are redefining cultural survival as a vast exercise in information management.

Box 4.3

Case study of intangible heritage in Africa

Munjeri (2003), the former vice-president of ICOMOS, argues that tangible and intangible heritage are not necessarily inextricably linked. The example of Benin in West Africa is used to show that although there was massive slavery and slave trade in the city of Ouidah from the seventeenth to eighteenth centuries, there is no tangible evidence of slavery. Although some sites have remained that recall slave activity, such as plants, lagoons, plantations etc., these tangible reminders are likely to disappear, but the intangible legacy remains in people's consciousness, oral histories and some historical documents, etc.

The ICOMOS cultural itineraries or themed routes, such as the Slave Route, were supposedly composed of 'tangible elements of which the cultural significance comes from exchanges and multi-dimensional dialogue across countries or regions'. While the pilgrim route of Santiago de Compostella (Spain) may meet this definition, the Ouidah case is testimony that this would not apply in non-material heritage societies.

Munjeri (2003) also cites examples of Ouidah's temples, which are tangible evidence of traditional religious practices. However, it should be noted that Ouidah's most important worship practices do not take place in such temples. Instead, a room, a tree or a corner of a wall could have greater value in terms of religious practice.

In some African societies cultural heritage is much more about values than edifices. This means that Africa may seem to lack any kind of monumental 'built heritage'. However, local people believe that if a building collapses, traditions can continue to be celebrated. Westerners may be mourning the loss of the physcial fabric but, to Africans, the spirits are simply moving house to settle elsewhere!

(after Munjeri 2003)

Heritage interpretation

Schouten (1995: 25) is very positive about the creative potential of heritage interpretation to enliven history, stating: 'History and historical reality are black boxes: we do not know what they contain, but with an input of imagination and good research, the output can be marvellous. Interpretation is the art that makes history "real."' History has a dynamic quality to it, and will vary according to our perceptions and interpretation of it within the present. Tilden (1977: 8) defines 'interpretation' as 'An educational activity, which aims to reveal meanings and relationships through the use of original objects, by first-hand experience, and by illustrative media, rather than simply to communicate factual information.' Use is made of a wide range of tools, which are becoming increasingly high-tech and interactive. Emphasis is often placed on the educational purpose of interpretation, as well as the entertainment function. Light (1995: 139) states that '[a]t the heart of interpretation is informal education. Interpretation is designed to communicate the significance of heritage places, in a manner appropriate to visitors engaged in leisure activities during their leisure time.' This combination of learning and fun has been referred to by Urry (1990) as 'edutainment', a concept that has become central to the leisure and tourism industries. Uzzell (1989: 3) states cynically that '[i]nterpretation has been regarded as a novel way of pepping up tired tourist attractions and giving them a value-added component.' This suggests that interpretation is serving to enhance heritage sites and to make them more 'fun' for the visitor. This is perhaps not problematic in itself, but there is a danger that the inherent meaning or nature of the site will be compromised in some way. For example, Hems (2006) states:

> Heritage may be a powerful mirror; it is also a distorting one, through which past events and experiences can be reduced to a kind of nostalgic dressing-up or bland description.

She goes on to say that interpretation is an 'exciting, if not dangerous activity' (Hems 2006), as it is mainly rooted in the experience of the present, rather than the recreation of the past. Schouten (1995) argues that the visitor is looking for an experience rather than the hard facts of historical reality, which can be provided through interpretation. Clearly, the non-expert visitor cannot necessarily construct a meaningful and entertaining experience for him- or herself, and is generally reliant on the guide, curator or audio tour for an interpretation of what is being visited. Puczkó (2006: 232) states:

> Interpretation, by definition, can or should have an impact on visitors in such a way that they react to the stimuli in the desired form (e.g. appreciation, enjoyment and understanding).

Tilden (1977: 9) sees the role of interpretation as being a way of encouraging visitors to take a less unquestioning and passive approach to their visit: 'The chief aim of interpretation is not instruction but provocation.' Uzzell echoes this, and also stresses the need for visitors to engage with and learn from the heritage:

Plate 4.1 Telling the story of wine making, Loisium, Austria

(Source: László Puczkó)

> If interpretation is to be a source of social good then it must recognise the continuity
> of history and alert us to the future through the past. Interpretation should be
> interesting, engaging, enjoyable, informative and entertaining. But now and again it
> has to be shocking, moving and provide a cathartic experience.
>
> (Uzzell 1989: 41)

It is argued that heritage interpretation should provoke a reaction in its recipients.
Kavanagh (1996: 13) states that 'museums are places where memories and histories
meet, even collide, and that . . . can be an emotional experience' (see Box 4.4).

Box 4.4

Case study of Robben Island, South Africa

In 1999, Robben Island was designated one of South Africa's first World Heritage Sites, and it
was inscribed mainly because of its intangible heritage. Deacon (2004) notes that in South
Africa after 1994, intangible forms of heritage became politically acceptable in an attempt to
project new interpretations onto the colonial landscape. Robben Island Museum (RIM) officially

commemorates 'the triumph of the human spirit over adversity', relating mainly to the period of political imprisonment between 1961 and 1991, when Robben Island was most notorious as a political prison for the leaders of the anti-Apartheid movement, including most famously Nelson Mandela.

In 1997 the Robben Island Museum Council mandated the Museum to pursue the following tenets:

- To maintain the political and universal symbolism of Robben Island.
- To promote Robben Island as a platform for critical and life-long learning.
- To manage the Robben Island Museum in a manner that promotes economic sustainability and development.
- To conserve and manage Robben Island's diverse natural and cultural resources in an integrated manner.

Oral histories of the anti-Apartheid struggle were especially valued and Robben Island Museum established an extensive oral history project with former political prisoners and employed former prisoners as tour guides. The guides tell visitors who ask them why they would want to come back and work in their former prison that it is a way of coming to terms with the past. However, it frequently seems to be a somewhat emotional experience for them.

Robben Island has also become a site of pilgrimage for many visitors. Makhurane (2003: 3) explains why:

> Robben Island has been characterized as a place of emptiness, barrenness, pain and suffering. Without a doubt, the spirit of the people who were incarcerated there and the positive energy, which they generated in their attempts to overcome an oppressive social and political order, is what transformed the Island into a site of pilgrimage.

Ownership of and access to heritage

Gathercole and Lowenthal (1994) discuss in detail the Eurocentric and exclusive nature of historical interpretation, as do Jordan and Weedon (1995). Postmodern interpretations of the past clearly favour plural histories over so-called 'grand narratives'. Historical narratives have traditionally been dominated by white, Western males, hence excluding and marginalising minority, ethnic and gender groups. There are therefore key debates within the heritage field surrounding 'ownership' and use of heritage. This includes a focus on cultural politics and the power struggles that seem to govern the interpretation and representation of heritage. Walsh (1992: 79) sees heritage as inherently elitist: 'The public heritage is undoubtedly an extremely narrow and selective concept founded on a dismissal of the richness and variety of what different groups consider to be *their* heritage.' He goes on to be even more critical of the hegemonic and ideological structure, which determines whose heritage is of value:

> The aim of heritage would appear to be to select only that which pleases the sensibilities of a narrow group of people. Those who decide what is worthy of preservation and how it should be preserved, are basically deciding what is worth remembering.

Jacobs (1996: 35) similarly sees heritage as a kind of accolade for which different groups compete: 'Heritage is not in any simple sense the reproduction and imposition of dominant values. It is a dynamic process of creation in which a multiplicity of pasts jostle for the present purpose of being sanctified as heritage.' Lowenthal (1998: 250) refers to the 'adherents of rival heritages [who] simultaneously construct versions that are equally well-grounded (and equally spurious)'. Gathercole and Lowenthal state:

> The past is everywhere a battleground of rival attachments. In discovering, correcting, elaborating, inverting, and celebrating their histories, competing groups struggle to validate present goals by appealing to continuity with, or inheritance from, ancestral and other precursors. The politics of the past is no trivial academic game; it is an integral part of every peoples' earnest search for a heritage essential to autonomy and identity.
>
> (Gathercole and Lowenthal 1994: 302)

Everybody, not surprisingly, wants their history to be recognised, as well as being given the freedom and resources to interpret it. Merriman (1991) argues that the past belongs to everyone, and that everyone should have access to the past. He perceives museums to be the principal means by which people can gain access to their history; however, he also criticises the failure within the sector to maximise public access to that history. His survey work reveals that the main barriers to access are based on cultural factors (e.g. people's perceptions of museums) rather than structural factors, such as physical access, transport, time and money. This suggests that people feel excluded from their history, and that there is a need to increase cultural empowerment or cultural capital. Only certain groups (mainly more highly educated people) tend to visit museums, and Merriman argues that museum and heritage visitation is often based more on status affirmation than orientations to the past. He draws on Bourdieu's (1984) notion of the accumulation of cultural capital, which helps to distinguish between social classes. Walsh comments on the problems of so-called 'democracy':

> The idea that democratic access is improved through the market is a deception. It assumes a context of democracy in which all members of the public have equal and unrestricted access to both capital and cultural capital, access to the latter being enhanced by greater access to the former. The market is by its very nature undemocratic.
>
> (Walsh 1992: 179)

As well as the questions that have been raised about people's access to their own past, it is contentious as to which aspects of the past should be selected for presentation to the public. As stated above, Western imperial societies often tend to idealise or romanticise the past and view it with a sense of nostalgia. Equally, we idealise or glorify the past to reflect society in a positive light. Lowenthal (1985: 332) states:

> We alter the past to 'improve it' – exaggerating aspects we find successful, virtuous, or beautiful, celebrating what we take pride in, playing down the ignoble, the ugly, the shameful. The memories of most individuals, the annals and monuments of all people highlight supposed glories; relics of failure are seldom saved and rarely memorialised.

Lowenthal highlights one of the most interesting aspects of heritage interpretation, which is our tendency to distort the past and to be selective in our representation of past events. It is common in more 'Eurocentric' interpretations of history to ignore the past of indigenous or ethnic minorities, and to focus solely on the 'glory' of colonial history. Merriman (1991) describes museums in particular as being part of the broader ideological and hegemonic structure which has traditionally determined whose heritage is important or worthy of preservation, and whose is not.

The new museology

In the days before international travel became so accessible, museums traditionally served as a form of surrogate travel. Even with increased travel, the advent of the DVD and virtual tours on the Internet has helped to make museums even more accessible without ever leaving the comfort of the PC. MacCannell (1976: 84) describes modern museums as 'anti-historical and un-natural', and it could indeed be argued that many collections do appear to be rather disparate or displaced. Hewison (1987: 84) is unequivocally negative about museums in Britain, describing them as 'symbols of national decline'. This is perhaps overly pessimistic and something of a generalisation, especially given the diverse nature of museums, as illustrated in this comment by Boniface and Fowler :

> Museums are wonderful, frustrating, stimulating, serendipitous, dull as ditchwater and curiously exciting, tunnel-visioned yet potentially visionary. The real magic is that any one of them can be all of those simultaneously.
>
> (Boniface and Fowler 1993: 118)

The character of a museum is determined largely by the nature of its collections. Kirschenblatt-Gimblett stresses the importance of the presentation of collections:

> Fragmentation is vital to the production of the museum both as a space of posited meaning and as a space of abstraction. Posited meaning derives not from the original context of the fragments but from their juxtaposition in a new context. As a space of abstraction exhibitions do for the life world what the life world cannot do for itself. They bring together specimens and artifacts never found in the same place at the same time and show relationships that cannot otherwise be seen.
>
> (Kirschenblatt-Gimblett 1998: 3)

However, she later rather cynically cites Washington Matthews (1893) as having said that 'a first-class museum would consist of a series of satisfactory labels with specimens attached' (ibid.: 32), which implies that interpretation is becoming more important and more interesting than the objects themselves! She backs this up later by saying: 'The question is not whether an object is of visual interest, but rather how interest of any kind is created' (ibid.: 78). Walsh makes a similar statement, but implies that there is a certain bias, not only to the selection of objects but also to their interpretation:

> In a museum display, the object itself is without meaning. Its meaning is conferred
> by the 'writer,' that is, the curator, the archeologist, the historian, or the visitor who
> possesses the 'cultural competence' to recognise the conferred meaning given by
> the 'expert.'
>
> (Walsh 1992: 37)

This brings us back to Bourdieu's (1984) idea of cultural capital, and Merriman's (1991) discussion of access. But the question is: How far are museums responding to criticisms of elitism and exclusivity? Simpson suggests that museums must become focused increasingly on people rather than collections if they are to evolve. This is not just in terms of access, but also in terms of 'authorship':

> The traditional role of the museum must change, if it is to adapt to the needs of
> contemporary society, from that of an institution primarily concerned with artifacts
> and specimens to one which focuses upon people as creators and users of the
> artifacts in their collection.
>
> (Simpson 1996: 265)

Kirschenblatt-Gimblett (1998) believes that museums are experiencing a crisis of identity, and are finding it increasingly difficult to compete with other attractions. They are struggling to shake off their perceived image of being boring, dusty places full of defunct things – effectively 'dead spaces' rather than 'life spaces'. Merriman's (1991) research suggests similarly that people perceived museums to be old-fashioned, musty and dead. He argues that museums should be effectively 'peoples' universities', highlighting the potential of museums as a positive, democratic social force. Walsh criticises the apparent standardisation of museum services:

> There should not be an emphasis on only one form of representation. A true
> democracy will offer many and varied forms of museum service. The danger is that
> we are in fact moving towards an homogenised monopoly of form, which in itself is
> an attack on democracy.
>
> (Walsh 1992: 183)

Urry (1990) is much more positive about the changing nature of museums, especially the proliferation of plural histories (e.g. social, feminist, ethnic, industrial, populist) that are being increasingly represented. He argues that museum displays have become much less 'auratic', and he is largely positive about the replacement of 'dead' museums with 'living' ones. However, it could be argued that museums have not yet gone far enough in their representation of plural histories. As stated by Porter (1988: 104), 'museums have been slow to take up issues such as racism, class bias, and sex discrimination, either as employing institutions, or as a medium which propagates a particular and pervasive brand of history'. For example, Porter supports Horne's (1984) contention that traditionally museums have been patriarchal and that representations of women tend to be stereotyped. Carnegie (1996) is critical of the representation of women as mere 'home-makers', rather than being recognised for the roles they played in key industries (see Box 4.5).

Box 4.5

Case study of the International Museum of Women

The International Museum of Women is based in San Francisco, and was originally founded as the Women's Heritage Museum in 1985. For over 10 years, the Women's Heritage Museum produced several exhibitions, hosted public programmes, sponsored an annual book fair, provided teacher resources for Women's History Month, honoured unknown women from local history and recreated historic events.

Mission

The mission of the International Museum of Women (I.M.O.W.) is to value the lives of women around the world.

Goals

1 To be an organization that honours and values women, past, present and the futures they are creating.
2 To accurately incorporate women into the historical record through both global and gender perspectives.
3 To contribute to a culture where all women have a voice and participate fully in the societies they inhabit.
4 To build global understanding by fostering international dialogues and promoting social, economic, cultural, and political equality.

In 2005, I.M.O.W. embarked on a strategy to create an innovative twenty-first century museum with innovative global online exhibitions which would engage women from all around the world. In 2006, I.M.O.W.'s strategy culminated with the launching of *Imagining Ourselves: A Global Generation of Women*, I.M.O.W.'s first interactive, multi-lingual online exhibition that connected more than a million participants around the world. In addition, local events are frequently held to encourage the attendance, education and support of local women.

In 2008, a second global online exhibition was created called *Women, Power and Politics*, which was available in four languages – Arabic, English, French and Spanish. It focused on the stories of women who had harnessed politics and power to transform women's lives and society through online exhibitions, online community-building tools, and a live speaker series.

(International Museum of Women 2009)

Simpson is largely positive about the future of museums in terms of the adoption of alternative perspectives:

> Museums are changing in many ways: their image as dusty, stuffy, boring and intimidating storehouses is slowly giving way to recognition that museums can be authoritative without being definitive; inclusive rather than exclusive; exciting, lively and entertaining while still being both scholarly and educational.
>
> (Simpson 1996: 5)

Ross (2004) suggests that museums have been forced to change because of political and economic shifts and market forces, which have been decisive in bringing about a new climate of audience awareness. He sees the trend towards greater accessibility and wider public participation as progressive, as it dispels elitism and makes museums more representative. Museums have to be more responsive to their public, to diversify and to target niche markets.

However, Appleton (2006) suggests that turning museums towards the visitor in this way is not just a change of direction or embellishment of what went before; instead it is a total reversal of the meaning and purpose of the museum. If a museum puts the perceived needs of people before its collections, then the collections lose their importance and value. However, Hooper-Greenhill (2000) describes the concept of the 'post-museum', which still holds and cares for objects, but which concentrates more on their use than further accumulation. The post-museum is also interested in intangible heritage, even if tangible objects from a culture have been largely destroyed. The post-museum represents something of a 'feminisation', which is responsive, nurtures partnerships and celebrates diversity. Black (2005) also suggests that museums should engage in audience development strategies which encourage under-represented groups to participate in museums. The European Museum of the Year award (established in 1977) goes to museums which manage to serve the general public the best.

Swarbrooke (2000) criticises museums for focusing increasingly on 'soft' history in an obvious attempt to avoid controversy and conflict. Urry (1990) also suggests that

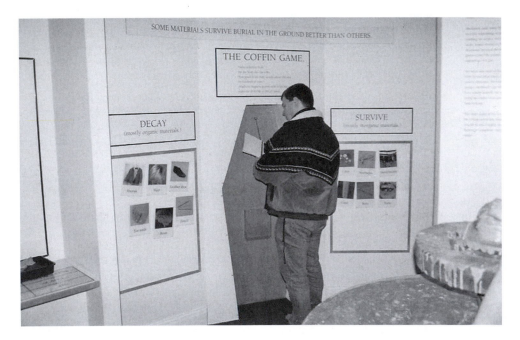

Plate 4.2 Museums can be fun

(Source: László Puczkó)

our emphasis on 'artefactual' history ignores or trivialises a whole variety of social experiences, such as war, disease, hunger and exploitation. Similarly, Kavanagh (1996: xiii) states: 'In the acceptance of alternative narratives is the recognition that if history in the museum is to be valid intellectually and worthwhile socially, it has to find ways of admitting to and dealing with the darker side of ourselves and our pasts.' This may well be true; this is therefore perhaps an appropriate point at which to consider some of the more 'dissonant' and 'darker' forms of heritage that may or may not be represented adequately in our museums and heritage sites.

Dissonant heritage and 'dark' tourism

Graham *et al.* define 'dissonant' heritage as:

> the mismatch between heritage and people, in space and time. It is caused by movements or other changes in heritage and by migration or other changes in people, transformations which characteristically involve how heritage is perceived and what value systems are filtering those perceptions.
>
> (Graham *et al.* 2000: 93)

Dissonance basically refers to the discordance or lack of agreement and consistency as to the meaning of heritage, who 'owns' it, and who should be allowed to interpret it, and in what ways.

As mentioned earlier in this chapter, the process of heritage interpretation is problematic, as it is difficult to offer the visitor a truly objective depiction of historical reality. It usually requires those heritage site managers and museum curators to select and display selected aspects of the heritage, often of a group to which they may or may not belong. If the heritage managers concerned are not members of the group whose heritage is being interpreted, this raises the question of ownership. To whom does the heritage belong, and who should have the right to interpret and present it to others? This may not be a problem in cases where the particular group can no longer claim ownership (i.e. they are an ancient civilisation, or there are no remaining survivors). As Blakey (1994: 39) writes, 'Archaeologists speak for a past that cannot represent itself . . . archaeological views of the past are reshaped by changing cultural biases'; however, the feeling of 'disinheritance' may become a crucial issue if a group feel that their rights to their heritage have been usurped by others.

A good example of disinheritance might be the strong sentiments of the Jewish community in Poland, where it was felt that the Polish communists had provided a distorted interpretation of the Holocaust, especially at the site of the concentration camp in Auschwitz. The Jews felt 'disinherited' because, in their view, the Polish had represented the events as being a national or a European tragedy rather than a Jewish one (historical evidence shows that 90 per cent of the victims who died in Auschwitz were Jewish). The visitor to Auschwitz could view a number of exhibitions which were devoted to the plight of different nationalities, including other minority groups, such as gypsies or homosexuals. Although it was important to represent each of these groups, it arguably distorted the scale of the Jewish tragedy. This situation does raise another important question about representation and the perspective of history offered to visitors. Whose experience or perception of events should be viewed as the most valuable or the most important, and how should it be represented? Should the perspective of the 'victim' always be given priority (in this case the Jewish community during the Holocaust), or is the perspective of the 'observers' (in this case, the non-Jewish Polish community) or the 'perpetrators' (here, the Nazis) equally as important to the 'true' representation of historical events (Tunbridge and Ashworth 1996)? In theory, if we hope to depict historical events as objectively as possible, then all three perspectives should be given equal priority, and would be included in a display or exhibition of those events. In such a case, however, the potential offence or upset that might be caused would no doubt lead to a very different representation of events. As well as the sensitivities around Holocaust tourism, Jewish tourism has also proved to be challenging in Poland and elsewhere (see Box 4.6).

Box 4.6

Case study of Jewish heritage tourism

With the weakening of the Communist regime in the late 1980s, and its demise in 1989, there was a reawakening of interest in what Polish historians have called 'missing a part of our history'. Unfortunately, anti-Semitism is still rife in Central and Eastern Europe, but Jewish heritage tourism to Poland is booming, and the phenomenon known as 'roots tourism' for Jews, which means travelling to Eastern Europe to discover their family history, has grown steadily since the 1980s. Many of the visitors are Israeli or American, and these nationalities also fund much of the development of the Jewish quarters.

It is estimated that there are a few hundred Jews still living in Krakow, about 200 identified as Jewish community members. Before the war, 56,000 Jews lived in Krakow and some 70 per cent of properties in Kazimierz (the Jewish quarter in Krakow) had Jewish owners. However, most perished or never returned to Poland after the war. Currently, 17,000 residents make their homes in Kazimierz, though few are Jews, says Walczak (Krakow Development Forum). Now, only one synagogue is in use. Nevertheless, the history of the quarter is still seen as an intrinsic part of its identity and character. Even though it is a 'Jewish area with no Jews', Walczak says, 'the heritage should be preserved'.

Krakow therefore has a Jewish Heritage Route, which is a walking tour of the main buildings and synagogues. There are 'Schindler's List' tours, visiting the sites where the Stephen Spielberg movie was made in 1993, and organised trips to Auschwitz/Birkenau. Many enterprising non-Jewish businesspeople have been capitalising on the renewed interest in Krakow since the filming of *Schindler's List*. Another vivid manifestation of Poland's interest in Judaism is the Krakow Jewish Culture Festival. Every year, thousands of people gather at Kazimierz, the old Jewish quarter of Krakow, to attend workshops on subjects like Jewish cooking and Hassidic dancing. But the main attraction of the festival is music: klezmer bands arrive from around the world to perform. The festival was founded in 1988 by Janusz

Makuch and Krzysztof Gierat, both of whom came from traditional Catholic homes. Due to the festival's success, Kazimierz has become even more of a tourist attraction. Asked to explain the festival's popularity, the festival director told the *New York Times*: 'You cannot have a genocide and then have people live as if everything is normal. It's like when you lose a limb. Poland is suffering from Jewish phantom pain.'

However, there is some debate about whether events like the Krakow festival reflect genuine interest in Jewish life. Even though it marks the growing appeal of Judaism, the festival invokes an image of Judaism with which many Jews are uncomfortable. 'The festival is promoting Jewish stereotypes we are not happy with,' says Piotr Pazinski, editor of the Jewish–Polish monthly *Midrasz*. 'It celebrates the popular, even anti-Semite image of the long-nosed Chasids dancing to a whining violin. It has nothing to do with actual Jewish culture and thought.'

(after Alon 2008; Cabot 2009)

A similar development is starting to take place in Vilnius in Lithuania, despite the resistance from local people who do not want a 'Jewish Disneyland', but instead want to get on with their own lives. Vilnius was known as the 'Jerusalem of Northern Europe' before the Holocaust, but now there are only two synagogues (Németh 2008b).

A heritage of guilt is perhaps being developed for the wrong reasons and for the wrong people.

Just as the interpretation of heritage usually disinherits someone in some way, there are always aspects of the past which will be dissonant or distasteful to certain individuals or communities. Much of this will depend very much on individual sensibilities. Not every tourist will want to make the pilgrimage to a concentration camp such as Auschwitz, or to First World War trenches in France or Belgium, or to a site of genocide such as the 'Killing Fields' in Cambodia. Those who do usually have their own particular motivations for doing so. Some visitors may have experienced a personal loss; others feel a sense of collective tragedy, especially if they are part of a certain community; some visit for educational purposes; some may just have a morbid fascination with the darker side of human nature, arguably a dubious motivation, but one which seems to be common to many visitors to such sites.

What are the implications for heritage site managers of this kind of heritage of atrocity, and to what extent is it acceptable to interpret such sites for the purposes of tourism? We are not referring here to tourism attractions which are purpose-built for leisure and entertainment (e.g. chambers of horrors, museums of torture and so on). Many sites of atrocity, such as concentration camps, massacre sites, battlefields or cemeteries serve as memorials to historical events and are visited as such, often for educational purposes. Within Europe, citizens are generally encouraged to learn about their collective history, however distressing it may be, whereas in other societies a more selective version of history may be taught.

Visits to military heritage sites, such as battlefields, war museums, battleships and so on, are also becoming more and more popular, especially in Europe. However, demand for this kind of tourism is also growing internationally. For example, many visitors to Thailand now visit the River Kwae bridge and Death Railway, and Vietnam affords the visitor a plethora of war-related 'attractions' such as the Cu Chi tunnels and Ho Chi Minh Trail.

It should be pointed out, however, that our perceptions of historical events and our approach to heritage interpretation are affected greatly by temporal and spatial factors. It is interesting that we are quite happy to create entertainment through battle re-enactments of the Battle of Hastings, whereas it would be considered extremely insensitive and distasteful to re-enact the trench warfare of the First World War for the purposes of entertainment. While wars and disasters are still within living memory, we cannot feel detached from the historical reality of the situation. Equally, the closer to home an historical event seems to be, the more likely we are to be sensitive to its interpretation. The historical events which are being depicted in the museums and exhibitions of Europe are still very prominent in the European collective memory, and people are sensitive to their interpretation in a way that a non-European might not be. Tourists are presented with a certain interpretation of a historical reality. In many cases this may be their only visit to a site, and their impressions of that site and their understanding of a country or region's heritage will be influenced largely by the nature of the interpretation of the site. It should therefore be managed carefully and sensitively.

Ethnic, indigenous and minority heritage

The notion of disinheritance should perhaps be discussed in more detail, as we have so far talked about the concept of a 'collective' history or heritage without really defining what is meant by this. To what extent does the interpretation of national heritage marginalise regional, ethnic or indigenous minority groups? As stated by Tunbridge and Ashworth:

> The shaping of any heritage product is by definition prone to disinherit non-participating social, ethnic or regional groups, as their distinctive historical experiences may be discounted, marginalised, distorted or ignored. This, it has been argued, is an innate potentiality and a direct consequence of the selectivity built into the concept of heritage. Choice from a wide range of pasts implies that some pasts are not selected, as history is to a greater or lesser extent hijacked by one group or another for one purpose or another.
>
> (Tunbridge and Ashworth 1996: 29)

Following the First World War, the fall of the empires in Europe meant a shift from imperial to national heritage, meaning that minority heritages were often seen as a threat to national integrity, so they were either ignored, discouraged, disinherited or removed. Gathercole and Lowenthal (1994) suggest that indigenous and ethnic minorities tend to cherish their monuments and sites as being bastions of community identity, especially as they have usually been forced to relinquish their land, religion, language and autonomy under colonial rule. Clearly, many groups are not able to represent themselves because of lack of funds to establish a museum or exhibition, or to interpret a heritage site. Coupled with the frequent destruction of non-European artefacts because of their apparent 'worthlessness', and the displacement of objects from their native lands, indigenous minorities rarely have the political leverage and economic wherewithal to reclaim and represent their heritage.

There are often arrogant assumptions that indigenous peoples need to be educated about their own cultural background and history. Worse still, there were frequently Eurocentric and elitist historians who believed that indigenous cultures were not worthy of representation. For example, the eminent historian Hugh Trevor-Roper (1965: 11) declared: 'Perhaps in the future, there will be some African history to teach. But at the present, there is none, or very little. . . . The history of the world, for the last five centuries, in so far as it has been significant, has been European history.' In addition to being deeply patronising, this comment is indicative of an intensely subjective and selective approach to the study of history which has dominated for centuries. As Gathercole and Lowenthal (1994) so brilliantly outline in *The Politics of the Past*, there is a heritage of Eurocentricity which has suppressed and undermined the history of colonised communities, a history which clearly pre-dates that of the colonising nation. It is not uncommon to hear people declare that Australia, New Zealand or the USA have little or no history, and few heritage sites compared to European countries, discounting, of course 40,000 years of Aboriginal, Maori or Native American Indian history. These important issues are discussed in more detail in Chapter 5.

The validity of history and its conversion into heritage is often questioned unless there is written documentation of its significance. This is problematic in itself, as clearly the working classes, ethnic minorities, women and other marginalised groups in society have traditionally not had access to the form of education that would be required in order to produce written documentation of their experiences. There may be fragments and remnants of physical evidence, or possibly oral histories, but the depiction of the past and the representation of its citizens has traditionally been dominated by educated, Western, white males. Hence, the distortion of historical accounts has sadly been inevitable for most of our documented past. Historians such as Trevor-Roper deemed much of the world's history to be 'irrelevant' and unworthy of serious study. Recent developments in history have perhaps been even more dangerous as historians have tried to omit or distort historical evidence in an attempt to construct an alternative narrative. For example, the revisionist historian David Irving tried to convince the public in the late 1990s of 'die Auschwitzluge' (the lie about Auschwitz). Luckily, his ideas were publicly and definitively disproved.

The development of ethnographic museums and galleries is well documented in museum studies literature. Durrans (1988) explains how ethnographic museums originally emerged as adjuncts of European expansion and colonialism; consequently representation of ethnic groups was often overtly or covertly racist or patronising. He describes how Western museums and art galleries tend to display ethnic objects in isolation, disconnected from any social context. This is in accordance with the aesthetic 'auratic' conventions of the West, whereas ethnographic museums focus more on an object's original meaning, function and purpose. Kirschenblatt-Gimblett (1998: 18) discusses in some detail the problems of displaying ethnographic collections, stating, 'Like the ruin, the ethnographic fragment is informed by the poetics of detachment.' Some interpretation may therefore be needed, as the cultural meanings attached to objects, events or traditions cannot usually be predicted from the objects alone. However, such interpretation needs to be managed carefully and sensitively, involving the appropriate ethnic community in its development.

Another problem of ethnographic museums has been the often illegal or forceful acquisition of cultural property. Although ethnographic museums are increasingly taking an ethical stance, often refusing to acquire material that has been smuggled out of the country of origin, repatriation of ethnic objects is still a sensitive and controversial issue. Simpson (1996) notes that this is particularly significant when ethnic and indigenous groups whose culture is still thriving today seek the return of their cultural property. Such objects are often symbols of their cultural identity, their future survival and cultural continuity. However, the fossilisation of ethnic and indigenous cultures is still not unusual. Cummins (1996: 92) describes how 'in many cases, museums still continued to portray African art and material culture as if it were purely ethnographic relics of the past, rather than evidence of a sentient people and a living culture'. However, there are some growing examples of good practice, as the case study in Box 4.7 shows.

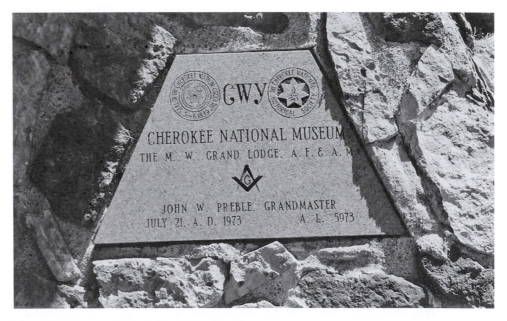

Plate 4.3 Museum dedicated to Native Americans

(Source: László Puczkó)

Box 4.7

Case study of the National Museum of the American Indian

The National Museum of the American Indian is the sixteenth museum of the Smithsonian Institution. It is the first national museum dedicated to the preservation, study, and exhibition of the life, languages, literature, history, and arts of Native Americans. Established by an act of Congress in 1989, the museum works in collaboration with the Native peoples of the Western Hemisphere to protect and foster their cultures by reaffirming traditions and beliefs, encouraging contemporary artistic expression, and empowering the Indian voice.

The museum's extensive collections, assembled largely by George Gustav Heye (1874–1957), encompass a vast range of cultural material—including more than 800,000 works of extraordinary aesthetic, religious, and historical significance, as well as articles produced for everyday, utilitarian use. The collections span all major culture areas of the Americas, representing virtually all tribes of the United States, most of those of Canada, and a significant number of cultures from Central and South America as well as the Caribbean. Chronologically, the collections include artifacts from Paleo-Indian to contemporary arts and crafts. The museum's holdings also include film and audiovisual collections, paper archives, and a photography archive of approximately 90,000 images depicting both historic and contemporary Native American life.

The National Museum of the American Indian comprises three facilities, each designed following consultations between museum staff and Native peoples. In all of its activities, the National Museum of the American Indian acknowledges the diversity of cultures and the continuity of cultural knowledge among indigenous peoples of the Western Hemisphere and Hawai'i, incorporating Native methodologies for the handling, documentation, care, and presentation of collections. NMAI actively strives to find new approaches to the study and representation of the history, materials, and cultures of Native peoples.

(Smithsonian Institution 2009)

Conclusion

This chapter has attempted to provide an overview of some of the fascinating and complex issues surrounding the development of the heritage and museum sectors, and the role cultural tourism plays within this development. It is clear that the postmodern recognition of the need for a departure from traditional, elitist and exclusive interpretations of history has led to a number of significant changes in the way in which the past is represented through heritage. Although it could be argued that the development of the cultural tourism industry has exacerbated the commodification of heritage, and the 'heritagisation' of the past, it has also led to an increase of interest in the histories and heritage of regional, ethnic, indigenous and other previously marginalised groups (e.g. women and the working classes). The future success of the sector is arguably dependent on a more inclusive, democratic and multicultural approach to both the interpretation and representation of history. Only then will society recognise the diversity and multiplicity of cultural groups that have contributed not only to its past, but also to its present and future.

5 ▶ Indigenous cultural tourism

> We are not myths of the past, ruins in the jungle, or zoos. We are people and we
> want to be respected, not to be victims of intolerance and racism.
>
> (Rigoberta Menchu Tum 1959–)

Introduction

This chapter analyses the growth of indigenous cultural tourism in a range of
environments, focusing in particular on fragile or remote locations. It is clear that
cultural tourists are becoming increasingly interested in the culture, traditions and
lifestyles of indigenous peoples, tribal and ethnic groups. Cultural tours or treks
involving visits to or overnight stays with tribal peoples or villagers are becoming
more and more popular, especially in some of the emerging destinations of the world
such as South-east Asia and Central America. Those tourists who venture in search
of traditional and ethnic cultures in remote locations are often motivated partly by an
anthropological desire to learn more about communities under threat from global
forces, but also to satisfy their need for cultural experiences of a diverse nature.
The impacts of this increasingly widespread form of cultural tourism are significant,
both for the communities who are the object of the tourist gaze, and for the local and
national economies that stand to benefit from tourism development. The inevitable
consequence of increased tourism is often the gradual erosion of the social fabric,
acculturation and irreversible destruction of natural habitats. This form of tourism
can easily become a kind of cultural voyeurism in which the local indigenous
population is reduced to little more than a human zoo. However, if managed carefully,
indigenous cultural tourism has the potential to benefit local communities
considerably. Cultural tourism may be seen as a means of increasing the profile of
indigenous peoples and to bring economic benefits. It can also lead to a renewal

of cultural pride and community cohesion if managed carefully. This chapter aims to discuss ways in which the potential benefits of cultural tourism can be maximised for indigenous communities.

What is indigenous cultural tourism?

The terminology used to describe the kind of tourism where tourists visit local people in their natural habitat has been variously referred to as 'ethnic', 'tribal', 'native' or 'Aboriginal'; however, Butler and Hinch (2007) prefer to use the umbrella term 'indigenous'. Indigenous groups are described as being distinct in terms of their culture and identity relative to dominant groups in society. This may include their traditions, their language, their political systems and institutions, and their ties to natural environments and territories.

Indigenous tourism implies visiting native people in their own habitat which is different from that of the tourist, whereas ethnic tourism could refer to engaging in the cultural activities of a minority group within the tourist's own society. For the purposes of this book, a distinction is made between indigenous cultural tourism and ethnic cultural tourism. The former refers to the lifestyles and traditions of tribal groups living within fragile and remote environments, often in post-colonial developing countries, whereas the latter refers to the arts and culture of ethnic minority groups, immigrants and diasporas living largely within post-imperial Western societies. For example, Shaw (2007) notes the increasing importance of 'ethnoscapes' in cities, which are largely inhabited by diasporic groups and ethnic minorities. Maitland (2007) also suggests that many visitors are attracted to areas on the fringes of cities or districts where development is organic, and experiences are spontaneous and more authentic.

Indigenous cultural tourism usually involves visiting native or indigenous people, such as tribal groups or ethnic minorities, in their 'natural environment'. This may be an area that is a designated cultural landscape, a national park, a jungle, a desert or a mountainous region. More often than not, it will be a remote and relatively fragile location that is not easily accessible to the average tourist. Land issues have been one of the most controversial aspects of indigenous people's lives; therefore many groups have been shifted from what was once their traditional homeland. In addition, now that the frontiers of modern tourism have been pushed to the limit, no area of the world is technically out of reach, which has serious implications for both the natural environment and the fragile cultures of indigenous groups.

Many tour operators are now capitalising on the exoticism of indigenous, ethnic and tribal groups. Activities such as hilltribe, mountain or desert trekking are becoming increasingly popular. Even without face-to-face contact with indigenous groups, tourists are keen to purchase indigenous arts and crafts as souvenirs, as well as enjoying the cultural displays and performances that seem to constitute an integral part of the tourist experience.

The following list suggests a typology for indigenous cultural tourism and the kinds of activities and destinations that are becoming increasingly popular among tourists:

- Hilltribe and mountain trekking (e.g. Thailand, Vietnam, Peru, Chile, Nepal, China, India).
- Wildlife tourism and national parks (e.g. Kenya, Tanzania, South Africa, Botswana, Namibia).
- Rainforest and jungle ecotours (e.g. Brazil, Ecuador, Costa Rica, Indonesia, Malaysia).
- Desert trekking (e.g. Tunisia, Morocco, Egypt, Mongolia, India, Middle East).
- Arctic and northern periphery tourism (e.g. Canada, Alaska, Scandinavia, Greenland, Iceland).
- Village tourism (e.g. Senegal, Mali, Indonesia, Malaysia, South Pacific islands).
- Cultural heritage tourism (e.g. New Zealand, Australia, North America, Hawaii).
- Arts and crafts tourism (e.g. Guatemala, Mexico, Lapland, Mali, Panama).

The profile of indigenous cultural tourists is changing rapidly. In the past, the market was composed largely of allocentric tourists; that is, adventurous or intrepid individuals seeking the unexplored and the untouched. Although many activities such

Plate 5.1 Maasai, Kenya

(Source: Georgina Smith)

as hilltribe, mountain or desert trekking are still dominated mainly by the independent backpacker market, other forms of indigenous tourism (e.g. cultural heritage, arts and crafts, and village tourism) are now starting to form part of mainstream tourism packages. In fact, wildlife tourism on indigenous tribal lands in countries such as Kenya and Tanzania has almost become a mass tourism phenomenon. The ubiquitous cultural performances, displays and arts and crafts markets also indicate the growing significance of indigenous culture for the tourism product (see Box 5.1).

Box 5.1

Case study of Maasai tourism in Tanzania and Kenya

Kenya and Tanzania are two of the most popular tourism destinations in Africa, and also two of the best places in the world to view wildlife. They are also home to the indigenous Maasai tribal people, who are semi-nomadic pastoralists whose life centred traditionally on herding cattle. The creation of the Maasai Mara Wildlife Reserve in Kenya led to local land being taken away from the tribal groups who used the land for grazing their cattle. It is gradually being recognised that it is becoming almost impossible for the Maasai to maintain their traditional culture and lifestyle. Weaver (1998) describes how the colonial legacy of the park system in Kenya has led to the curtailment of many traditional activities.

Van der Duim *et al.* (2006) describe how the Maasai are still seen as quintessentially African, a mysterious and exotic community untouched by Western influence. This is, of course, something of a stereotyped view. The establishment of cultural 'manyattas' (something similar to a reservation) means that tourists can go on a wildlife safari and also visit Maasai in their 'natural habitat'. Tourists usually pay an entrance fee, and are then welcomed with song and dance, a talk about Maasai culture, a tour around the manyatta, and demonstrations of Maasai lifestyle (e.g. fire-making, handicrafts, warrior rituals). However, these cultural manyattas can seem more like museums as most of the activities are simulated and many villages are modern reconstructions.

There have been some efforts to provide more benefits for Maasai people. One programme in Tanzania is the initiative of the Dutch development organisation known as SNV which has been directly involved in Tanzania's community development programmes, especially in the rural areas. The main goal is that indigenous communities should directly benefit from tourists who visit their areas. Cultural tourism allows local people such as Maasai, Pare, Sambaa, Wa-Arusha, Gogo, Nyakyusa and Wazaramo and Sukuma by the side of Lake Victoria to offer tours that show their culture, their sacred places of worship, and economic activities such as farming, pastoralism and fishing. Visitors can also visit clinics and primary schools. The income generated is used by local people for specific development programmes, such as the building of dispensaries, schools and cattle dip sites. Although there are still problems of gender inequality (i.e. women receiving less revenue than men despite doing the same or more work), such projects can raise incomes, enhance self-esteem and increase cultural pride.

(Van der Duim, Peters and Akama 2006; Introducing Africa 2009)

The environments in which indigenous activities take place are clearly diverse, usually fragile and often remote. Although this chapter is concerned principally with the cultural dimension of tourism, the environmental issues are significant, since they impact greatly on the lifestyles and traditions of indigenous peoples. Issues relating to land ownership are central to their struggle for survival and, in many cases, tribal groups have been forcibly moved from their homeland so that a national park, hotel complex or golf course can be developed. The environmental impacts of tourism activities such as trekking are well documented. Such environments cannot easily withstand large groups of tourists, especially as they are often home to numerous indigenous tribal groups who then become part of the tourist landscape.

Ecotourism is a form of tourism that was more concerned originally with environmental than with cultural issues, but its development has inevitably encroached on the lifestyle, traditions and culture of indigenous peoples, who often reside in the visited areas (e.g. rainforests, jungles, mountain regions). It encourages the use of indigenous guides, local products and local resources. Many tour operators have jumped on to the ecotourism bandwagon in an effort to declare themselves 'green' or 'ethical' (see Box 5.2 opposite). Of course, ecotourism can be a relatively sustainable form of tourism if it is well managed and small-scale.

It is clearly difficult to generalise about the impacts of tourism activities on the host community of the destination. This will depend largely on the stage of tourism development, the degree of previous local exposure to external influences, the size and structure of the indigenous community, and the nature of their lifestyle, culture and traditions. Throughout this chapter a number of examples are given to illustrate some of the impacts of tourism on different indigenous groups, as well as discussing some of the measures that have been taken to protect their interests. The following section demonstrates why it is necessary to support and protect such groups.

A profile of indigenous peoples

It is important to understand some of the factors that have impacted on the lifestyles and traditions of indigenous peoples in both the pre- and post-colonial eras. The ongoing plight of indigenous minorities is more often than not a consequence of the colonial process whereby many communities were subjugated, disempowered or persecuted. European colonisers tended to assume an innate superiority over native people, many of whom had lived on the land for thousands of years before their arrival. This made them feel entitled to the best land, the right to enslave the local people, or to convert them to a more 'civilised' way of life or religion. Land was often taken from the native peoples by force. Despite their struggles they were

Box 5.2

Case study of rainforest ecotourism in Latin America

Zeppel (2006: 1) writes about indigenous ecotourism, which she describes as 'nature-based attractions or tours owned by indigenous people, and also indigenous interpretation of the natural and cultural environment including wildlife'. She focuses in particular on the Pacific Islands, Latin America, Africa and South-east Asia.

To give an example, Latin America has 13 million indigenous people in Central America and over 15 million in South America. They can represent more than 50 per cent of the population (e.g. in Bolivia – 66 per cent or Guatemala – 60 per cent). They mostly live in highland regions, rainforest and rural areas. In Latin America, the indigenous people are referred to as *Indigenas*, Indians and Amerindians.

Ecotourism ventures can help to provide a means of preserving natural and cultural resources, and a way of making a living. The southern countries of Chile, Argentina, Paraguay and Uraguay have few indigenous ecotourism ventures, but there are many in Central America, Costa Rica and Belize. Ecuador has one of the most developed indigenous ecotourism developments. This includes jungle ecolodges, rainforest tours, canoeing, trekking in the Andes, visiting Indian villages, and participation in rituals and traditions (e.g. ceremonies, face painting, fire making, dancing).

Tourism development has often provided a good economic alternative to logging, mining and agriculture; it can help to support schools and improve healthcare, as well as strengthening indigenous cultures. Conservation NGOs and other donor agencies help Indian groups to develop ecotourism projects and to preserve their environment, especially rainforests. Some of the barriers to development include remoteness, communication, access to tourist markets, community training and funding. A final problem is that the growth of so many Indigenous ecotourism ventures in Latin America may not be matched by market demand.

(after Zeppel 2006)

---

usually outnumbered, and sometimes subjected to intense violence. Colonisation also brought new and dangerous diseases such as smallpox which wiped out whole families. Indigenous culture and religious beliefs were usually suppressed, and local people's children were sometimes taken away from their families by force to be educated by the white colonisers or to be married to a non-indigenous person in order to 'purify' the race.

In more recent decades, other factors have taken their toll on the lives and traditions of indigenous peoples. Mining, deforestation, road building and civil war are all responsible for threatening the long-term survival of tribal peoples, and many are still subjected to racism, persecution and violence. The legacy that remains for many

Plate 5.2 Rice harvesting in Kerala

(Source: Melvyn Smith)

indigenous people is more often than not one of poverty, deprivation and social exclusion. Frideres (1988) describes the culture of indigenous people as 'a culture of poverty', and gives the example of the socio-economic characteristics of indigenous Inuit people in Canada as having higher rates of unemployment, suicide and incarceration, and lower income and education levels than non-indigenous peoples. Butler and Hinch (1996) suggest that this profile is often typical of indigenous people throughout the world, and that tourism is viewed consequently as a potential means of supporting community development and enhancing socio-economic status. In some cases, cultural tourism can have a positive impact, albeit small, on the revitalisation of local indigenous culture.

One example of the plight of indigenous peoples is that of the Native American Indians, who were present in North America as far back as 200,000 BC. Until the first explorers arrived in the fifteenth century and the first settlers came in the 1600s, they led a relatively peaceful life in harmony with nature and were self-sufficient. Settlers brought with them fatal diseases, enslaved, kidnapped or massacred the people, and prohibited their spiritual or religious practices. Their children were often abducted and sent to boarding schools far away. Despite their valiant revolts, the Native Indians were unable to stop their lands being taken away from them, and by 1776 they were forced to cede over 90 per cent of their ancient homelands. By 1871

Plate 5.3 Native American Indian settlement in the Petrified Forest, California

(Source: Károly Novák)

this figure had risen to 99 per cent. The Indians were forced to live in reservations, often in squalid conditions, and many were filled with despair.

Throughout the next century, the Native Indians remained determined to continue the traditions of their ancestors, but it was not until the 1980s that a revival of interest in their culture, heritage and traditions began to manifest itself, partly among the tribes themselves, and partly supported by the government and tourism development. During the 1990s, many tribes began to rediscover their heritage and to explore ways of celebrating it. The development of cultural tourism has been one of the ways in which Native Indian culture is being revived. Native American cultural centres are being developed throughout North America and parts of Canada to provide a space for exhibitions, performances or demonstrations. Tours are conducted around the reservations and gift shops sell handcrafted goods. Native American museums and cultural centres can help to reaffirm cultural identity by providing a means of preserving aspects of culture such as artefacts, languages and skills. They can also provide a venue for community education and activities (Steele-Prohaska 1996; Simpson 1996).

The Native Indian story is not unique. Many indigenous peoples suffered a similar fate, and only their courage, determination and resilience have prevented the complete annihilation of their culture and traditions. Although nothing can compensate for the atrocities of the past, such groups are now accorded more political support and there is more recognition of the plight of indigenous peoples. Cultural tourism can often help them to gain support for the preservation of their culture and traditions.

The role of charities and action groups in support of indigenous peoples

Indigenous issues are highly politicised because the majority of ethnic and tribal groups are fighting for their cultural survival in an increasingly globalised world, usually without access to adequate political or legal protection and support. It should be noted that many of the conflicts that affect indigenous peoples constitute human rights abuses. Consequently, a number of international and national organisations are working for and with indigenous peoples to protect their interests. Not all of these organisations are chiefly concerned with the impacts of tourism on the lifestyles and traditions of native peoples, but tourism is only one of the many factors that threaten the well-being and future of indigenous groups.

One of the highest profile organisations devoted to indigenous peoples is Survival International, which is the only worldwide organisation supporting tribal peoples through public campaigns. It was founded in 1969 in response to massacres, land theft and genocide in Brazil's Amazonia. Survival has supporters in 82 countries, and it works for tribal peoples' rights through campaigns, education and funding. This includes letter writing, lobbying politicians, disseminating information and supplying legal advice. Tribal peoples are given a platform from which to both defend and represent themselves. Much of Survival's work aims to contest the notion that tribal peoples are relics and that they are inevitably going to die out or be assimilated because of 'progress'. Survival is an autonomous organisation that refuses national government funding in order to ensure freedom of action. Although it is not the organisation's main preoccupation, Survival is involved in some tourism-related campaigns, often in support of Tourism Concern – another high-profile organisation which campaigns at both international and national level against the exploitation of indigenous peoples. Many of the campaigns relate to land-use conflicts, the displacement of traditional industries, water consumption, the sex tourism industry or cultural conflicts. They have also established a Fair Trade in Tourism Network which fights for equitable and ethical trading rights for disadvantaged communities in poorer regions of the world.

Other organisations such as the World Council of Indigenous Peoples and Cultural Survival also protect the rights of indigenous peoples. Again, much of their work is based on research, dissemination of information, campaigns, education, conferences and, most importantly, supplying a strong support network for indigenous groups worldwide. It is worth noting that there are many other national and regional groups that campaign on behalf of indigenous, ethnic or tribal groups, for example, in North America or Australia. Many of these organisations work closely with the international organisations, and can be accessed through linked websites.

The majority of these groups are campaigning for indigenous rights, autonomy and the control or freedom to develop tourism in a way that befits best the needs of the local community. The following sections explore in more detail some of the issues relating to indigenous community tourism.

A community-based approach to indigenous cultural tourism development

The importance of a community-based approach to tourism development has clearly been recognised over the past two decades, increasingly in the context of the sustainable tourism debate. It is clear that few communities have equal access to political and economic resources, especially Aboriginal peoples and indigenous minorities who are often politically, economically and socially disadvantaged. Community-based tourism can offer such communities the chance to move towards greater political self-determination, but only if local control is maximised. As stated by Butler and Hinch (1996: 5), tourism should be planned and managed so that 'indigenous people dictate the nature of the experience and negotiate their involvement in tourism from a position of strength'. In their later publication, Butler and Hinch (2007) suggest that indigenous peoples had at least made some inroads into self-determination and involvement.

Zeppel suggests:

> Successful community-based ecotourism requires the empowerment of community members through local participation and control of tourism decision-making, employment and training opportunities, and increased entrepreneurial activities by local people.
>
> (Zeppel 2006: 284)

Indigenous groups have sometimes had no control over tourism development whatsoever, but, as discussed above, charities, action groups and other political organisations are trying to ensure that consultation and involvement are maximised. This may include an advisory role at the planning stage, joint or sole management of key tourism initiatives, and employment in or ownership of tourism-related businesses. However, as outlined by Butler and Hinch (1996), many tourism ventures are dominated by non-indigenous groups with strong ties to the global tourism industry. It illustrates clearly the complexity of developing a form of tourism that is acceptable to the local indigenous community and which is at the same time economically viable and environmentally sustainable (see Box 5.3).

Box 5.3

Case study of indigenous tourism in Alaska

Today Alaska Natives (or indigenous Alaskans) represent approximately 16 per cent of Alaska's residents, and are a significant segment of the population in over 200 rural villages and communities. Many Alaska Natives have retained their customs, language, hunting and fishing practices and ways of living since 'the creation times.' Alaska's Native people are divided into eleven distinct cultures, speaking twenty different languages. In order to tell the stories of this diverse population, the Alaska Native Heritage Center is organized based on five cultural groupings, which draw upon cultural similarities or geographic proximity. With cultural tourism growing nationwide, many of Alaska's 227 Native village corporations are counting on their unique lifestyle and spectacular scenery to provide economic opportunities.

Alaska's Silver Hand Program also protects indigenous artists and guarantees consumers that items bearing the Silver Hand identification seal are authentic—made in Alaska, by native artists. The Alaska State Council on the Arts, a continuing partnership between the public and private sectors, champions an enriched atmosphere for lifelong participation in Alaska's rich artistic diversity. For students, artists and all Alaskans, the Council seeks to:

- Advocate arts programs that reflect and sustain the cultural identities of the people of Alaska.
- Promote the perpetuation and recognition of Alaska Native Arts.
- Demonstrate that the arts are central to the vitality of communities and citizens.
- Provide informational and educational services.
- Facilitate the development of Alaska's cultural resources.
- Match resources with needs.

(Alaska Wilderness Recreation and Tourism Association 2009)

However, despite government support, there have still been some problems with Native tourism development. For example, Haakanson (2009) who is director of the Alutiiq Museum, highlights some of the difficulties of developing indigenous tourism in Alaska (and which are typical of elsewhere too). First, few tourists have any knowledge of remote indigenous cultures, and therefore promotion is a big challenge, especially with limited resources. Second, indigenous groups do not always agree among themselves what they want from tourism (or even if they want it at all). Third, tourists are not anthropologists, and the majority simply want to have fun, relax, sleep in a warm bed, and not to work very hard while learning something new. As a tourist they get only a bird's eye view of Native life, and most are not truly interested in living this way themselves. One example is given of the cultural camp on Kodiak Island, Alaska which did not fit into the normal expectations of visitors for an expensive remote stay at an exotic locale. As stated by Haakanson (2009):

> Most visitors expect a warm bedroom, not bunkroom, limited number of bugs, nothing dead to see or strange foods you had to look at and then eat. This may appeal to us but it was too much for visitors and more than they expect to see or experience.

Although modern tourists clearly enjoy the culture and heritage, they often do not like the lifestyle that comes with it!

The final problem is that indigenous peoples have frequently been told to forget the past and to embrace modern living. However, as a result of heritage conservation and tourism development, they are now being told to protect and preserve their traditions. This means living in two worlds simultaneously, one traditional and one modern.

Indigenous involvement in and attitudes to cultural tourism development

The extent of indigenous involvement in and control of cultural tourism development is variable, and will depend very much on the context in which development is taking place and the degree of local support. Although indigenous peoples are still rarely given complete control or ownership of tourist sites or attractions, there have been definite moves towards consultative, joint or co-operative management. Co-operative arrangements can be highly beneficial as long as indigenous peoples are treated as equal partners. However, ultimately, the majority of indigenous peoples are likely to be seeking the kind of empowerment that enables them to move towards sole ownership and management of tourism venues and initiatives. However, better support is often needed in terms of funding, education and business skills training. As discussed earlier in the chapter, international agencies are keen to ensure that indigenous people are given the support they need to become involved at all levels of tourism development and management, but there is still a long way to go.

Accessibility of the site and its location are key considerations. There is clearly no point developing cultural tourism in a location that is inaccessible to tourists. Equally, tourists have to know that the site exists, and therefore marketing is a major consideration. The interpretation of history and heritage should be undertaken by the people themselves in ways that they consider to be appropriate. It is assumed generally that cultural tourists want to experience the authentic culture of the local environment and its people, and will go to great lengths in search of the ultimate authentic experience. This may involve pushing the frontiers of tourism further and further, and visiting the most remote locations. Selwyn (1996) explores the concept of the tension between the quest for the 'authentic Other' and the quest for the 'authentic Self'. It is not unusual to hear of tourists who want to spend time with native peoples in an attempt to 'find themselves'! This is particularly true of the hippy tourists who first went to countries like India in the 1960s and 1970s. However, it is evident that some tourists are not so much seeking authenticity, but are actually in search of a romanticised vision of 'primitive' or native living. Those who are keen to escape the trappings of the globalised, material world will relish the notion of spending some time in a remote village without running water and electricity. Ironically, the villagers themselves might be just as keen to procure Western goods such as Coca-Cola, Nike trainers and satellite TV.

Tourists are increasingly being encouraged to take organised treks into the hilltribe country of northern Thailand in the region of Chiang Mai and Chiang Rai. Most of the trips involve a two- or three-day trek with a local guide through jungle areas and include overnight stays in tribal villages. The activities offered are mainly hiking, bamboo rafting and elephant riding. The tribal groups visited depends on the routes taken, but it is the usual practice to visit at least three different tribal

---

Box 5.4

Case study of tribal tourism in Papua New Guinea

The Independent State of Papua New Guinea is a country in Oceania occupying the eastern half of the island of New Guinea and numerous offshore islands (the western portion of the island is a part of the Indonesian provinces of Papua and West Papua). It is located in the southwestern Pacific Ocean, in a region defined since the early 19th century as Melanesia. It is one of the most diverse countries on Earth, with over 800 indigenous languages and at least as many traditional societies, out of a population of just under 6 million. It is also one of the most rural, with only 18 per cent of its people living in urban centres. The majority of people, whether they be from the Highlands to the Coastal regions, remain dependent on subsistence farming and live in small villages.

The country is also one of the world's least explored, culturally and geographically, and many undiscovered species of plants and animals are thought to exist in the interior of Papua New Guinea. Very few people have visited, often because they are concerned about safety and security. It traditionally had high crime rates. Zeppel (2006) adds that high transport and tour costs and tribal fighting have limited the growth of tourism.

The PNG Tourism Promotion Authority has made renewed efforts to revitalise itself and its product, promoting great surfing, fishing, diving and trekking and a resurgent interest in wartime history. The slogans include: 'Like every place you've never been' and 'PNG: where tourism is not an industry'. A few tour operators offer eco-adventure tours, which take visitors to remote rural villages to experience aboriginal tribes' cultural and natural environments. Village homestays and guesthouses are also becoming more common.

However, the island is full of remote island communities who have been exposed to very little western influence. Some tribes are still cannibals (they are among the last people in the world to practice cannibalism). There have been stories of tribal tours which are not only very expensive and time-consuming, but dangerous too. Some tribes were so hostile to tourism that they blocked the rivers with logs and even shot at tourists on rafts with bows and arrows! However, anthropologists have suggested that many tribes are keen to negotiate their relationship with the world and tourists within their system of strongly held beliefs. The diversity of tribes means that it is impossible to generalize about the needs and wishes of indigenous peoples in PNG. Development therefore needs to take place on a carefully and sensitively negotiated tribe-by-tribe basis.

(Eirne 2007)

---

groups. There are at least seven or eight different indigenous groups living within this area of Thailand. Many are subsistence farmers (e.g. rice, corn, livestock, opium), and some are involved in local crafts production (e.g. textiles, embroidery, silversmithing). Most groups have their own dialect, and the majority practise the animist religion. Opium addiction is common, and this is not helped by the fact that some tourists view opium-smoking as one of the highlights of the trip. Some tourists may even travel to an indigenous area only because of a desired drug experience. For example, Grunwell (1998) writes about 'ayahuasca tourism' in South America. Ayahuasca is a hallucinogenic drug which can actually be procured outside the region, but many tourists want to experience the Shamanic rituals that go with it (see Box 5.5).

Box 5.5

Case study of ayahuasca tourism in South America

Many native Amazonians revere ayahuasca, believing it to be a sacred plant, imbued with a living spirit that speaks to them when they enter into discourse with the brew. In many authentic milieus, ayahausca is a purgative, a substance taken to cleanse and heal the body and mind. In common parlance, it is an hallucinogetic drug! The early missionary reports generally claimed it was demonic, and great efforts were made by the Roman Catholic Church to stamp it out. However, Peruvians regard ayahuasca as an herbal tonic rather than an illegal drug. It is a valued part of Peruvian spiritual and economic life. The government tourist agencies sponsor ayahuasca festivals, the product is openly sold in markets, and even Peru's president once participated in an ayahuasca ceremony.

Ayahuasca tourism takes place in the villages, rainforests and jungles of Peru, Columbia, Bolivia and Brazil, and attracts visitors from all over the world, especially from Europe, the US and Australia. Although ayahuasca is more widely available than just in this region, many people travel here from all over the world just to use it. It provides them with an extremely novel, exotic experience, and it is also a cultural and spiritual one, as the substance is usually taken within a tribal setting in the presence of a local shaman. Stuart (2002) suggests that 'Shamanism' came into vogue in the 1990s, with some Europeans and North Americans travelling to South America to find the wisdom, and the brews of other traditions. He also cynically states that 'Ayahuasca tourists are often bewildered by the fact that almost every shaman claims to be the only person in all of Amazonia who knows how to properly brew the magic potion.'

Advertising ayahuasca tourism is achieved through a number of media, primarily periodicals and the Internet. Most internet sites are devoted to a single group, offering tours either through Amazonia, or the use of a compound for ayahuasca sessions. Adverts for ayahuasca tourism can be found in periodicals such as *Magical Blend* and *Shaman's Drum*. Some tour groups venture into the wilderness to visit encampments of indigenous groups, experiencing ayahuasca in a supposedly authentic setting. Others visit mestizo shamans (more accurately, healers known as ayahuasqueros) or operate out of compounds organised around ayahuasca tour groups. This is clearly quite a powerful experience for most visitors, and it has been cited by many (including the pop stars Sting, Paul Simon and Tori Amos) as being quite disturbing, and not something to be taken lightly. Ayahuasca can have adverse interactions with various prescription medicines, particularly some medications used to treat AIDS, depression and psychiatric disorders.

(adapted from Grunwell 1998; Stuart 2002)

The cultural representation of indigenous peoples

The establishment of museums, cultural centres and performance space is a good way of exhibiting local culture. The development of arts and crafts initiatives is also an increasingly popular way of maximising economic benefits for communities. The following section explores some of these issues in more depth.

Ali states:

> The 'struggle over the relations of representation' though it is not yet over, echoes strongly the legacy of empire in its 'us' and 'them' colonial relations. A politics of representation is altogether a more complex, more interesting and more open challenge for the future.
>
> (Ali 1991: 211)

Museums and galleries have been subject to criticism in recent years because of their inadequate or inaccurate representation or interpretation of black, indigenous and minority cultures in exhibitions. As stated by Creamer (1990: 132), 'a white, Western, colonizing ideology has provided the intellectual framework for interpreting indigenous cultures the world over'. Simpson refers to the concept of 'scientific colonialism' whereby anthropologists have claimed that cultural colonialism continues to control the representation of indigenous arts and culture, especially in museum collections and exhibitions:

> Indigenous groups in Australia, New Zealand and North America, while unique and diverse, share certain similarities with regards to their treatment historically at the hands of colonial powers, their status as disempowered minority communities in their own countries, and the history of their treatment by anthropologists and museum interpreters.
>
> (Simpson 1996: 80)

Ethnic minorities tend to be under-represented in the arts and museum world, as they have traditionally lacked the power and control to determine exhibition content and interpretation. Hence, interpretation of indigenous collections or exhibitions is often left in the hands of non-indigenous peoples who may or may not understand fully the culture and traditions they are depicting. Traditionally, the culture of indigenous peoples has been fossilised in museum exhibitions or viewed with nostalgia, implying that it has vanished or disappeared, rather than being dynamic and ongoing. As stated by Dann (1996: 366), 'museums emerged as warehouses of assembled artefacts rather than representations of living cultures'. However, museum exhibitions are now focusing increasingly on the 'truth' of indigenous and colonial history, as well as attempting to represent and interpret indigenous traditions and culture more accurately.

Indigenous lifestyles and traditions have often been romanticised or described as 'exotic'. Jordan and Weedon describe how Australian Aborigines are typically perceived in the West, a description that could apply easily to many other indigenous groups:

> Most images in the West of Australian Aborigines are of 'primitive', 'tribal' people – the uncivilised 'dying race' of the anthropologist, *National Geographic* and documentary films; the dark-skinned savages of cultural evolutionist texts; the scary nature-people of 'Crocodile Dundee'; the 'stone age artists' of Australian travel brochures. The images are of naked primitives with their boomerangs, stone axes and spears, their ancestral sites and secret rituals, their traditional songs, dances and Dreamtime stories, their bark paintings and body decorations – living in harmony with nature, blending into the flora and fauna.
>
> (Jordan and Weedon 1995: 489)

They remark that this is clearly a romanticised vision of the exotic native of the white Western imagination. It stands in stark contrast to the reality of the large groups of uprooted, oppressed and demoralised Aborigines who are living in shanty towns plagued by poverty and alcoholism.

Whittaker (2000) comments on the way that postcards over the past century have traditionally depicted indigenous people in a stereotyped, exoticised or eroticised way. The patronisingly benevolent and covertly racist depiction of the 'noble savage' is perhaps the best-known example of this. Most postcard production has pandered traditionally to a white, Eurocentric mythology of the 'Other'. Because indigenous peoples were perceived increasingly as a dying breed, the capturing and fossilising of cultural images was deemed imperative:

> The world's indigenous people provided a limitless reservoir for a traffic in images. The myth of the time was that there is a world of types, a veritable smorgasbord of racial, ethnic and indigenous people. Deeply-rooted beliefs about colonial entitlements, sanctified by science and its closest lieutenants, truth and reality, kept these types prisoners of the roving camera. The task of scientist and layperson alike was to document and preserve the huge variety of peoples, surely a global mission to record each and every 'type' and 'species' and 'culture'.
>
> (Whittaker 2000: 428)

Dann (1996) comments on the way in which the 'Other' has been traditionally depicted in travelogues. Images of natives are often overtly seductive, exotic, quaint or cute relative to the traveller's own culture. Although little interaction is depicted between host and guest, locals are usually depicted as being in a subordinate position. In some cases local people are shown to be exploitative, hostile or something of a nuisance; in other cases they are marginalised or deemed irrelevant. Dann (1996: 366) comments on this 'new' form of tourism: 'Even in the very act of sightseeing, attractions become ways of remaining out of contact with destination peoples.'

However, at the other end of the spectrum are those tourists who are keen to spend as much time as possible in close contact with local people and to experience authentic culture. Increasingly, images of native peoples are being used to attract tourists. Kirschenblatt-Gimblett (1998) notes, for example, that Australia and New Zealand tend to identify their uniqueness as tourist destinations with the indigenous, a fact that is becoming increasingly apparent in their national marketing campaigns. Similarly, Power (1997: 54) emphasises the significance of aboriginal arts to the cultural tourism product in Australia:

> Today it is the visual arts that offer Aboriginal Australia its greatest empowerment in our efforts to have our culture recognised locally, nationally and internationally. Foreign statistics reveal that at least 60% of all visitors to Australia cite an interest in Aboriginal culture as one of the reasons they come down under.

However, arts tourism has not always been viewed as a positive development in indigenous contexts, especially with regard to Aboriginal arts. For example, Fourmile states:

> Much Aboriginal artistic endeavour is commercially driven, aimed at the tourist dollar . . . with an enormous current emphasis on Aboriginal cultural tourism, one senses that much of the revival and maintenance of aspects of Aboriginal traditions will be dependent on, and therefore modified to suit the needs of tourism.
>
> (Fourmile 1994: 75)

She also notes that tourists tend to be selective in their interest in Aboriginal arts, preferring dance groups or crafts to music, drama or literature.

The growing interest in indigenous culture and arts and crafts tourism raises important questions about concepts such as authenticity and commodification. Richards (1999) describes how culture, crafts and tourism are becoming inseparable partners. Arts and crafts production can play a central role in the local economy of indigenous communities, and tourism can help to support and strengthen the continuation of local cultural production. The kinds of souvenirs that might be purchased depend very much on local resources and traditions, but may include textiles, carvings, pottery, paintings and jewellery, among others. It is noted that the authenticity of arts and crafts is considered to be very important for the majority of cultural tourists. Tourists want to be assured that the product they are buying is made by a local craftworker, and reflects traditional methods and a design which is characteristic of the local area. Of course, the commodification and mass production of tourist souvenirs is widespread, but many craftworkers are now using government-approved stamps of authenticity to protect local production and to reassure tourists seeking authentic products.

Nevertheless, the proliferation of pseudo-traditional art forms is sometimes a cause for concern, especially among indigenous peoples who are keen to preserve their traditions. Local arts and crafts production is increasingly under threat in many parts of the world, and although tourism can lead to a revival of traditions that might otherwise be lost, numerous examples of cultural change are inherent in the art forms that are produced. Graburn's (1976) work on the changes in Fourth World arts and the commercialisation of cultural traditions is still one of the most comprehensive studies on this subject. Schadler's (1979) work on arts and crafts in Africa is also worth consulting, as he outlines many of the modifications that have been made to traditional and tribal art forms in response to the demands of tourism. Mathieson and Wall also cite numerous examples of the changes that have taken place within traditional art forms over time. They show the three major phases of change in traditional art forms resulting from outside contact:

> 1 The disappearance of traditional artistic designs and art and craft forms, particularly those with deep religious and mythical affiliations. This is followed by;
>
> 2 The growth of a degenerate, unsophisticated replacement which develops in association with mass production techniques. This is often followed by;
>
> 3 The resurgence of skilful craftsmanship and distinctive styles incorporating the deeper cultural beliefs of the host society. This phase is a response to the deleterious impacts evident in Phase 2 and also to the gradual decline in the symbolic meaning of traditional arts which also occurs in the second phase.
>
> (Mathieson and Wall 1992: 165)

This is a largely positive model, implying that the final outcome leads to a resurgence of interest in traditional designs and production methods, although there are still concerns about changing production methods, the quality and authenticity of the products, and the nature of the tourism market. However, De Vidas (1995: 81) makes the point that '[i]nstead of dwelling on the dialectic of the maleficent or beneficent effects of tourism on visited societies it will be more pertinent to focus upon their social, economic and cultural reorganization in response to that access.' Indeed, more recent studies of arts and crafts tourism have tended to focus on the needs of local artists, producers and craftspeople and the protection of their interests. As the demand for crafts tourism grows, the role of the intermediary is becoming problematic for the distribution and sales of arts and crafts products, as it can easily lead to the exploitation of local people. Fair trade initiatives (e.g. Tourism Concern's Fair Trade in Tourism Network) are therefore being set up in order to protect local producers from exploitation, and more emphasis is being placed on local training needs (see Box 5.6).

The performing arts are increasingly forming an integral part of the indigenous cultural tourism experience. This may be in the form of music, singing, dancing, festivals or rituals. Local festivals in particular are a big draw, especially in countries such as India which are renowned for their colourful celebrations of life, religion and spirituality. More often than not, they represent an authentic cultural experience for

---

Box 5.6

Case study of Aboriginal arts tourism in Australia

A 2007 press release on behalf of Australia's tourism minister, Paul Henderson, stated that a new travel initiative would be launched in the Northern Territory based on Aboriginal art trails. The Northern Territory is home to Australia's largest population of Aboriginal people.

This initiative aimed to attract more visitors to the Northern Territory by developing partnerships between Aboriginal artists and tour operators throughout Arnhem Land and Alice Springs. 'The Art Trails will take art-lovers to meet artists and visit Aboriginal art centres to learn more about Aboriginal art and culture, and add to their art collections by purchasing directly from communities,' Mr Henderson said. The Northern Territory is home to about 5000 Aboriginal visual artists – about 70 per cent of all indigenous visual artists in Australia, giving the Northern Territory a significant competitive edge in targeting overseas travellers for niche tours.

The Government committed A$160,000 to the initiative. The Aboriginal art tours aim to provide a new market for the Territory's indigenous tourism industry, as well as delivering economic benefits directly back to the artists and their communities. Aboriginal art has become an important source of income for remote communities and visitors can buy directly from galleries and centres along the trail (Tourism NT 2007).

Many Aboriginal communities have an open community art gallery or centre, where the Aboriginal artists, old and young, gather to create their art, tell a story and maintain the connection with traditional customs. At some galleries and centres visitors can sit with the artists, learn how they create the art and share their stories of tradition and creation of the landscapes. De Brito (2008) visited the Irrkerlantye Community Arts Centre, where the Centre's director states: 'This place is as much about passing on tradition, telling stories and engaging with the mainstream as it is about selling paintings.' She says, 'We're certainly not the sharp end of the art market,' referring to artists such as Clifford Possum Tjapaltjarri whose work recently sold for more than AU$2.4m.

---

the visitor, as they are neither staged nor adapted to suit tourists' tastes. However, the same cannot be said for many other kinds of cultural performance and display. The growing interest in indigenous arts and culture can help to support cultural continuity or the revival of traditions; however, it can also compromise the authenticity of the art form:

> Whenever tourism becomes an important component of the local economy there is an increase in interest in native arts and crafts. However, it is the cultural components that have value to the tourists that have been preserved or rejuvenated and not necessarily those which are highly valued by the local culture. This type of cultural awakening has sometimes made host populations more aware of the historic and cultural continuity of their communities and this may be an enriching

experience. In other cases the new appreciation of indigenous culture, the revival of
ancient festivals and the restoration of cultural landmarks have emerged in ways
which pose long-term threats to the existence of culture in its original form.

(Mathieson and Wall 1992: 175)

Turner and Ash (1975) suggest that the majority of tourists have a fairly limited
sensual and aesthetic sense; therefore indigenous culture sometimes needs to be
presented to them in a simplified format which then compromises the art form. The
implication here is that tourists are not apparently 'sophisticated' enough to appreciate
the more complex art forms of indigenous communities (they refer to the example of
Balinese culture and art). Many tourists do want simply a taste of local culture, not a
lengthy performance of dancing, singing or music which requires considerable
concentration or phenomenal endurance. For example, the Kathakali story-plays in
southern India would traditionally be performed all night for a Hindu audience in a
temple. However, most tourists are quite content with a performance lasting one-and-
a-half hours in a theatre or cultural centre. The same is true of some Maori
performances. Tahana and Oppermann (1998) note, for example, that Maori cultural
shows tend to be modified to suit the needs of the clientele in hotels, unlike the more
traditional performances in the *marae*. This does not necessarily make the experience
a simplified or 'inauthentic' one, nor does it have to compromise the integrity of the
artists. The cultural experience is simply condensed. Tourists rarely understand local
dialects; therefore translations might be provided of songs or plays, or some kind of
interpretation offered. This is surely educational and informative rather than being
an over-simplification. It is unrealistic to expect the majority of tourists to gain an
in-depth understanding of indigenous cultural and art forms in the short time available
to them, especially given that they may be experiencing a whole host of other
attractions and events. This does not imply that they are necessarily superficial and
gullible. This depends very much on the type of tourist, the context in which they find
themselves, the kind of experience they are expecting, and the kind of product that is
being offered to them.

Conclusion

This chapter has provided an overview of the post-colonial status of indigenous
peoples in a range of environments. Clearly, this account is by no means definitive,
but it is evident that the majority of tribal and ethnic people have suffered a similar
fate. However, over the past few decades, indigenous peoples have increasingly been
afforded the kind of political, legal and economic support that is imperative to their
future survival. Rather than being perceived as a dying species, there is a growing
appreciation of their resilient and dynamic culture and tradition, and a recognition of
the need to protect it. Although land use remains perhaps the most controversial and
unresolved issue, a great deal of progress has been made in other areas of indigenous

development. Tourism may be viewed as one of the most positive forces for change in terms of economic benefits, conservation measures and the protection or revitalisation of cultural traditions. The key concepts of local empowerment, self-determination and control need to be adhered to, but if tourism is managed responsibly and ethically, its contribution to the cultural survival of indigenous peoples can be invaluable.

6　The arts, festivals and cultural tourism

To the world of tourism, the arts bring style, culture, beauty and a sense of continuity of living.

(Zeppel and Hall 1992: 29)

Introduction

The aim of this chapter is to analyse the relationship between the arts and cultural tourism, which has arguably been somewhat fraught in the past, with rather different philosophies governing the two sectors. Traditionally, there was a general lack of communication between arts and tourism organisations and a poor understanding of respective activities, priorities and objectives. Arts organisations were not always well informed of tourism trends and markets, just as tourism organisations sometimes failed to understand the needs of the arts. However, both the visual and performing arts sectors are increasingly providing visitors or tourists to a destination with a whole range of colourful exhibitions or spectacles to observe, admire or participate in. This is true particularly of destinations where vibrant local cultural events such as festivals or carnivals draw in the crowds. Many such events serve as an assertion or expression of the culture and identity of minority groups, such as ethnic communities. There are therefore a number of sensitive issues surrounding the presentation of such events, and the interrelationship between performers and their audience. This chapter focuses partly on the importance of ethnic and minority arts to the cultural tourism industry; therefore the historical and political backdrop of post-colonialism and emergent multiculturalism serves as the overarching theoretical framework. There is also some analysis of changing perceptions of art and its relationship to more democratic interpretations of culture.

Reconciling the arts and tourism

Past research in cultural tourism studies has often focused on the relationship between tourism and heritage management. Arts tourism has tended to receive less attention, with the exception perhaps of festivals and events. Past studies often focused on the tensions or conflicts between the two industries (e.g. Tighe 1986; Turner 1992; Varlow 1995). For example, Turner (1992) suggested that there tended to be a lack of understanding of respective priorities of the arts and tourism industries in the past, especially with regard to the concept of entertainment. Whereas tourism is often viewed as being focused on merely entertaining or amusing visitors, the arts are perceived as having an apparently more cerebral or educational role. He is also slightly cynical about the motives of some organisations for seeking financial support through tourism: 'there are those who suggest that "entertainment" only becomes "the arts" when it needs a subsidy' (Turner 1992: 109). However, he does also recognise the potential benefits of collaboration, as do Zeppel and Hall, who state:

> In commercial terms, the arts revitalize the tourism product, sharpen its market appeal, give new meaning to national character, and permit much tighter sales and promotional efforts. Simply stated, the arts, as an element of tourism, improve the product and strengthen its appeal, making tourism saleable.
>
> (Zeppel and Hall 1992: 29)

Tourism is also important for the arts in the sense that it generates substantial revenue in terms of attendance figures and ticket sales at events and attractions, and museums and galleries are often heavily dependent on financial support from tourists. In addition, tourism can broaden the market for the arts, and increased publicity can lead to the possibility of sponsorship opportunities, which are growing in importance in a climate of waning financial support.

As stated by Myerscough (1988), the arts can act as a magnet for destinations, encouraging people to stay and spend money in the local economy. Tourism can help to broaden and diversify arts markets, and to raise the profile of lesser-known events. Whereas many arts events tend to attract a local audience, tourism tends to be national or international in its scope. Many arts venues and events are becoming increasingly reliant on commercial sponsorship as public sector support declines. Consequently, new sources of revenue are always being sought. However, arts organisations are often wary of diversifying audiences too much, fearing that tourism may in some way compromise the artistic integrity or authenticity of the event. The programming of arts schedules is often not compatible with the more mainstream interests of tourists; therefore arts organisations are sometimes forced to compromise to please their target audiences. Arts organisations are perhaps right to be sceptical in such cases, as it means the potential dilution, commercialisation or trivialisation of art forms.

Hughes (2000) discusses the relationship between the arts, entertainment and tourism and provides some useful and comprehensive definitions of cultural and arts tourism, and an in-depth analysis of audience participation and the potential for audience development through tourism. He recognises the importance of developing arts tourism, but he is also realistic about the limitations. He suggests, for example, that the impact of the arts on local economies is often exaggerated, and that developing arts-related tourism is not always in the best interests of the arts: 'It may be naïve to assume that commercial organizations will forgo revenue and profit in the cause of artistic integrity and creativity and of stimulating new, experimental and minority-appeal artistic creations' (p. 197).

In destinations where arts tourism development is flourishing, tourism organisations tend to view the arts as an attractive way of boosting the cultural tourism product. Art museums and galleries are a big draw for tourists, particularly in large cities. For example, there appear to be a number of 'must-see' international art museums and galleries, particularly in Europe, such as the Louvre in Paris, the National Gallery in London, the Prado in Madrid and the Uffizi in Florence. These are clearly unique collections of some of the world's most beautiful and valuable pieces which can be seen only in those cities. In contrast, the performing arts are often more global in the sense that opera, ballet, classical music, theatre plays and musicals tend to be movable feasts, and can often be viewed in the tourist's own country or city. The increasing

Plate 6.1 Crowds gather in the Louvre to admire the Mona Lisa from a distance

(Source: László Puczkó)

globalisation of the arts, particularly in the urban context, is an interesting phenomenon. Many art forms that started out as small-scale, local traditions have now become globally available and universally popular. Flamenco dancing is a good example. Many community festivals or events have also started to attract national and international audiences, despite having traditional roots. Some examples of these are given later in the chapter.

It is generally recognised that arts tourists tend to be the kind of people who regularly visit arts attractions or venues at home (Richards 1996; Hughes 2000). The profile of arts tourists tends to be broadly similar to that of more general cultural tourists. They usually have relatively high levels of education, income and cultural competence. However, participation in the arts is a hotly debated issue in arts management literature. For example, it has long been recognised that the contemporary arts scene in Britain tends to be dominated by predominantly white, middle-class, middle-aged audiences. In addition, minority and ethnic arts activities tend to be underfunded and less supported than mainstream arts. There is still arguably a certain snob value attached to the arts which is linked partly to the nature of so-called high art forms, but also to the host institution, its location and its pricing structure. For example, many large arts venues such as Covent Garden Opera House in London have been criticised in the past for not facilitating access to a broader range of potential audiences. Barriers to access clearly need to be overcome before the arts can truly become democratic in their audience development, and funding and support need to be increased for minority activities (see Box 6.1).

Box 6.1

Case study of KUMU – European Museum of the Year 2008

In 2008 the KUMU Art Museum in Tallinn, Estonia was declared the winner of the European Museum of the Year Award. There were altogether 140 candidates, and a short-list of 38 who were given the opportunity to introduce their museums at an event held in the National Museum of Ireland in Dublin.

KUMU abbreviates from Estonian 'KUnsti MUuseum' (art museum). The designer was a Finnish architect Pekka Vapaavuori, who won the competition in 1994. It was constructed between 2003 and 2006. KUMU presents both permanent collections and temporary exhibitions. The main collection covers Estonian art from the 18th century onwards, including works from the occupations period (1941–91) and shows both Socialist Realism and Nonconformist art. Temporary exhibitions consist of both foreign and Estonian modern and contemporary art.

The museum's website describes how

> The history of this museum is also the history of a new country reaching independence and reflects the events which led up to it. The establishment of such a large museum at a time of transition was questioned, but as a working museum rooted in a diverse society,

which influences all its activities, it has been aware from the beginning of its responsibility to reach out to groups which do not normally visit art museums.

For example, the museum has paid special attention to the Russian minority, which is particularly important in the context of Estonian society. Another important aspect is the museum's skill in having gathered a collection which represents a crucial aspect of the Estonian cultural heritage, and then integrating it into the wider European cultural network.

The museum is described as an excellent example of how to communicate with visitors, which sometimes proves a problem for modern art museums. Its holistic approach illustrates the importance of museums and arts in the complex process of mass communication, and the overall excellence of its building, its exhibitions and management contributed to its winning of the much-coveted European Museum of the Year award.

(ARTe Media 2009)

In terms of motivation, the high arts (e.g. opera, ballet, classical concerts) often tend to attract audiences who are motivated partly by the prestige value or social status of attending such a performance (Dimaggio and Useem 1978; Zeppel and Hall 1992). Compare this with the genuine and spontaneous delight that spectators and participants often take in a festival, carnival or rock concert, and it is not difficult to see why certain arts events are more popular with tourists and the general public than others. They are more inclusive, since barriers to access such as the need to accumulate cultural capital, a better education or a higher income level have been removed. In addition, many such events are staged or performed by local, often ethnic artists, and because they have a strong community focus they are often free to the general public. A democratisation of the arts is clearly called for.

Democratising the arts: values, policies and politics

The increasing democratisation of the arts over the past few decades has emerged as a response to a perceived elitism and inherent racism within cultural policy making in many Western societies. Before the decolonisation of Western empires, the major preoccupation within cultural studies, particularly in the UK, was with class issues and the value of so-called mass or popular culture. As discussed earlier in this book, theorists such as Raymond Williams challenged the prevailing notion that so-called 'high culture' was in some way superior to the culture of the masses. However, since decolonisation, emphasis has been placed increasingly on issues of cultural diversity, diaspora, expressions of identity and hybridisation.

At this juncture, it would perhaps be of some interest to discuss the relationship between the arts and culture, as the terms are not necessarily synonymous, although Lippard (1990: 14) suggests that they are inextricably linked: 'When culture is perceived as the entire fabric of life – including the arts with dress, speech, social customs, decoration, food – one begins to see art itself differently.' Proponents of the 'Culture and Civilisation' movement of the nineteenth century argued that Culture (with a capital 'C') should be ennobling or civilising, leading to personal advancement or enlightenment. Although cultural critics like Matthew Arnold declared that this cultural enlightenment would transcend social divisions such as class, gender, religion or ethnicity, Jordan and Weedon (1995) argue that the basic tenets of such Liberal Humanist theories were quintessentially Eurocentric. Not only did they advocate the high culture and grand narratives of white, European males, but they took little account of the barriers to access to cultural education and the accumulation of cultural competence required to appreciate such dominant cultural forms. Although in countries like Britain a form of liberal, mass education had developed towards the end of the nineteenth century, the definitions of what constituted 'worthwhile' culture were (and still are) largely tenuous and essentially elitist. As argued by Bourdieu (1984), 'artistic value' is normally placed upon forms or objects for which a high degree of cultural competence is required. Artistic value systems therefore become somewhat arbitrary.

There has been much debate about whether culture should be defined as a 'whole way of life' or as 'the arts and learning'. Williams (1958) makes a case for both definitions having equal validity. Problems arise, however, in a climate of limited support and resources for culture, when decisions have to be made about whose culture should be funded; whose culture should be given a space or a voice; and how those cultures should be interpreted or represented. These decisions are fundamentally political, but they are also commercially driven increasingly by the demands of the marketplace and the power of the consumer.

If we consider for a moment the concept of art as opposed to culture, we are dealing predominantly with the works of creative expression of an artist or artists, rather than the whole way of life of a people. Lewis suggests that although definitions of art are more or less arbitrary, it makes sense to use a functional definition of art as:

> a cultural practice that involves the creation of a specific and definable object – a play, a video, a piece of music for example. The function of that object is as a self-conscious, personal or collective expression of something. This distinguishes bingo from ballet.
>
> (Lewis 1990: 5)

There have been numerous fierce debates about what constitutes valuable or worthwhile art. For example, controversies abounded over Damien Hirst's sheep in formaldehyde and Tracey Emin's bed. Both pieces of art were, in accordance with Lewis's (1990) definition, a personal and creative expression of something by the artist in question. He also notes that (in accordance with the Surrealists) art generally becomes art when an artist says it is! Yet, the general public railed against this apparent insult to what they deemed to be 'art' in much the same way as the

Impressionists faced public derision in the late nineteenth century. Now, of course, Impressionist art is some of the most publicly and commercially valued of any artists in the history of Western painting. However, the image of the starving artist in the attic, which characterised artists like Van Gogh during his lifetime, has never afflicted the likes of Damien Hirst or Tracey Emin, the market value of whose art is astronomically high. This is a sad irony for the artists of the past, but arguably a coup for the artists of the present. One gains the impression that Damien Hirst has had the last laugh when it comes to the apparent 'commercialisation' of his art. In many ways, his attitude resembles that of Andy Warhol who was one of the first artists to blatantly fuse art and commerce, aestheticising everyday household objects (e.g. soup cans) and drawing on popular cultural influences like Hollywood to inspire his art. Other pop artists have been similarly influenced by cartoons, comic strips and advertising (e.g. Lichtenstein, Rauschenberg). But the relationship between artist and commodity culture is arguably always somewhat uneasy, especially where the needs or desires of the marketplace start to dictate the nature of cultural production. Rockwell (1999: 94) suggests that what we may end up with is 'demotic desolation, with mass taste, whipped along by overpowering commercial interests, nearly obliterating high art'. But he emphasises again their interdependence:

> To separate the older 'high' arts from the younger mass arts denies both their best chance for healthy growth. The high arts lose vitality, while American demotic culture, writhing and heaving with mindless bestial energy, is cut loose from refining guidance.
>
> (Rockwell 1999: 101)

There was clearly a fear in the USA that popular culture would somehow absorb high art, a feeling that was intensified in the 1950s. The idea was developed that the arts should be useful rather than beautiful, hence the shift from 'auratic' art to art being mass produced or used as a tool (perhaps for community development or regeneration, for example). Benjamin contested that the 'aura' of a work of art, which was linked to its authenticity and ritual aspects, would effectively be destroyed by mechanical reproduction. The extent to which this compromises artistic integrity is debatable. The reproducibility of the arts is perhaps harmless in the case of CDs or books, but the endless reproductions of great masterpieces as cheap prints or souvenirs has arguably detracted from the appeal of the originals somewhat.

It is difficult to conclude how far art appears to be defined increasingly by its market value rather than by its aesthetic appeal or, indeed, whether this matters. The concept of aesthetics has always been philosophically problematic. For example, although philosophers like Kant argued in favour of a universal or objective notion of aesthetics, it is difficult to define or describe this apparent 'truth'. Therefore, aesthetics is regarded more generally as a subjective notion, hence any aesthetic judgements made on pieces of art will be biased according to the eye of the beholder. Of course, it has not helped that in the history of Western art, the beholder has usually been a white, middle-class male.

Multi-cultural and ethnic arts

The same Eurocentric and ethnocentric biases as described in the context of art have also extended to broader cultural policy making; thus minority groups – especially ethnic minorities – have rarely been given the chance to represent themselves or their interests adequately. This is not unique to post-imperial societies where immigration from the former colonies has been widespread, but it also affects countries such as the USA or Australia where the 'first peoples' have been similarly marginalised. For example, as noted by Lippard:

> Ironically, the last to receive commercial and institutional attention in the urban artworld have been the 'first Americans', whose land and art have both been colonized and excluded from the realms of 'high art', despite their cultures' profound contributions to it.
>
> (Lippard 1990: 6)

Khan's (1976) work on ethnic minority arts suggests that ethnic contributions enhanced the UK's cultural provision considerably. By showcasing their culture, minority groups were able to assert their identity. Carlson (1996) similarly suggests that cultural performance can allow traditionally marginalised groups to explore relationships between self and society, as well as issues relating to objectification, exclusion and identity. Candida-Smith's (2002) work also sees performance as a memory trigger, which is linked to memories of traditional ways of life. This might be an important point to note in the case of diasporic cultures, where there is often a strong sense of both 'over here' and 'over there' (i.e. 'back home') (Kaur and Hutnyk 1999). Jermyn and Desai (2000) optimistically state that barriers to ethnic participation in the arts are gradually being removed. However, Mowitt (2001: 8) is more cynical, suggesting that there is a great deal of tokenism in government support for ethnic minorities: 'In a global white world, a little local color goes a long way'. Lippard (1990) outlines the key problem with discourse in ethnic art, in that it tends to be *about* the Other, rather than *by* the Other. Appropriation of ethnic cultural forms is not uncommon in the programming, interpretation and representation of art. In addition, audience development for ethnic and minority events can be contentious, with claims that Caribbean carnivals and similar events are becoming 'whitewashed' or over-touristed (e.g. Errol 1986); see Box 6.2.

Even once they have found a voice and claimed a space, many minority artists may need support in casting off the shackles of their oppressive past and finding new forms of expression and appreciative new audiences. Cultural tourism can partly afford them this opportunity, but not without some challenges for ethnic and diasporic groups. For example, Ferguson (1998) describes how the globalisation of the media has led to the fragmentation of cultural representation, which is then reconstituted and usually referred to as cultural hybridity. The Parekh Report (2000: 27) suggests: 'The process of mixing and hybridisation will increasingly be the norm where rapid change and globalisation have made all identities potentially unstable.' The report suggests that

Plate 6.2 Masked man in India

(Source: Georgina Smith)

Box 6.2

Case study of Black History Month

Black History Month was established in the USA by the Harvard-educated African-American scholar Dr Carter G. Woodson in 1926. It was thought that such a month was necessary in order to celebrate and acknowledge the achievements of African-Americans and to keep alive their heritage, traditions and histories.

In England, Black History Month is celebrated in the month of October. It was first celebrated in 1987. The introduction of Black History Month was facilitated by the former Greater London Council. The first Black History Month celebrations formed part of the African Jubilee celebrations organised by London's Race Equality Unit. From the London boroughs the interest in Black History Month soon spread to other cities like Bristol, Leeds, Manchester, Nottingham and Birmingham.

The Black History Foundation organised the first Black History Fair in the UK on 8 December 2007 at Birmingham's Millennium Point. Following the Black History Month of October 2007, this event aimed to further promote awareness of Black heritage and culture in the UK. Due to the national interest, the Fair attracted exhibitors from all across the UK, representing a variety of organisations, from community theatres to Black history researchers and health awareness organisations. Some of the Black History Month events in Birmingham have included:

- Exhibitions displaying the work of Black artists and photographers.
- Literature and poetry reading.
- Talks on Black history.
- Music and drama performances.

Many regions and cities in the UK now organise special events for Black History Month (the same is true in the USA). It is noticeable that many of these events address sensitive and dissonant heritage, such as slavery, while others focus on celebration, for example carnivals. Black History Month (2009) lists examples for 2008 in the UK:

East of England: Hidden Heritage: The Archive centre

South East: The Historic Dockyard exhibition

South West: Devon and the Slave Trade

East Midlands: Slave Narratives – Nottingham Castle and Sankofa Project

North West: Fight To End Slavery: A Local Story At Touchstones Rochdale

North East: Spice Roots – Gateshead Council Arts Development Team

Yorkshire and Humberside: Doncaster African Caribbean Community Display

Scotland: The Slave Trade And Dumfries And Galloway: The Stewartry Museum

Wales: Everywhere in Chains: National Waterfront Museum Bicentenary Programme there is too much emphasis on separating 'ethnic' traditions from the 'western' canon, and on conserving the past rather than promoting new creativity in the present. Brah (1996: 181) suggests that the notion of diaspora was always discussed along a 'majority/minority' axis, but that this is no longer appropriate: 'Diaspora space as a conceptual category is "inhabited" not only by those who have migrated and their descendants but equally by those who are constructed and represented as indigenous.' Thus the children of first-generation immigrants have become indigenised, and are often searching for a new identity.

Carlson (1996) provides an interesting analysis of the significance of performance for traditionally marginalised groups, such as women, homosexuals and ethnic minorities. Tensions between self and society might be explored, including issues relating to objectification, exclusion and identity. In some ways, the development of larger audiences for local, small-scale, traditional or minority performances and events is helping to raise the profile of such groups. Carnivals are a good example, as are jazz festivals which are now universally popular. Many jazz festivals now attract large numbers of international tourists, despite jazz music traditionally being a marginalised form of music belonging to poor, Black communities.

More often than not, the political and social status of immigrant and ethnic groups is uncertain, and their power to represent themselves and their interests is limited. Complex relationships of dominance and suppression tend to govern the extent to which such groups are granted political or cultural autonomy and support. Priorities in policy making and funding tend to favour initiatives and projects that represent national interests, and usually those of white, middle-class society. For example, it is clear that many national organisations such as the Arts Council of England have struggled to accept a more inclusive and democratic definition of minority and ethnic arts and culture. Such groups may consequently feel under-represented, misrepresented or stereotyped, and hence unable to develop a clear sense of cultural identity.

Within contemporary British cultural studies, identity construction and representation have become recurrent themes, with racial and ethnic issues gaining significance from the mid-1980s onwards. Black writers and theorists such as Hall, Gilroy and Mercer have focused extensively on such issues in their work. In her seminal report, Khan (1976) emphasises the importance of the ethnic arts and cultural activities that Britain tends to ignore. Owusu (1986) took this work further, focusing particularly on black communities. Hewison (1997) discusses the various ways in which 'subcultures' (e.g. ethnic, women, youth and gay groups) challenged the prevailing cultural hegemony in the 1970s in Britain. More recent reports have accorded such issues greater priority. For example, Jermyn and Desai (2000) discuss how barriers to ethnic minority participation in the arts could be removed, and the Arts Council of Great Britain has devoted considerable attention to such issues in its recent policy documents.

These debates are not, of course, confined to the UK and Europe, although the nature of cultural politics in these countries is influenced largely by their imperial pasts. It is recognised that there are a large number of international cities that have become more and more ethnically diverse, with second- and third-generation immigrants playing a key role in all aspects of cultural and arts development. This is particularly true of large cities in the USA, as well as Canada, Australia and New Zealand. However, it is also worth noting the increasingly globalised and culturally diverse nature of many Asian and South American cities (e.g. Tokyo, Singapore, Rio de Janeiro).

One of the key challenges within the arts and cultural industries is the need to create activities, exhibitions and collections with which the maximum number of a country's culturally and ethnically diverse population can identify and participate in. This includes the appropriate interpretation and representation of indigenous and ethnic collections in museums and galleries; the provision of space and funding for ethnic and minority performing artists; and the support of local festivals and special events. The development of cultural tourism can variously support or compromise the nature of many festivals or events depending on how it is managed.

Festivals, events and tourism

Kirschenblatt-Gimblett (1998) writes extensively about performing culture, noting that the European tendency has been to parcel each art form separately, splitting up the senses, and ensuring that art is experienced with sustained attention and the minimum of distractions and noise. Festivals, however, offer a whole host of sensory experiences and the performance spaces are not hermetically sealed. It is a form of ethnographic, environmental performance. Festivals are described as the perfect entrée for the tourist seeking to engage with the destination and to penetrate the quotidian.

Festivals have been a cultural phenomenon for hundreds of years, dating from when a festival was traditionally a time for celebration and relaxation from the rigours of everyday existence. Traditionally, festivals were first and foremost religious celebrations involving ritualistic activities. For example, in Ancient Greece, festivals afforded an opportunity to worship deities, and prayers were offered for a good harvest or success in battle. In late-mediaeval times in Europe, festivals took on a more secular identity, and adopted a growing tendency to celebrate the greatness of men and their artistic achievements. Often, festivals would serve as a means of reaffirming or reviving a local culture or tradition, and would offer communities the chance to celebrate their cultural identity. Picard and Robinson (2006) suggest that during the Grand Tour of the eighteenth and ninteteenth centuries, festivals gave animation to 'foreign' townscapes and landscapes. Festivals also aim to support and promote local artists and to offer a concentrated period of high-quality artistic activity.

Adams (1986) notes that festivals and tourism have had a long history of mutual benefit. Festivals have proliferated since the growth of mass tourism in the post-war period with the explicit intention of encouraging tourism. Picard and Robinson (2006: 2) suggest that festivals 'whether as "traditional" moments of social celebration or as constructed and highly orchestrated events, have been absorbed into the expansive stock of "products" that tourists desire'. Rolfe (1992) demonstrates that over 50 per cent of arts festivals in the UK originated during the 1980s, and that this growth was at least partly aimed at increasing tourism in many tourist cities. Today, although many festivals aim to cater primarily for the local community, they succeed nevertheless in attracting tourists, and many new festivals are created with a tourist audience in mind. Since the late 1960s, the number of newly created festivals has increased significantly (Picard and Robinson 2006). The aim of many festivals is to enhance the image of an area and to 'put it on the map'. Hughes (2000) notes, however, that many festivals which did not set out to attract tourists, have done so anyway. Festivals clearly have a higher concentration of visitors in areas of a country that are already established tourist destinations, and the majority of festival organisers therefore design the programme content with the attraction of tourists in mind.

Plate 6.3
Sziget Festival, Hungary

(Source: Georgina Smith)

Kirschenblatt-Gimblett (1998) suggests that festivals are the ideal way for tourists to engage with a destination and to experience everyday life practices. Zeppel and Hall state:

> Festivals, carnivals and community fairs add vitality and enhance the tourist appeal of a destination. Festivals are held to celebrate dance, drama, comedy, film and music, the arts, crafts, ethnic and indigenous cultural heritage, religious traditions, historically significant occasions, sporting events, food and wine, seasonal rites and agricultural products. Visitors primarily participate in festivals because of a special interest in the product, event, heritage or tradition being celebrated.
>
> (Zeppel and Hall 1992: 69)

Tourism can even help to revive festivals and events which have been discontinued. For example, the Venice Carnival was discontinued in 1769, but was revived in 1980 as a community and tourist festival, partly in order to address problems of seasonality as it traditionally takes place in February.

However, MacLeod (2006) suggests that there has been a growth in what she terms 'placeless festivals', which are dislocated in terms of place and identity, and have little or no connection to the specificities of local cultures and communities. These festivals correspond more to the notion of a '"global party" with an emphasis on conviviality and consumption' (MacLeod 2006: 232). Examples might include world-famous carnivals such as Notting Hill or the Edinburgh Festival. Although such events might appear to be culturally embedded from the perspective of their founders or local residents, for tourists they are largely placeless, global spectacles.

Festivals can take numerous forms, for example:

- Carnivals
- Arts festivals (e.g. dance, theatre)
- Music festivals
- Food and wine festivals
- Religious festivals
- Circuses
- Mega-events (e.g. Olympic Games Cultural Olympiad)
- Cultural events (e.g. European Cultural Capital)

Music festivals, especially pop and rock festivals such as Glastonbury in the UK, are popular with young audiences. WOMAD (World of Music, Arts and Dance) is a global festival which aims to bring together and to celebrate the music, arts and dance of a diverse range of countries and cultures throughout the world. It has taken place in many different countries since its inception in 1982. Morley (2000) suggests that World Music festivals have helped to undermine the cultural hegemony of white 'Britpop' and allowed commercial marketing opportunities for non-white, non-Western music. Food and drink festivals, such as the Munich Bier Fest, have always attracted large numbers of people but now wine festivals are becoming equally if not better attended. Whereas music festivals tend to be somewhat globalised (i.e. inviting mainly internationally known artists), food and drink festivals can help to showcase and sell local products to tourists. Religious festivals are often colourful enough to attract tourists, but care must be taken that the religious and spiritual significance is not compromised by tourists' presence who may not understand the significance of certain rituals, or may behave inappropriately. Circuses are travelling shows or may be a permanent feature of a destination. One of the most popular and spectacular in recent years has been Cirque du Soleil, which originates in Canada, but which offers a multi-cultural spectacle of exceptionally high quality. The artistes are from different countries and represent the best of their profession. Sporting events are also growing in popularity, and may include cultural activities. For example, all Olympic Games are now required to run a parallel Cultural Olympiad (see Box 6.3).

Box 6.3

Case study of London's Cultural Olympiad

It was stated on the London 2012 official website that 'the London 2012 Games are not just about sport. They will also celebrate cultures, people and languages – in London, the UK and around the world'. The Cultural Olympiad divides into three sections:

1 **Ceremonies** – extraordinary live spectacles watched on television by one in three people around the world. This includes the Torch Relay. There will be educational programmes for young people and the chance to take part as a volunteer. The Opening and Closing ceremonies will draw on the UK's creative industries, which have a worldwide reputation for excellence.

2 **Major projects** – a number of major cultural projects featured in the London 2012 bid, forming the backbone of the Cultural Olympiad. These major projects were phased over the four years leading up to the Games:

- Artists Taking the Lead – bringing artists together with local communities to create a major piece of artwork in each nation and region of the UK.
- Sounds – bringing together different organisations, musicians and communities through a range of muscial genres.
- Discovering Places – introducing a new generation to the hidden places and spaces of the UK.
- Somewhereto – empowering young people to find ways to access the spaces they need for sport, dance, music, making art or films.
- Stories of the World – celebrating the collections in museums around the UK and displaying them in new ways and in unexpected venues.
- Film Nation – helping more young people make and deliver stories digitally.
- Unlimited – a world celebration of disability arts, culture and sport.
- World Shakespeare Festival – including major collaborations between leading UK and international theatre companies as well as non-professional theatres in the UK.
- Festival of Carnivals – creating a chance to welcome the world in spectacular style in outdoor spaces, culminating in five major carnivals in London and around the UK in 2012.

3 **Inspire mark projects** – local and regional events featuring in the UK-wide celebration.

The London 2012 UK-wide cultural programme will feature a mix of projects in which a whole range of communities are taking part. Project organisers were invited to take part and to introduce inspiring ideas, whether large or small. It was stated that chosen projects would be granted the right to use the 'Inspire mark' on various project materials, such as posters, brochures and website. The Inspire mark is part of the London 2012 brand family. It recognises that a project has been 'inspired by London 2012' and reflects the values of the Olympic and Paralympic Movements.

(London 2012 official website 2009)

Festivals can become the quintessence of a region and its people. There are, of course, problems of authenticity, compromising of artistic integrity, or trivialisation of culture: 'The more ethnographic festivals and museum exhibitions succeed in their visual appeal and spectacular effect, the more they re-classify what they present as art and risk appealing to prurient interest' (Kirschenblatt-Gimblett 1998: 73). Getz (1994) points out that authenticity means something different for traditional as opposed to created events. In the case of traditional events, authenticity must belong to the community presenting the event. Repetition of the performance or event to meet the demands of audiences does not necessarily imply that the value of the event is being compromised. This depends very much on the perceptions and expectations of the performers and their audiences.

It is often difficult to reconcile differing priorities, especially in the case of festivals that were initially developed as community events, but which have since become re-orientated towards tourism. Festivals arguably share quite a few of the criticisms directed at tourism, as they 'internalize many of the tensions common to cultural tourism development including the dialectic opposition between culture and economy . . . local and global cultures' (Richards 1996: 31). With the growth of the importance of events, many community festivals have rapidly evolved, becoming visitor attractions and targeting tourist markets. Several authors suggest that there is a fundamental distinction between community-orientated and tourism-orientated events (Arnold 2001; Evans 1996; Hall 1992), with doubts raised over the sustainability of the latter. With the evolution of festivals into economic tools (Chacko and Schaffer 1993; Joppe 1996), the financial dimension can often take over social, cultural and educational objectives. Festival activities do not only lose their local roots but become repetitive and unchallenging under the pressure of sponsors and the mass visitor market (Arnold 2001; Rolfe 1992).

On the positive side, festivals and events are full of animation, vibrancy and spontaneity. They are often multi-locational so they can be taken *to* people wherever they may reside, or to areas of high tourist concentration. Programming is fluid and flexible and can be adapted to the local environment, its communities and their cultures. In terms of socio-cultural impacts, festivals can play a key role in local community development, as they tend to be more socially inclusive than other forms of culture, and are often viewed by festival directors and residents alike as expressions of cultural diversity and identity. In the context of regeneration, festivals can contribute to the democratisation of culture, celebrating diversity, animating and empowering communities, and improving quality of life.

However, festivals are usually temporary, fleeting or elusive experiences, which can fail to sustain or support cultural continuity if they are not repeated. This is why festivals are ideally repeated annually. Another problem is that as festivals become increasingly 'international', they often lose their roots and connections to specific localities. Small community festivals are often described as being more engaging for local people than large mega-events, but they generally fail to attract tourists and are therefore unlikely to be commercially viable in the long term unless extensive local funding is available. Quinn (2005) notes the need for better research and more holistic management if festivals are to succeed in providing positive benefits for locations and their inhabitants. Issues of appropriation and local ownership are complicated by the desire or need for increased publicity, political and financial support, and tourism development. However, these are paradoxically usually essential to the future continuation of many festivals and events.

Ethnic festivals and carnivals

Representation is clearly a key issue when planning festivals. Representation of the diverse cultural activities and art forms of different community groups is an important consideration, but it is perhaps the quality of the events that is most significant when programming festivals. The involvement of women in ethnic festivals is particularly worth mentioning, as it is significant that festivals are perhaps the most family-orientated and child-friendly of any cultural or arts events. Many Asian and Muslim women are often less able to participate in cultural events outside the home than other groups; therefore festivals can afford them an ideal opportunity for participation and involvement. This might include preparation of costumes or catering, for example. In addition, festivals can play a political role. Marschall (2006: 155) describes how the National Women's Festival in Durban, South Africa has been used to empower women and transform their societal role: 'The festival uses creative means of expression to foster awareness of the women's plight.' This can include poverty, lack of proper healthcare, domestic violence, rape and HIV/AIDS.

Carnivals

Bakhtin (1965) is the one of the main theorists associated with the concept of carnivals. He describes carnivals as being 'Rabelaisian' in nature, whereby participants and spectators are released from the constraints of everyday life to engage in sensuous, hedonistic and licentious pleasure. Sampson (1986: 34) writes of the typical Trinidadian Caribbean carnival as being:

> An aphrodisiac – a gigantic, erotic road and stage show – a breezing, reeking melodramatic atavism. It is high and low musical drama, peppered by mild emotions, lascivious designs and gushing alcohol. It's the Alpha and Omega of mass hysteria: unrestrained jollity; carefree carnality; and calculated (sometimes spontaneous) crazy behaviour. It's an upsurge where for two fleeting days the players can enjoy in fantasy what is denied to them in reality.

Miles (1997) describes the 'polyphonic' nature of carnivals and festivals, suggesting that it is the ideal forum for representing a multiplicity of perspectives and the expression of ethnicity. Alleyne-Dettmers (1996) traces the history of carnival, which is often based on historically and culturally specific models born out of the oppressive context of European imperialism, colonisation and slavery. This is particularly true of Caribbean carnival, which is now a particularly vibrant event throughout the region. The biggest carnival in the world in Rio de Janeiro combines the cultures of the colonial Portuguese rulers with that of African slaves and native Indians, resulting in a rich, colourful, hybridised form of Afro-Brazilian culture which is expressed through one of the biggest and best-known cultural events in the world. Large numbers of tourists are keen to experience the carnival of these countries, to enjoy the spectacle, and to free themselves from the constraints of their everyday lives.

European carnivals are perhaps more sedate, less frenzied affairs; however, they are equally popular with both residents and tourists alike. In Europe, the history of carnival can be traced back to the concept of Carnivale in Italy and the masquerade balls of the sixteenth century, where the masked Mardi Gras derived partly from the 'Commedia dell'Arte'. Nowhere in Italy was this phenomenon as spectacular as in Venice, where the Carnival which was abandoned in 1769 was revived in 1980 for tourism purposes and to address seasonality.

Kirschenblatt-Gimblett (1998: 77) suggests that tourism can sanitise the carnival experience by aestheticising it and treating it ahistorically: 'Carnival represented is carnival tamed.' There have recently been concerns about the Notting Hill Carnival in London, which has become more and more popular with Londoners and tourists alike, now attracting around 2 million tourists. Some have argued that the event has outgrown the local area and should be moved to central London. Unfortunately, the event has also sparked violence, including numerous arrests and even murders. However, the event clearly has its roots in what was once a predominantly Afro-Caribbean area of London, and removing it would be something of a wrench for local communities, as it would displace a cultural event with clear links to the area's heritage. Notting Hill has already been the focus of a controversial gentrification process which was exacerbated by the success of the film *Notting Hill*. There appears to be some discontent and disillusionment among the local Afro-Caribbean population who feel (perhaps rightly) that the area is being taken over increasingly by white, middle-class communities, and this includes the Carnival.

Box 6.4

Case study of Rio Carnival

Although Carnival is celebrated in towns and villages throughout Brazil and other Catholic countries, Rio de Janeiro has long been regarded as the Carnival Capital of the World. The Rio Carnival is not only the biggest carnival but also one of the most interesting artistic events in the world. Foreign visitors number around 500,000 every year.

Rio Carnival is a four-day celebration, which takes place 40 days before Easter. It is a hedonistic event where people dance, sing, party and generally have fun. There are many parties that take place before, during and after Carnival all night and all day.

Almost all of the music played during the Rio Carnival is samba. It is a uniquely Brazilian music originating from Rio and a dance form that was invented by the poor Afro-Brazilians. The word samba comes from the Angolan world semba referring to a type of ritual music. The word had a variety of meanings to the African slaves brought to Brazil during the seventeenth, eighteenth and nineteenth centuries. It meant to pray or invoke the spirits of the ancestors and the gods of the African Pantheon. As a noun, it could mean a complaint, a cry or something like 'the blues'.

Some of the most involved groups in Rio Carnival are the poorest neighbourhoods, the so called favelas. The favelas are shantytowns or slums, in which houses are made of cardboard or other scraps, and they are often without water, electricity and sewage system. However, no matter how bad a situation the favelas' residents are in, they join in the festivities and they actually 'make' the Carnival in Rio. Carnival means a great deal to them because for once during the year, they can go out and have as much fun as they can.

Gays and drag queens also come and help out and become very involved in Rio Carnival. For everyone, this is a time to come together as a whole and have fun together. Brazil becomes a most tolerant society.

The official website for the Carnival describes how:

> They may try to organize it, glamorize it, televise it, even industrialize it but Rio Carnival is something that comes deep from the fun-loving soul of the Rio people. It does not depend on any authority or sponsor to happen. Carnival in the streets is a living proof of this passion. It's free, and everybody's welcome to participate.

(Rio Carnival 2009)

Melas

The term 'mela' is derived from a Sanskrit word meaning 'gathering', and is used to describe a range of community events in the Asian subcontinent. The cultural activities included in melas incorporate (among others) music, dance, fashion, food and sometimes film. In recent years, melas have become an increasingly prominent feature within the cultural calendar of many Western European countries, particularly in Britain. Melas have gradually developed from small-scale community-based events in India to national celebrations of diasporic cultures in Western countries. Like

Caribbean carnivals, melas have come to symbolise all that is 'colourful' about diaspora, transforming ethnicity into a cultural showcase for growing numbers of white and tourist audiences. This similarly engenders fears of cultural dilution, distortion and 'othering'.

In comparison to African Caribbean carnivals, it could be argued that melas are less overtly political in their origins. Whereas carnivals were generally born out of the oppressive context of imperialism, colonisation and slavery (Alleyne-Dettmers 1996), melas appear to be predominantly celebrations of community cultures. However, it would be misleading to suggest that melas are depoliticised events. There are concerns about appropriation, especially in areas where local governments are keen to hijack melas in order to add local colour to their promotion, and internal conflicts among different Asian groups are common. As a result, sometimes white directors are appointed to mediate! This is true of the Edinburgh Mela, for example (see Box 6.5).

Box 6.5

Case study of the Edinburgh Mela

The Edinburgh Mela has been running for more than fifteen years. Positioned within the summer festival season, over the last weekend of the International Festival, the Mela inevitably draws a mixed audience of locals and tourists. A large percentage of the visitors to the Edinburgh Mela are white. The Edinburgh Mela sought to produce a programme of events, which addressed the following key concerns.

- Melas could enhance the self respect of all people in minority communities, but especially young people
- There is the potential in Melas for inclusion allowing all generations to come out and enjoy themselves together
- Awareness through living in a culturally diverse Scotland that new approaches were required to bring about recognition and celebration of that diversity
- Growing awareness of the hybrid nature of south Asian culture and the diversity of south Asian culture in a changing UK and world context
- Methodology from the start that stressed networking, partnership and collaboration, and that built in opportunities for members of the community to achieve both group and individual development
- Growing aspiration of achieving recognition as a major festival in its own right and becoming a significant player in the local, regional, national and international infrastructures
- Working together across cultures towards racial equality and harmony

(Edinburgh Mela Artistic Policy Document 2003)

Interestingly as the artistic policy highlights, the Edinburgh Mela is also concerned with Scottish traditional culture and music and the Mela features major fusion events. There has been a split in the Festival board between those who believe that the Mela should remain a showcase for traditional culture rather than popular culture and those who wish to use the Mela as a forum for renewing interest in, or indeed gaining the interest of, second-generation Asians and in this way ensuring musical traditions are not lost as a consequence of a different way of life.

This raises several points worthy of consideration. Is the inclusion of Scottish traditional music in the mela a reflection that Scottishness is part of the dual identity of Scotland's Asian diaspora, or does it in fact highlight the minority nature of such music within Scotland, where popular culture or high cultural art forms, as exemplified by the International Festivals, hold sway? Is this fusing of Scottish and traditional Asian music a way of fusing identities or is it in fact keeping Scottish traditions (or a version of what is deemed to be Scottish traditions) alive in an increasingly changing society?

(after Carnegie and Smith 2006)

It is clear that ethnic events can help to reinforce a sense of cultural identity and community cohesion, but that the over-commercialisation of such events (for example, for the purposes of tourism) can somehow detract from the original purpose and meaning of the event. Hence communities must be given control of the organisation and development of such events if they are to retain their local and ethnic significance.

The final section of this chapter takes a brief look at the growth in popularity of gay arts events, many of which are becoming more mainstream and tourism-orientated, but which also face the threat of misappropriation.

The growing popularity of gay arts events

In the early 2000s, Richard Florida (2002) devised his own ranking systems that rate cities by a 'bohemian index', a 'gay index', a 'diversity index' and similar criteria. The gay index is linked to Florida's argument about the economic advantages associated with attracting the 'creative class' to cities, which will lead to revitalisation, regeneration and economic success.

Kolb (2007) is cynical about Florida's claims, sardonically commenting:

> Thank god those gays have such a good eye for design and interior decorating, for building rehabilitation and kitschy stores, for gourmet food and fine living. Thank god they make neighborhoods consumable by all, indicate where cities should spend their money and where new firms should locate.
>
> (Kolb 2007)

However, it often does seem to be the case that gay-friendly cities and destinations really do seem to be much more vibrant, diverse, tolerant and creative. It is nevertheless important also to note that many destinations are far from being gay friendly. These include most Muslim countries where it can be illegal to be openly gay, many parts of Africa, which have introduced new anti-homosexuality laws in recent years (e.g. Zanzibar in 2004), and much of the Caribbean. Amnesty International once described Jamaica as 'suffering from an appalling level of homophobia'. The couples-only resort chain Sandals, with several locations in Jamaica, lifted its banning of gay couples only in 2004, and the Cayman Islands famously denied docking to an Atlantis Events all-gay cruise in 1998 (Free Library 2005).

Nevertheless, elsewhere gay events are becoming increasingly popular both with the gay and mainstream markets. Chapter 8 analyses briefly the way in which a number of gay spaces have been created in cities, often as part of urban regeneration schemes. Many of these are centred on the strength of the 'pink pound', and can therefore be some of the most gentrified areas in a town. A good example of this is Manchester's Gay Village, which has become the main focus of the city's vibrant nightlife. Indeed, a number of cities both in Europe and internationally can claim to have a gay quarter which has a thriving evening economy, not to mention daytime leisure and retail provision. This is certainly true of London, Madrid, Amsterdam, San Francisco, Sydney, Rio, to name but a few. Buenos Aires was chosen to host the 2007 International Gay and Lesbian Football Association (IGLFA) World Championship because of its tolerance of homosexuality, considered to be greater even than that of Rio in Brazil (Mail and Guardian Online 2006). Many English seaside towns are also actively promoting gay tourism as a means of establishing a new image or identity. Examples include Brighton, Blackpool and Bournemouth, which have all been promoted as gay destinations by the national and local tourism agencies. Sitges in Spain has also been a popular gay destination for many years, as well as some parts of the Canary Islands (e.g. Gran Canaria).

The increasing popularity of gay areas, especially with women and heterosexual couples, has sometimes led to concerns about the 'de-gaying' of certain spaces, in much the same way that Notting Hill Afro-Caribbean residents are concerned about the increasing white, middle-class presence. This is certainly a contentious issue, but it is perhaps symptomatic of the growing popularity of gay culture and events. The most significant examples of gay cultural events that draw a mainstream and tourist audience, as well as a gay one, are the Gay Pride or Mardi Gras events. Originally, such events were highly politicised, and the marches which accompany such events still tend to be so. These were largely a forum for the gay community to present a united front, and to express and assert their identity and rights publicly. However, in most cases, the lively celebrations that follow are becoming more of a public party than anything else. Indeed, the London Gay Pride event was criticised by some in 2001 for being too depoliticised and commercial, especially as it attracted such a large number of heterosexual revellers. The Gay Mardi Gras concept is quite well developed in Britain, and usually involves a day of concerts, dance tents, funfairs and food stalls. London's is still the biggest event, and it has consequently become ticketed rather than free. In other cities where the events are relatively new, such as Birmingham, they are still free (see Box 6.6).

Box 6.6

Case study of Manchester's LGBT

The city of Manchester in England is one of the most gay-friendly cities in the country, mainly due to its Gay Village which was developed in the 1990s. This area consists of a number of bars, cafés, nightclubs and gay businesses. As a result, Manchester has frequently been promoted as a gay tourism destination in the UK alongside other cities like London, Brighton and Bournemouth. The Village also featured in the popular TV series *Queer as Folk* in the late 1990s.

In addition, Manchester has a yearly Lesbian, Gay, Bisexual and Transgender Festival (LGBT), which extends beyond the Gay Village into other parts of the city which are then closed to traffic for the afternoon. The LGBT is similar to other Gay Pride Festivals or Mardi Gras. However its origins were less about politics and more about support for and awareness of HIV issues. The early events were used to raise funds for a local hospital ward that cared for people with HIV. By the late 1990s, however, no funds were being raised for charity, and ticket sales had to be used for operational costs including safety. This was mostly a result of changing ownership and organisation. By 2002 the Mardi Gras (as it was then called) became more politicised in response to restrictions placed by the city council and police and alleged homophobia, and a 'weekend of gay pride' was called for, including a protest march.

Although it is not known how many tourists come to the LGBT, it attracts up to 80,000 visitors and up to half a million people watch the parade through the city centre. There has never been a conscious policy to attract tourists; however, Manchester's existing reputation as being gay-friendly and fun is likely to attract large numbers of gay and straight tourists alike. There are still concerns about the 'de-gaying' of the space and the 'depoliticisation' of the increasingly politicised Mardi Gras, This may mean a need to reduce the tourism element in the future if the Village and the Festival are to retain their meaning for the gay community.

(after Hughes 2006)

Conclusion

As well as discussing the importance of the visual and performing arts for tourism, this chapter has demonstrated the especially important role festivals and special events play in the development of cultural tourism. Festivals and events are often more accessible to the masses than other art forms, as they provide an open forum for the celebration of life and the continuity of living. In many cases they can also be an expression of local community culture, traditions and identity. Although care must be taken by the community to ensure that the authenticity and enjoyment of their celebration is not compromised by tourism, it is clear that new audiences can often be created for ethnic and minority cultural events. As many of these events may previously have been threatened or marginalised politically or financially, tourism can help to raise their profile and encourage support. Although such events tend to be free for locals and tourists alike, hence encouraging access and participation, they can also make a significant contribution to the local economy. As discussed in the early part of this chapter, the relationship between the arts and tourism is not always a harmonious one; however, it is interesting to note that in the case of certain art forms, such as minority and ethnic events, tourism can make a positive contribution to cultural continuity.

7 The growth of creative tourism

Creativity is a central source of meaning in our lives . . . most of the things that are interesting, important, and human are the results of creativity . . . [and] when we are involved in it, we feel that we are living more fully than during the rest of life.

(Csikszentmihalyi 1997)

Introduction

This chapter focuses on the growth of creative tourism, which has been developing partly in response to the increasing emphasis placed on creative industries throughout the world. There is no doubt that creativity became one of the main buzzwords for the early 2000s; however, there is still some confusion about how to differentiate between culture and creativity. This has remained one of the major problems for the development of the so-called cultural and creative industries, which feature prominently in many economic and tourism development strategies, as well as being catalysts for regeneration. Whereas cultural tourism was traditionally seen as a rather passive form of consumption, whereby tourists enjoyed heritage sites or artistic spectacles, creative tourism is about more interactive forms of activity which are closely linked either to a location and its people, or to some of the more technologically advanced industries. Therefore, we see a twofold development of creative tourism in different parts of the world, which is based either on the traditional practices of indigenous communities, or which is connected to more contemporary experiential industries. This chapter provides an overview of the development of the cultural and creative industries, followed by a discussion of the use of the creative industries in regeneration and tourism strategies.

The history and development of the cultural and creative industries

Hesmondhalgh (2007) suggests that if we define culture as a 'whole way of life', as in the theories of many anthropologists and cultural studies experts, then it could be argued that almost all industries are cultural industries, as they are involved in the production and consumption of culture. Conversely, if more elitist views are taken (e.g. those of Matthew Arnold in the nineteenth-century 'Culture and Civilisation' tradition), culture is defined in a too aesthetically narrow way as mainly the arts or 'high' culture. There was traditionally a tension between commercialised so-called 'mass' or 'popular' culture, and more artistic activities or products for an educated elite. The work of radical sociologists like Bourdieu (1996) explained how in the nineteenth century there was a division between large-scale commercial cultural production and small-scale creative or artistic production.

By the 1940s, however, critical theorists like Adorno and Horkheimer (1979 [1947]) argued that cultural items were produced in a similar way to any other consumer goods. They linked the idea of what they called the 'culture industry' to mass culture, arguing that the products were of a standardised or homogenous nature, and that artistic integrity had been compromised by production methods. Adorno and Horkheimer also believed that individuals and groups were manipulated into pursuing certain activities by capitalist corporations and governments. They drew on Marx, arguing that the nature of cultural production within a capitalist industry results in a standardised commercial, mass-produced commodity. They deemed that the cultural industries served to reduce or eradicate the distance between art and life, lulling audiences into passive consumption and predictable responses, rather than shocking or provoking them. It is worth noting that dramatists such as Brecht had addressed this notion of bourgeois complacency in his use of the *Verfremdungs* (or Alienation) effect. There is also the notion that people no longer responded spontaneously to works of art, but evaluated them only according to their value in the marketplace. Hence exchange-value largely replaces use-value, a theory that is derived from Marx's concept of commodity fetishism. People become enslaved by, rather than emancipated by, art and culture, surrendering their autonomy.

Rockwell (1999) suggests that the Frankfurt School (of which Adorno and Horkheimer were a part) may have reacted strongly to seeing the Nazis and Stalinists crush artistic freedom in the name of the masses, hence likening the manipulation to a form of subtle totalitarianism. Adorno reflected later in his essay of 1967 'Culture industry reconsidered' (see Adorno 2001), on why he and Horkheimer had replaced the concept of 'mass culture' with 'cultural industry'. They believed that the products of mass culture did not emanate from the people themselves, but were administered by a central hegemonic authority. The Italian neo-Marxist Gramsci argued in his theory of hegemony that cultural producers were able, through various means, to win continually the consent of the masses. MacDonald (1994: 30) also states: 'The Lords of *kitsch*, in short, exploit the cultural needs of the masses in order to make a profit and/or to maintain their class rule.' However, the ideas of Adorno and Horkheimer were largely rejected by French sociologists in the 1960s and 1970s (e.g. Morin 1962; Huet *et al.* 1978; Miège 1979), who saw new processes of cultural production using industrialisation and technology as being innovative rather than commodified. They also preferred to talk about 'cultural industries' in the plural to show that they were not unified, but instead were very different from one another in terms of their production.

In 1982, UNESCO published *The Culture Industries: A Challenge for the Future of Culture*, which took Adorno and Horkheimer's essay as a starting point. It pluralised the concept of 'the cultural industries', re-emphasising the fact that consumer demand was dictated largely by powerful corporations, and that artistic creativity and spontaneity were being subordinated. UNESCO was also concerned at the way in which the entertainment industry was contributing to global inequality, undermining cultural diversity, and standardising or homogenising culture (Negus 1997). The threat of increasing globalisation and deregulation had perhaps fuelled these concerns. Hewison (1987) views the heritage industry in much the same way as Adorno and Horkheimer viewed the cultural industry: as an artificial history imposed on the public by marketing managers from above. Nevertheless, he supports the view that the public are largely manipulated in their choice and consumption of culture.

It can be seen, therefore, that the historical concept of the 'cultural industries' has been highly politicised, and there is still some discomfort amongst academics, even practitioners, with the idea of 'culture' and 'industry' being sandwiched together. Although the debates have moved on considerably in recent years as a result of postmodern theory, it is interesting to note the continuing resistance in many cultural circles (e.g. museums, galleries) to the introduction of any form of commercial venture such as a shop or café, visitor centre, interactive technology, etc. However, with the growth of the so-called 'creative industries', this stance is becoming very quickly outmoded, even obstructive to cultural development. Garnham (1990) argues that artist-centred strategies should be replaced by subsidised 'creators' policy which focuses on distribution and the reaching of audiences. This is perhaps why the terminology started to change.

Defining the cultural and creative industries

Hartley (2005) suggests that the use of the term 'cultural industries' has proven to be somewhat limited in the policy context because it fails to combine art and culture, culture and creativity, and it does not take into consideration social, technological and cultural changes adequately. He describes how:

> The idea of the CREATIVE INDUSTRIES seeks to describe the *conceptual and practical convergence* of the CREATIVE ARTS (individual talent) with Cultural Industries (mass scale), in the context of NEW MEDIA TECHNOLOGIES (ICTs)

within a NEW KNOWLEDGE ECONOMY, for the use of newly INTERACTIVE
CITIZEN CONSUMERS.

(Hartley 2005: 5)

This takes us back to Adorno and Horkheimer's idea of the cultural industries being
about mass consumption, whereas the creative arts or industries are more about
individual practices. However, there seems to be some confusion here between the
supply of cultural products and the creative *talent* that goes into making them. This is
a question of input and output, which has important implications for defining which
sectors are 'cultural' and which are 'creative'. Many more industries are creative if we
talk about *input*, as creativity can inspire any form of design (e.g. software,
technology, transport), and creative thinking can be used in all businesses, as well as
professions, such as teaching, law, medicine, banking, accountancy, etc. (e.g. see
Florida 2002). However, most of the *outputs* from these professions could not be
described as specifically 'cultural' (assuming we are not using the anthropological
notion of culture as a whole way of life, but more as artistic practices).

Hartley (2005) suggests that the notion of creative industries has been created out of a
combination of the cultural industries and the creative arts, largely as a result of
political and technological change. The core of 'culture' is still creativity, but
creativity can also be produced, consumed, experienced and enjoyed in many more
and different ways. Thus, creative industries are broader and less focused on
traditional, 'artistic' understandings of culture. This is fine until we reach the point as
described by Hölzl (2007) where 'the creative percentage of statistically defined
industries can range from 0% to 100%'. Florida (2002) suggested that around 30 per
cent of all employed citizens in the USA are part of the creative class (but this
includes financial planners, doctors, lawyers, teachers, engineers etc.), whereas, in the
UK, it has been estimated at more like 7 per cent because so-called 'knowledge
workers' were excluded (DCMS 2001). Hesmondhalgh (2007: 147) considers
Florida's category of culture to be 'absurdly broad-ranging'.

One of the most appropriate definitional frameworks arguably comes from Australia:
this is the categorisation which is mainly adopted in this chapter along with that of the
Department for Culture, Media and Sport (DCMS) in the UK. NOIE (2002) in Australia
lists the sectors belonging to the cultural and creative industries respectively (see Table
7.1). It is arguably still difficult to place certain sectors in definite categories (e.g. the
arts, which can be publicly subsidised or not, or can be educational and entertaining at
the same time). Here it can be seen that although there are overlaps in the area of music
and the performing arts, these sectors vary according to the type of music or art form
(e.g. classical versus pop music; ballet versus folk or street dance, etc.).

In terms of tourism development, the performing arts have always been popular, but it
is interesting to note the increasing interest in other creative industries such as
architecture, film and TV, and design. Visitors may even enjoy attractions or
exhibitions based on advertising or publishing, and interactive software is increasingly

Table 7.1 Defining the cultural and creative industries

Cultural industries (Defined by public policy function and branding)	Creative industries (Largely characterised by nature of labour inputs 'creative individuals')
Museums and galleries	Advertising
Visual arts and crafts	Architecture
Arts education	Design
Broadcasting and film	Interactive software
Music	Film and TV
Performing arts	Music
Literature	Publishing
Libraries	Performing arts

Source: NOIE 2002

being used in many cultural venues. The latter part of this chapter discusses this development in more detail.

The DCMS in the UK included a few more categories in its analysis of the creative industries, which was one of the pioneering mapping exercises in this field in 1998. It describes the creative industries as being 'those industries which have their origin in individual creativity, skill and talent and which have a potential for wealth and job creation through the generation and exploitation of intellectual property' (DCMS 1998):

- Advertising
- Architecture
- Art and Antiques Markets
- Crafts
- Design
- Designer Fashion
- Film and Video
- Interactive Leisure Software
- Music
- Performing Arts
- Publishing
- Software and Computer Services
- Television and Radio

The addition of the crafts and fashion industries are important for tourism, and visitors also enjoy antiques markets and even auctions.

The EU is currently working towards a common definition of cultural and creative industries in order to facilitate research. See Table 7.2 for the differentiation made in 2006.

Table 7.2 EU definitions of cultural and creative industries

Core arts	Cultural industries	Creative industries	Related industries
Visual arts, performing arts, heritage	Film and video, TV and radio, video games, music, books and press	Advertising, architecture, design	PC, MP3 player, mobile phone

There is no reference to the 'Creative Professionals' or 'Knowledge Workers' of Florida (2002) (e.g. financial planners, doctors, lawyers). Instead, the focus is rather on what Florida describes as the 'Super-Creative Core', which comprises about 12 per cent of all US jobs. This group is deemed to contain a huge range of occupations (e.g. architecture, education, computer programming) with arts, design and media workers making a small subset. The EU definition may be even narrower (for example, excluding education).

An overview of cultural and creative industries policy

In the past, government support always tended to be for the so-called 'high' arts and culture, i.e. those that were considered to be worthwhile by an elite group of people (usually white, European males). As argued by Bourdieu, 'artistic value' is normally placed upon forms or objects for which a high degree of cultural competence is required. This was certainly true of what we have now defined as the 'cultural industries', such as the visual arts and museum collections. On the other hand, those sectors which were deemed to be 'low culture' or mainly for the masses and their entertainment (i.e. popular music, cinema), were generally not state-subsidised. For example, at one time, the Arts Council of England refused to support jazz music as it was seen as a 'popular amenity'.

In the 1970s and 1980s, public policy started to include media industries in discourses about culture, so popular commercial industries like film, TV and music were also branded as cultural industries. Postmodern theory also influenced policy making from the 1980s onwards, as did radical social politics of gender, race, class and so on. There was a need to recognise the inherent elitism of cultural policy and to embrace broader, more multi-cultural understandings (at least in the UK, USA and much of Western Europe). The Greater London Council (GLC) in the early 1980s challenged elitist and idealist notions of the arts. In addition, the privatisation of many industries and the decline in state subsidy meant that romantic notions of non-commercial approaches to art needed to be readdressed. This led to a very strong orientation towards 'audience maximisation' (Garnham 1990) and a shift in policy thinking in the UK which democratised cultural activities and forced cultural producers to become more consumer-orientated.

The Greater London Council started a trend which continues today, and that is the use of cultural industries in urban regeneration (discussed further in Chapter 8). At this time, the terminology used was 'cultural industries', but by the late 1990s there was already a shift to the use of 'creativity' and 'creative industries'. Cultural industries were used as a tool for economic and social regeneration in Europe in the 1980s and 1990s. The DCMS (2004) describes regeneration as 'the positive transformation of a place – whether residential, commercial or open space – that has previously displayed symptoms of physical, social and/or economic decline'. Several approaches were used, such as the development of cultural or creative quarters with a concentration of cultural attractions, businesses or activities. Large museums or galleries were built as catalysts for further development. Festivals or mega-events were organised to attract visitors and enhance image. Artists could also work with communities or contribute to local initiatives. By the 2000s, much more emphasis was being placed on creativity and the creative industries, especially in cities (e.g. Landry, Bianchini). Definitions were much broader than those discussed above, and tended to include concentrations of design, media, entertainment and technology, businesses or 'creative clusters', which served as catalysts for further regeneration and investment.

By the 2000s, the term 'creative industries' seemed to fit better the new landscape of globalisation, experience economy and information technology. Support-in-kind became available for creative industries clusters and networks from government sources in the UK and elsewhere (e.g. USA, Australia, New Zealand, Taiwan, Hong Kong). In the UK, cultural and creative industries policy making was led by the DCMS which produced a 'Creative Industries Mapping Document' in 1998.

The use of the term 'creative industries' meant that the government could take the traditionally subsidised sectors (e.g. the arts, crafts) and link them to the supposedly booming commercial sectors (e.g. music, television). Broadening definitions also meant that the estimated economic value of the combined cultural and creative industries would be much greater. This was important given the growing trend in Europe since the 1990s of privatisation and the need for culture to achieve something other than its own ends – i.e. to create jobs or income, attract investment, enhance image, help social cohesion and so on. No more art for art's sake! Interestingly, this also meant a shift back to the idea of artist-centred creativity (but supported-in-kind and not financially subsidised) rather than audience-orientated culture. It is worth noting that the DCMS excluded heritage and museums from the list of creative industries, although it is recognised that they have a supporting role to play. This means that although the cultural industries have technically become a subset of the creative industries, separate research is needed to take into consideration cultural sectors which have been excluded or are now marginal in definitional or policy terms.

Differentiating the cultural and creative industries

Although the definitions of cultural and creative industries have moved closer together in many policy documents, often to the exclusion of the cultural industries altogether, they have some very different characteristics which need to be taken into consideration in policy making, research, support and funding. This section demonstrates some of those differences using mainly the DCMS (1998) and NOIE (2003) categorisations.

Although this is arguably a generalisation, it provides a useful starting point for debate. Cultural industries tend to consist of 'core' cultural sectors (e.g. the arts – visual and performing, heritage, museums, festivals and cultural events), which have cultural products as an *output*. Cultural industries are often based on tangible products such as works of art, museum collections (although performing arts and festivals can be more experiential). These are often consumed passively by the public. Creative industries, on the other hand, tend to have creativity as an active *input*, but the resulting product is not necessarily described as 'cultural'. There may not even be a tangible product, rather a means of accessing information. Creative industries tend to be based on global production and distribution, whereas cultural industries are more national or local (e.g. museum or art collections, theatre by national dramatists, folk festivals). Cultural sectors tend to have a traditional, educational, intellectual remit, and as a result, can seem somewhat didactic. Creative industries, on the other hand, can seem more modern, imaginative, interactive and entertaining. Many cultural venues make (too) little use of new technology, whereas creative industries are usually

Table 7.3 Major differences between the cultural and creative industries

Cultural industries	Creative industries
State subsidised	Privately funded
Not-for-profit	Commercial
More output-focused	More input-focused
Usually tangible	Often intangible
Product-centred	Information-centred
Passive	Active
Traditional	Modern
Collective	Individual
Intellectual	Imaginative
Didactic	Interactive
Educational	Entertaining
Low-tech	Technologically advanced
National/local	Global
Art/artist-centred	Consumer-orientated

high tech. Because they are not state-subsidised, creative industries must be focused on their markets and thus consumer-orientated. Cultural industries have often managed to be art or artist-centred, and therefore somewhat visitor-unfriendly because the focus is on the value of the art and its preservation or continuity. However, state subsidy is diminishing and a more commercial orientation is being forced by policy makers, hence the growing overlaps between the cultural and creative industries.

Increasingly, however, policy makers and industry practitioners should be looking towards enhancing cultural industries development (and by association cultural tourism) by taking a more creative approach. This may include some of the following:

- Architecture and design: creative buildings and interiors can enhance the appeal of museums and galleries, and may even turn them into major landmarks or unique icons.
- Marketing and branding: many cultural industries need to adopt a more creative approach to marketing and branding so that they can compete in the global arena for tourists or even attract local visitors.
- Technology and interactive software: many cultural venues need to compete with high tech, sophisticated leisure and entertainment attractions, and may need to become more experiential and interactive.
- Commercial flair: many cultural industries lack commercial experience having been state-subsidised for so long. Creative entrepreneurs can help to develop commercial ventures (e.g. retailing, catering, events).

Cultural and creative businesses tend to be structured differently. Cultural industries' products and activities can mainly be described as public goods, and are therefore state subsidised in some way or are run by non-profit organisations. Creative industries' products and activities are largely private goods, and therefore they are subject to free market forces and have to be commercially orientated to survive. Traditionally, one of the reasons that state subsidy was needed was because the cultural industries were seen as being educational and providing some form of public service. Creative industries, especially media, were seen as being more entertainment-based and therefore less 'worthy'. Conversely, one could argue that the cultural industries fail to attract adequate audiences or visitors because they are viewed as old-fashioned or less attractive than more modern forms of leisure; therefore they would not survive without state support. Compare, for example, the number of people who are interested in opera and those who go to the cinema. This trend has serious implications for the heritage sites, museums and traditional cultural tourism attractions, which must modernise to survive. Therefore, cultural industries are increasingly under scrutiny from governments and are expected to meet certain targets in terms of their visitor management and access policies.

Creative environments and destinations

Florida (2002) demonstrates how the creative classes have contributed enormously to urban transformation and (re)development in the USA. His research shows that those cities that have the highest level of economic growth and innovation are those that score highest on what he calls the 'bohemian index' (the relative concentration of artists, writers, musicians and other artistic professionals), as well as the 'gay index' (the relative concentration of gays). He suggests that such people are open-minded, diverse and are therefore receptive to creativity. Many cities that claim to have successful cultural development have based their strategies on 'creative industries' (e.g. media, design, music, film, advertising). However, Florida states:

> The physical attractions that most cities focus on building – sports stadiums, freeways, urban malls, and tourism-and-entertainment districts that resemble theme parks – are irrelevant, insufficient, or actually unattractive to many Creative Class people. What they look for in communities are abundant high-quality experiences, an openness to diversity of all kinds, and above all else the opportunity to validate their identities as creative people.
>
> (Florida 2005: 35)

Florida's work suggests that people tend to gravitate towards locations which are more tolerant and open to new ideas. It is therefore important for governments to help develop creative quarters or clusters within a city or other environment in order to attract more businesses and workers, as well as investment. This might be done through subsidised rents for artists, tax-free loans on land or property, and other incentives to settle in an area (e.g. green spaces, good-quality infrastructure). Cultural spaces (e.g. libraries, community centres, galleries) should be provided where people can meet, network, interact, discuss ideas and exhibit work. Good technological infrastructure is essential, for example wireless internet points in public buildings or internet cafés. It is also starting to be recognised that environments where there is a university are likely to have high concentrations of cultural and creative people. They may be studying, working or living there. Policy makers need to consider not only the economic but also the social impacts of attracting creative industries. Creative societies tend to be more democratic and tolerant, as well as dynamic and innovative.

UNESCO has recently been at the helm of the so-called creative tourism movement, advocating that creative tourism should include more access to culture or history (but 'less museums and more squares'), and involves doing something experientially, and an authentic engagement in the real cultural life of the city:

> Creative Tourism involves more interaction, in which the visitor has an educational, emotional, social, and participative interaction with the place, its living culture, and the people who live there. They feel like a citizen . . . while creative tourism must be linked to culture, the particular cultural expressions will be unique to each place.
>
> (UNESCO 2006: 2)

UNESCO made the decision in 2004 to appoint a Creative City Network in a bold effort to uphold cultural diversity across the world. The idea is to focus on less tangible forms of culture, and to 'personify the polar opposite of the worst in Disney and populist tourism' (an interesting statement considering Disney was one of the pioneers of what some might call 'creativity'!). Cities can choose from the following seven themes:

- Literature
- Cinema
- Music
- Craft and folk art
- Design
- Media arts
- Gastronomy

They then apply to join the Creative Cities Network. Some of the benefits of joining the network include highlighting the city's cultural assets on a global platform; making creativity an essential element of local economic and social development; sharing knowledge across cultural clusters around the world; building local capacity and training local cultural actors in business skills; cultivating innovation through the exchange of know-how, experiences and technological expertise; and promoting diverse cultural products in national and international markets.

Box 7.1 lists the current members of the Creative City Network as described by UNESCO (2006) (in no particular order).

Box 7.1

The Creative City Network

Aswan, Egypt

Aswan was the first city of crafts and folk art to make the UNESCO creative city list. As a foremost hub of Nubian art, the historical Nile River city in Egypt is without peer, with a folk scene that thrives to the present day.

Santa Fe, New Mexico, USA

With strong Pueblo culture and influence from Mexico, Sante Fe has one of the most distinct arts scenes in North America. Another crafts and folk art destination, Sante Fe has a number of annual festivals, museums and councils that preserve what is a singular cultural scene.

Berlin, Germany

Berlin's appointment as a city of design in 2005 was no major surprise. After all, the city's contributions to the field are self-evident and the capital of Germany has been home to some of the most creative and innovative thinkers for generations.

Buenos Aires, Argentina

At the confluence of many different ethnic, cultural and social profiles, Buenos Aires is a prominent design center. From fashion to industrial design, the capital of Argentina has a rich landscape whose impact is felt across Latin America.

Montreal, Canada

A major hub of cultural pluralism in North America, vibrant Montreal is the third design city in UNESCO's eminent list. Capable of admission in a number of areas other than design, the city is nonetheless the most avant-garde and stylish on the continent.

Popayan, Colombia

Small in comparison to other destinations in the creative city network, Popayan is the first entry in the realm of gastronomy. With fewer than 300,000 people, Popayan's contributions to the cultural and political development of Colombia far outshine the diminutive population. More importantly, the preservation of authentic cuisine is what marks Popayan as special within the country and indeed, South America.

Edinburgh, Scotland

Edinburgh's entry as a city of literature must have been unanimous within UNESCO. It has several annual cultural festivals, symposiums and conferences on literary topics, in addition to native sons such as Sir Arthur Conan Doyle, Sir Walter Scott and Robert Louis Stevenson.

Melbourne, Australia

As the cultural capital of Australia, Melbourne is a lively literary city. With a vast publishing sector and more bookshops and libraries per capita than even Sydney, Melbourne was the second UNESCO city of literature.

Bologna, Italy

If ever there was a city with intense appreciation for classical and traditional music, Bologna would be at the top of the short list. In addition to festivals and a vibrant scene, this UNESCO city of music in Italy has taken enviable measures to preserve and protect the classics and share knowledge in the form of cultural exchange programs.

Seville, Spain

A global cultural capital, music is simply part of everyday life in exquisite Seville. There is a festival scene that includes opera and classical symphony to flamenco and traditional music.

Glasgow, Scotland

With national and international acclaim as a musical centre, from a historic and present-day vantage point, Glasgow provides Scotland with a second member on the UNESCO panel. A swirl of creative energy seems to emanate from the city, as it produces more than 125 live musical events per week, on average.

Lyon, France

Home to a flurry of cultural activity, Lyon was the first media arts city on the UNESCO list. Festivals such as the Nuits Sonores and Fête de la Lumière propelled the city's candidacy with the application board, in addition to notable innovations in the field of digital games. Lyon is also a notable hub of gastronomy.

(UNESCO 2006)

Plate 7.1 Berlin Parliament

(Source: Melyvn Smith)

Creativity is always required in destination development, even if this means presenting a destination's existing attractions and resources in new and different ways. Competition is intense and no destination can afford to rest on its laurels for too long. Many cities (e.g. industrial or global) have relatively few heritage attractions to develop and promote, thus the emphasis on contemporary, experiential and creative tourism becomes of pivotal importance. Creative cities arguably need creative governments and creative leadership (Florida 2002). They also need creative communities, who depend on that leadership for encouragement and support.

The development of creative tourism

Richards and Wilson (2007: 12) state: 'Whereas a few years ago "culture" was the key to urban regeneration, now "creative districts", "creative clusters" and the "creative class" are in vogue'. Richards and Wilson (2006) identify a number of forms in which creativity can be integrated into urban and tourism development. These are creative spectacles (e.g. festivals and events), creative spaces (e.g. creative quarters) and creative tourism. The latter, they argue, is based on the interaction and reflexivity of the tourist – that is, going beyond spectating. This builds on earlier work by Richards and Raymond, where creative tourism is described as:

> Learning a skill on holiday that is part of the culture of the country or community being visited. Creative tourists develop their creative potential, and get closer to local people, through informal participation in interactive workshops and learning experiences that draw on the culture of their holiday destinations.
>
> (Richards and Raymond 2000: 16)

In this case, creative tourists are more actively involved in the culture of the countries and communities they visit. They develop new abilities and interact with local people and, as a result, creative tourists get closer to the cultures of the countries they visit. This is especially important for those tourists seeking authentic experiences. UNESCO (2006) defines creative tourism as:

> travel directed toward an engaged and authentic experience, with participative learning in the arts, heritage, or special character of a place, and it provides a connection with those who reside in this place and create this living culture.
>
> (UNESCO 2006: 3)

Many different activities might be included in creative tourism: for example, cookery, wine making, painting, drawing, photography, wood or stone carving, pottery, sculpture, crafts, flower arranging, drama, music or dance. Some of these activities may be undertaken in specific landscapes: for example, painting or photography require good light, or certain forms of flora or fauna, people or culture. Local people may or may not assist in the process, depending on the nature of the trip: workshops can be run by indigenous people or local artists on cookery, carving, sculpture, pottery or crafts. Richards and Raymond (2000) describe a creative tourism experience in New Zealand where Maori people lead workshops on bone carving, wood turning, clay, felt making, winemaking and brewing, among others.

However, workshops can also be led by creative practitioners who are indigenous not to the region, and may accompany the tourists on a trip from their home country. This is common for painting or photography holidays, for example. Such holidays may be organised in small groups by tour operators who tend to focus on one form of creative activity. It is possible to enjoy both a creative activity and the local landscape and culture. But, in some cases, the creative activity may have little or no connection to the location or its people. This means that a second definition is needed for creative tourism in cases where the tourists do not interact with local people and the location is incidental. Here creative tourism may be defined as

> [e]xploring and expressing one's creative potential whilst on holiday. The activities and the relationship to the self are the primary focus. Context or setting is secondary.

Dance holidays are an interesting example of where the trip may or may not take place in the traditional 'home' of a dance form, and the teachers may or may not be local (see Box 7.2).

Box 7.2

Case study of dance holidays

Club Dance Holiday (a UK-based company) has been running dance holidays all over the world for almost ten years. The holiday includes a dance course with experienced dance teachers. The tuition includes choreography, technique and styling. Most holidays cater for all dance levels from complete beginners through to advanced. The number of classes included in the holiday vary depending on the specific holiday which is chosen.

Types of dance include Tango, Salsa, Ceroc, Ballroom and Latin, Bollywood, Swing, Flamenco, Belly Dancing, Line Dancing, Arabic, and more. Sometimes the dance holiday takes place in the so-called 'home' of the dance form, for example, Salsa in Cuba, Tango in Buenos Aires or Flamenco in Spain. However, many others take place in locations which are simply attractive but have no connection to the origins of the dance, for example, Bollywood holidays sometimes take place in Spain and might also be combined with Salsa. Line dancing or Irish dancing can take place in Berlin. This means that the 'authentic' origins of a dance form may be less important than other factors.

However, the company now tends to offer most of its holidays in Spain or Spanish speaking locations (e.g. Caribbean islands). This means that in many cases, the cultural and linguistic environment is appropriate for many of the dance forms (e.g. Latin, Salsa, Flamenco, Biodanza, Tango). It also implies that Spain and Spanish speaking countries are particularly popular with many UK (and other) tourists.

The available choice of dance forms on this kind of holiday relies very much on current leisure and lifestyle trends. For example, salsa has become almost universally popular at present. There has also been a big revival in Ballroom and Latin dancing due to the success of UK programmes like *Strictly Come Dancing* and its equivalent in other countries.

(Dance Holidays 2009)

Another way of engaging in creative tourism, apart from undertaking specialist workshops or booking a creative trip with a specialist tour operator, is to go on a holistic holiday. Smith and Kelly's (2006) research suggests there are hundreds of holistic retreats offering a range of body, mind and spirit activities, but many of these also offer creative activities. Holistic retreat centres (e.g. Skyros in Greece or Cortijo Romero in Spain) may include dance classes, drama workshops, writing courses, painting or singing, among other activities. The main quality of retreat centres is that the activities should have a therapeutic effect, for example enhancing well-being, helping to develop better skills of communication and self-expression, getting in touch with the inner self, etc. Although these impacts may occur during a creative holiday elsewhere, in an holistic retreat, emotional and psychological development is a specified outcome (see Box 7.3).

A third possible definition of creative tourism is more closely connected to earlier discussions about the creative industries:

Box 7.3

Case study of creativity and holistic holidays

Cortijo Romero is located in the southern part of mainland Spain near Granada. It is an holistic retreat centre that tries to cover all aspects of wellbeing and places its programmes in different categories, such as Bodywork, Psychological and Therapeutic, Creative/Arts, Dance, Meditation, Fun and Laughter, etc. Each category offers a range of courses (e.g. yoga, Flamenco dancing, writing, painting, singing). Courses are delivered by experienced, professional practitioners.

The centre offers organic vegetarian food as part of its product, engages in environmentally friendly practices, leads trips to the surrounding villages and national parks and teaches its guests Spanish language and cookery using local residents. Extra treatments of massage and other complementary therapies are available for visitors to purchase during their stay. This means that the company is committed to sustainable development and retains close links with local people and their culture.

Visitors to Cortijo Romero range in age from 18 to 80 but with an average age of around 45. Most come on their own, with the main aim of enjoying some personal space and engaging in self-development. The creative parts of the holiday can help them to return to activities that they have not done since they were a child, to learn new creative skills, to improve their sense of self-expression or communication, to build confidence, or simply to relax and enjoy the 'flow' of creativity.

One example of a creative week in Cortijo Romero is 'Kickstart your Creativity':

> If you want to do creative work but find it hard to get started, this session will give you the jump-start you need. If you lack confidence, it will make you braver. If you think you don't have any subject matter, you'll leave this week with your pockets bulging with ideas. Or, if you simply fancy a week of storytelling and creative writing, exercises, journalling, games and a lot of laughter, come along and discover just how creative and playful you can be.

(Cortijo Romero 2009)

> [e]njoying attractions and activities which are linked to the creative industries, and which tend to be interactive or experiential in nature.

This might include industries such as film and TV, fashion, design and architecture. However, in these cases personal creative input is limited and the experience is mostly passive or at best interactive. This definition therefore is more appropriate for what we might call 'creative industries tourism'. Architecture is becoming more and more significant, especially for cities, both as a marker of place identity and as an attraction for tourism. Klingmann (2007) describes architecture as being multi-purpose with an increasingly important symbolic value which goes beyond the functional. For example, architecture is frequently used as a catalyst for urban renewal. One has only to think about the success of buildings like the Guggenheim in Bilbao, where the architecture is arguably just as important (if not more so?) than the art collection.

Frank Gehry (the architect of the Guggenheim) also designed a wine spa in El Ciego in Spain, which is viewed as a significant landmark for the region. Klingmann (2007) also suggests that architecture functions as spectacle. At present Dubai's architecture is thought to be some of the most spectacular in the world, and much of the tourism industry is based on the promotion of its distinctive architectural icons. Architecture is used extensively in marketing and gives brand equity to destinations, all of which are searching for unique selling propostions. Architecture provides inspiration for local people and visitors alike. At a simplistic level, one might compare responses to aesthetic buildings (e.g. Roman, Renaissance) compared to functional ones (e.g. Communist), and witness the impact on the well-being of inhabitants of each environment. Architecture is also a talking point and provides controversy, and many communities are united in their hatred of a particular building (for example, in Budapest the new National Theatre was voted the ugliest building in the whole country in a national poll). However, tourists' curiosity will take them to locally controversial buildings, and visitors may also be united in their love of architecture; for example, many tourists enjoy Gaudi's architecture in Barcelona, or the modern architecture in Rotterdam (see Box 7.4).

Box 7.4

Case study of Rotterdam, City of Architecture 2007

Richards and Wilson (2006) describe how Rotterdam embarked on a policy of developing arts festivals and leisure events in the 1990s, which was subsequently supported by the development of new creative spaces and cultural clusters. For example, Rotterdam has developed a number of creative clusters which offer studio and performance spaces for artists at relatively low rents. This strategy was very successful in increasing visitor numbers. The city was also European Capital of Culture in 2001. Research by Hitters (2007) during the year of Capital of Culture showed that many visitors' main image attribute for Rotterdam is modern architecture.

In 2007, Rotterdam was City of Architecture. It has over a century of modern architecture within just a few square kilometres. Forty buildings in the city centre, representing a hundred years of modern architecture were selected in 2007 to take centre stage in a Sites and Stories programme. Apart from the already existing opportunities such as a visit to the Show-Cube, additional events were organised in and around the Sites and Stories buildings: from a guided tour in places that are usually closed to the general public to theatre performances on site. Apart from striking works of art on the outside of the buildings and a soundwalk through the city of Rotterdam incorporating all forty buildings, there were also excursions, theatre performances on site and many other events. Especially for children City Maps and Imaginary Maps were created as part of the Sites and Stories tour.

A bus-excursion alongside the highlights of Rotterdam Architecture gave an extensive view on the architectural developments of modern Rotterdam. From the construction of the post-war city, the highrise of the eighties and nineties till the ambitious plans on the Kop van Zuid (Southbank). This excursion took visitors alongside the spectacular highrise on the Weena, the unmistakable Schouwburgplein, the Museumpark, the developments on the Kop van Zuid, and of course the Cubehouses. They also visited the Van Nelle factory, one of the most remarkable examples of Het Nieuwe Bouwen (Dutch functionalism) in Rotterdam. The concept of light, air and space pervades the entire complex. The factory is an international milestone in the development of modern architecture.

(Rotterdam City of Architecture 2007)

Film and TV tourism have become increasingly important in recent years (Riley *et al.* 1998; Busby and Klug 2001; Beeton 2005). The term 'film and TV tourism' describes tourism visits prompted by viewing a location on television or at the cinema, for example, *Sex and the City* tours in New York or *Sound of Music* tours in Salzburg, Austria. This form of tourism also includes visits to places associated with film and television characters or celebrities. Harrison (2006) describes how around one-third of Americans are suffering from 'celebrity-worship syndrome'; therefore, visits to the homes of celebrities or tours of their favourite places might be included. Film and TV tourism has become so popular that VisitBritain produced a Movie Map (first in 1996) to give visitors information about film and TV locations and attractions, the Harry Potter craze being one of the latest successes. Capitalising on the success of the *Lord of the Rings* films, filmed in New Zealand, the New Zealand government put considerable resources into promoting film tourism (see Box 7.5).

Box 7.5

Case study of Lord of the Rings tourism in New Zealand

When the filming of the *Lord of the Rings* was announced, the NZ government appointed a 'Minister of the Rings'. This was an unprecedented appointment! Although the OECD questioned whether the return on investment for film tourism would be worth the input of resources, the NZ government took its chances and the results seemed to be fairly successful at least in the initial stages.

The government developed the slogan, 'The movie is fictional. The location isn't. Middle Earth is New Zealand.' This meant that visitors were asked to imagine that they were in fact in Tolkein's Middle Earth when visiting New Zealand. This is typical of the postmodern tendency of attractions developers and even tourists themsleves to confuse the fictional and the real. To make this development even more 'authentic', maps of 'Middle Earth' were published which could be used by film visitors. However, it seemed that there was actually little evidence of some locations, as many had been computer enhanced, while others were filmed in national parks and the sets had since been removed. This meant that there was only one remaining 'authentic' site – Hobbiton. Although this engendered a sense of pride in the local town (Matamata), the phenomenon is likely to be short-lived.

A *Lord of the Rings Location Guidebook* was reprinted twice in 2002 and five times in 2003, indicating the popularity of film tourism at this time. Air New Zealand even started announcing 'Welcome to Middle Earth' when landing, and artwork from the film was used on its aeroplanes.

Giant images of characters were placed around Wellington; for example, Gollum was located at the airport.

However, despite the *Lord of the Rings* fever apparently sweeping the world, it was estimated that only 0.3 per cent of visitors travelling to New Zealand were in fact travelling specifically for the film, although 9 per cent noted it as 'one reason'.

(after Beeton 2005)

The fashion capitals of the world are frequently cited as being Milan, Paris, London and New York. This means that many of the world's most prestigious fashion shows take place there, and there are designer shops in abundance. However, many Asian cities are also becoming popular with 'fashionistas', for example, Tokyo. Fashion is mainly globalised, although inspiration is clearly taken from a number of national or local cultures; however, most visitors who are motivated by fashion will simply follow the best catwalk shows and designers. Location may prove to be irrelevent, as the case study in Box 7.6 shows.

Box 7.6

Case study of a 'fashion island' in Dubai

As part of The World development in Dubai, an ambitious multi-million dollar project, there are plans to create the first 'fashion island'. Located off the coast of Dubai it will be called Isla Moda and will include a fashion resort, a luxury hotel, residential villas and hospitality facilities. The new luxury Hotel Moda will have around 250 rooms and serviced apartments, as well as fashion boutiques for those who love shopping holidays. There will also be luxury residential villas with sea views, private beaches and swimming pools.

Samira Abdulrazzak, CEO of the developer of Isla Moda, Dubai Infinity Holdings, says:

> Dubai is witnessing a boom in the property, tourism and retail sectors, and Isla Moda fits in ideally with this development. This first-of-a-kind project will cement Dubai's position as one of the top fashion and lifestyle destinations in the world . . . Isla Moda on The World will be the ultimate all-encompassing fashion experience, providing bespoke shopping, living, dining and entertaining.

Luxury holiday lovers will be attracted to Isla Moda by a range of services including a personal concierge. A style concierge will be on hand to offer advice on fashion and perfumes, while a design concierge will help create unique living environments including bespoke furnishings, art and multimedia technology. To draw in holidaymakers to Dubai as well as people looking for property in Dubai, Isla Moda plans to hold exclusive international events, including fashion shows and limited edition product launches attended by leading fashion designers. World-renowned fashion designers from each continent will be invited to design each element of the island, therefore the project will be truly global. It will be designed to represent the world's top fashion capitals, both countries and cities, will receive representation. Isla Moda won't be a country, but a 'city of fashion' instead.

> The fashion designer Karl Lagerfeld, who has been invited to design buildings as well as clothes, stated: 'Dubai is a fashion bud on the verge of blossoming into the next fashion hub of the world . . . Isla Moda has tremendous potential to be the style icon of the future.'
>
> (Trendhunter 2008; Freeman 2008)

Conclusion

It can be seen from this chapter that although it was initially difficult to differentiate between the cultural and creative industries, there have been many new developments in the field of 'creative tourism', which make it easier to define the concept. Three possible definitions are suggested: the first implies going to the 'home' of a certain creative activity, whether it be crafts, dance, cookery or music, and engaging with local people and culture(s); the second means that visitors can undertake creative activities, but these may be in environments where the location is largely incidental and there is little or no contact with local people; the third means creative tourism can involve the enjoyment of the creative industries such as architecture, film, fashion or design. These industries often tend to be more globalised, and therefore the destination culture may or may not be an essential factor. However, there seems to be a consensus that whichever definition we use, creative tourism should provide an experiential form of tourism. Many tourists now want to enjoy more active and interactive holidays, and creative tourism can provide them with the ideal opportunity. In the case of more culturally embedded creative tourism where location and local people are an integral part of the experience, authenticity seems to matter too. Both experience and authenticity are a major focus of Chapter 9.

8 ▶ Cultural tourism and urban regeneration

Most people now accept that you cannot breathe new life into cities, towns and communities without culture. Sometimes the cultural element alone becomes the driving force for regeneration.

(Jowell 2004: 5)

Introduction

The aim of this chapter is to analyse the role that cultural tourism can play in the regeneration of cities. Tourism, leisure and cultural activities have become as important as other service industries in compensating in part for economic decline and the loss of manufacturing industries. Cultural tourism can provide alternative sources of revenue for cities where traditional industries have declined, and whose economies, environment and communities have suffered as a result. The use of cultural events and 'flagship' initiatives is becoming a common means of transforming cities, attracting inward investment and enhancing image. A thriving cultural and tourism economy can often improve the socio-economic status of a city, contribute positively to local community life, and enhance image.

The role of regeneration in urban development

The term 'regeneration' is often viewed as being synonymous with 'revitalisation' (bringing new life to), or 'renaissance' (being reborn). It necessarily implies an initial *de*-generation. The Department for Culture, Media and Sport (DCMS 2004) describes regeneration as 'the positive transformation of a place – whether residential, commercial or open space – that has previously displayed symptoms of physical, social and/or economic decline'. This definition makes the point that the concept of regeneration is mainly applied to areas that are being *re*-developed after industrial decline, and does not really apply to those that are in the process of industrial development. Thus the term has generally been used in the context of developed Western countries (e.g. Europe, USA, Canada, Australasia). However, increasingly, the term is being applied to economic, environmental and social development programmes in all cities, including those in Asia such as Hong Kong, Tokyo, Hanoi, Kuala Lumpur and Bangkok (see Box 8.1). It also seems to refer to new cultural and creative areas of cities that may or may not be developed in previously degenerated zones.

Box 8.1

Case study of the regeneration of Shanghai, China

Since China adopted its open-door policy in 1978, many Chinese cities have been struggling with the challenges of urban regeneration, including the redevelopment of cities like Beijing and Shanghai. In the post-reform era, old dilapidated inner city centres and declining traditional industrial areas or abandoned docks were targeted. However, the development approach was largely economic and the success of projects was measured mainly by the level of investment and economic return. Old buildings were often considered as a burden for new development in Chinese cities, however, authorities and developers started to become aware of a different approach, based on the 'adaptive reuse' of buildings, which was inspired by pioneering works in European and American cities. In the beginning, these projects were limited to single historical buildings with high conservation value. For example, old villas and old apartments built in the early 1990s were transferred into restaurants, teahouses or hotels. Later the experiment was extended to bigger scale area redevelopment. By using a conservation-based approach to regeneration, it was possible to maintain the historical continuum of city life, which is hard to attain when replacing old buildings with new high-rise ones.

(Chen 2007)

The challenge of regeneration in Shanghai was partly to restore the grandeur of the colonial architecture, but also to create a model city and environment for the rest of the world to emulate. There had been little development since the 1940s as Shanghai had been neglected under Communist rule. In record time, Shanghai created a skyline which rivals New York's; however, this was often to the detriment of traditional buildings and communities. Many of the new towers also stand empty. However, attempts have also been made to revive the flourishing culture of Shanghai with the development of the Shanghai Museum, Shanghai Art Museum and Shanghai Opera. Despite the earlier over-zealous construction of modern buildings, there is now a movement to create an artistic as well as a greener, more sustainable city.

(Gilmore 2004)

Regeneration tends to be presented as an integrated process. For example, Bianchini (1993: 211) describes urban regeneration as 'a composite concept, encompassing economic, environmental, social, cultural, symbolic and political dimensions'.

Regeneration is often described as a process that aims to revitalise areas of cities that have declined using a range of tools (e.g. property, business, retail or arts development) to enhance an area. Urban regeneration strategies were largely developed initially in response to the post-war decline of cities, and the rising inequality, poverty, crime and unemployment that blighted inner cities, in particular. The de-industrialisation process and subsequent global economic restructuring in the late 1970s and 1980s also acted as a catalyst for the development of urban regeneration strategies for many cities in the USA and Western Europe.

Many policy and strategy documents for regeneration would still suggest that regeneration is synonymous with economic development. This is mainly because the need for regeneration usually stems from industrial or economic decline. The process consequently tends to be measured in economic terms, such as employment creation, multiplier effects or visitor expenditure. However, as concern for the supposed beneficiaries (i.e. the people living within target areas) of regeneration strategies has increased, the term appears to be more closely linked to the concept of 'community development'. Regeneration agencies are starting to consider the socio-economic or even socio-cultural impacts of regeneration, and although standardised measures for evaluation and monitoring have not yet fully emerged, there has clearly been a shift in priorities.

The urban regeneration process is a complex one, and the motivations for embarking on large-scale regeneration projects are varied (see Table 8.1). They may form part of a government's agenda for the economic or cultural redevelopment of former industrial cities that have fallen into decline; the enhancement of external image may be viewed as a means of attracting inward investment and tourism; or projects may be a way of initiating wider environmental improvements and infrastructure developments. A key factor in all of these motivations is that initial funding will hopefully have a cumulative effect, acting as a catalyst for further inward investment and the development of other initiatives.

There are many examples of apparently 'successful' regeneration schemes that are based on business or financial developments, physical, environmental or ecological

Table 8.1 Overview of different aspects and outcomes of regeneration

Regeneration as . . .

a 'panacea' for economic decline	a tool for social development	physical improvement	aestheticisation or beautification	a political or image-enhancing tool
Job creation	Housing	Conservation	Landscaping	Flagship buildings
Attraction of investment	Education	Environmental protection	Public art	Mega-events
Tourism development	Entertainment	Renovation	Animation	Branding

enhancement, or simply housing. However, the use of 'culture' has become more and more prominent in recent years.

The role of culture in regeneration

Regeneration had been a fascinating and controversial phenomenon for many years, but the interest in the role of culture within it grew exponentially throughout the course of the research. The Arts and Humanities Research Council (AHRC) in Britain was established in 1998 to further research on the importance of the arts and culture to enhancing quality of life and increasing the creative output of the nation: 'We welcome the acknowledgement of the importance of cultural and creative activities in enhancing and changing peoples lives, and in all areas of society and the economy' (AHRC 1998: 1). Culture is not mentioned as a tool for enhancing quality of life in the early days of Third Way politics in Europe (i.e. late 1990s), but later it becomes increasingly significant. For example, Giddens (2000: 5) quotes the sentiments of the (then) Italian prime minister, who said, 'Culture is the most important form of social inclusion, and I think we should invest in culture.' The Blair government in the UK followed suit by insisting that each local authority should develop a cultural strategy by 2002. The Department for Culture, Media and Sport started to issue policies that emphasised the contribution that the arts should make to social inclusion and neighbourhood renewal by improving communities' performance in health, crime, education and employment (DCMS 1999a and 1999b). Such instrumental cultural policies were used elsewhere in Europe to justify public expenditure on the arts.

An Institute of Ideas debate in 2001 (London, UK) entitled 'Can the arts create an urban renaissance?' suggested that regeneration agencies needed to think creatively now that culture rather than politics is often seen as being able to solve economic and social problems. The arts were viewed as being transformative, the 'glue of society', 'food for the soul' and 'even more spiritual than religion'. Nevertheless, the drive behind cultural regeneration is usually political, economic or commercial, and thus often seen as 'boosterist' or appropriated. The debate concluded that more artists should be involved in decision-making processes and regeneration needs to be more about people than the transformation of the city around them.

However, Belfiore (2002) suggests that research on the contribution of culture to regeneration and neighbourhood renewal remain paltry. Although the economic impacts of the arts had been analysed many years previously (e.g. see Myerscough 1988), the new government agenda in the late 1990s seemed to call for a more qualitative approach as the social dimension of regeneration became a focus of attention. The work of researchers and consultants like Bianchini, Matarasso and Landry provided social impact evaluation of arts projects, and although their work was criticised by Belfiore (2002) for being too short-term and superficial, it was arguably a significant starting point for more qualitative analyses of the role of culture in regeneration.

In 2004 the DCMS in the UK brought out the document *Culture at the Heart of Regeneration* for consultation, based on Evans and Shaw's (2004) report for the DCMS on *The Contribution of Culture to Regeneration in the UK*. Subsequent guidelines, such as Creative Cultures' (2004) *Guidance on Integrating Cultural and Community Strategies*, have emerged for local authorities. Examples of good practice are given from numerous local authorities. In the past few years, numerous strategy documents, toolkits and research projects have emerged in this dynamic field. For example, URBACT Culture Network (2006) produced an excellent study of the role of culture and creativity in urban regeneration, and IFACCA (2006) produced a document entitled *Arts and Culture in Regeneration*, which demonstrates shifts in thinking from large-scale icon-led regeneration to smaller scale community-based regeneration.

In the context of urban regeneration planning, the term culture seems to refer mainly to those developments and activities that form part of the deliberate and conscious production of space. It appears currently to refer to anything from architecture, heritage buildings and attractions, to the visual and performing arts, festivals and events, to entertainment and leisure complexes, shopping and sport. Table 8.2 considers the various roles of culture in regeneration.

Regeneration seems to require a somewhat instrumental approach fulfilling political and economic agendas, and the measurable outcomes are often the more quantitative ones. Therefore more intangible or qualitative elements (e.g. sense of place, identity, personal histories, everyday activities) are neglected or overlooked. Policy and practice have often failed to include those dimensions of culture which most reflect a local area and its people. The notion of culture as a force for social good is not backed up by consideration of culture as a way of life and is often secondary to political, economic or environmental considerations. Culture clearly needs to be articulated more widely and researched more qualitatively. Even the vocabulary used to describe culture often varies considerably between academics, policy makers, practitioners and the general public.

A critical analysis of the role of culture in regeneration

Evans (2005a) differentiates between approaches to regeneration, demonstrating examples of 'cultural regeneration', where cultural activities are integrated into a wider strategy; 'culture-led' regeneration, where culture provides a catalyst for further developments; and 'culture *and* regeneration', where cultural activities are less integrated and therefore play a more marginal role, often as a mere 'add-on'. In the latter two approaches, culture is generally seen as synonymous with the arts or

Table 8.2 Roles of culture in urban regeneration

Culture as a panacea for economic decline	Cultural industries can create jobs	Culture attracts investment and funding	Spending on culture boosts the (local) economy
Culture as political	Culture as an expression of diversity	Culture gives voice to marginalised minorities	Culture helps to create more accessible and safer spaces
Culture as a source for social good	Cultural activities can improve quality of life	Culture supports social integration and cohesion	Cultural activities can be educational
Culture as environmental enhancement	Culture supports conservation	Culture aestheticises space	Culture animates space
Culture as commercial or business opportunity	Culture as tourism product	Culture creates brands	Culture as entertainment
Culture as symbolic and prestige	Cultural flagship projects and events	Culture gives a sense of place and identity	Culture enhances internal and external image
Culture as everyday life	Culture as personal histories and heritage	Culture as everyday activities and practices	Culture as leisure and relaxation

heritage, with large flagship projects (e.g. museums, art galleries, mega events or festivals) acting as catalysts for further developments, often with little regard for the local area. In the case of cultural regeneration, however, there should logically be a better integration of new developments with the heritage, traditions, contemporary values and daily life of the local area.

'Grand projects' and 'flagships'

Some cities use cultural flagship projects or events as catalysts for the environmental, social, economic and cultural regeneration of an area by producing new spaces. This may include the development of new cultural attractions, such as museums, galleries or theatres, or cultural events, such as festivals and exhibitions. Cities clamour to host the next Olympic Games, the Expo or the European Cultural Capital initiative. However, the legacy of 'mega-events' and their contribution to urban regeneration is a subject that has concerned a number of researchers. Sandercock (1998) suggests that many governments have fast-tracked mega-projects, often short-circuiting established planning processes and isolating such developments from public scrutiny and democratic politics. Sudjic (1999) states that cities and governments are unfortunately not very good at hosting mega-events. The legacy is often one of high levels of debt, redundant buildings and a community that has been displaced or bypassed. However, they are high-profile events, which generate international publicity, and the host city often considers the prestige to outweigh other considerations. They can also boost the tourism profile of a city.

Such developments could technically take place in almost any city in the world, and attempts at engaging local people rather than tourists or visitors are often tokenistic. Heying et al. (2007) pessimistically conclude that '[a]s a lever for regeneration, the Olympics have perhaps passed a point at which they can work for the ordinary citizen.' 'Flagship' developments and attractions are therefore essentially icons and tourist attractions, but there are mechanisms that can be used to enhance local attendance and engagement. International art galleries such as Tate Modern in London have fairly extensive outreach and educational programmes, for example. Differential pricing or free passes for locals can encourage visitation. Residents may benefit indirectly from big events like Expos and Olympic Games if infrastructural improvements are made or new (affordable) housing is created. But all of this needs to be taken into consideration at the planning and consultation stages, where debates can be held about how best to balance the global and the local, the financially lucrative and the socially beneficial.

Jones (2000) suggests that a number of projects have failed for financial reasons, but also because they are largely inappropriate for the local community and cultural infrastructure. He cites the example of the Centre for Visual Art in Cardiff, which did not meet with the same success as the flagship rugby stadium or Cardiff Bay

Plate 8.1 Lisbon Expo site

(Source: Melyvn Smith)

Waterfront Development. He attributes this to a lack of local interest in modern art, suggesting that popular culture and sport generally tend to strike more of a chord with local audiences in Cardiff than high arts. Sheffield's National Centre for Popular Music perhaps failed because Sheffield does not have a particularly strong musical heritage in the way that Liverpool or Manchester do. Whereas Tate Modern has appealed to London audiences and international tourists alike, it should not be assumed that it is possible to reproduce such an effect elsewhere. The same is true of the Guggenheim Museum in Bilbao. Although many cities are now hankering after their very own Guggenheim, it is the uniqueness of the structure, its location and cultural context that partly shape its success (see Box 8.2).

Box 8.2

Case study of Greenwich, London: caught between two flagship projects

In 1999 Lord Falconer stated that 'Greenwich has become a globally recognised model for regeneration, regeneration for which the Dome has been a catalyst and is helping to bring prosperity to one of the poorest parts of London and to the UK as a whole.' At this time it was estimated that 12 million visitors would visit the Dome, of whom 2.5 million would be overseas visitors (BTA 1999), and that London would need 10,000 extra beds by the year 2000 to accommodate the influx (LTB 1997). The New Millennium Experience Company committed £1 million for training, employment and skills development for local people and local business, and Greenwich Borough Council estimated that as many as 25,000 jobs would be created in the local area in the following seven years (Sumner 1999).

However, in the same year Irvine (1999: 2) stated that 'the construction of few buildings in modern times has attracted as much scrutiny and hostility as the Millennium Dome in Greenwich'. By February 2000, the Dome had failed to meet visitor targets, attracting only 3 per cent of the 12 million visitors it needed to break even (Arlidge and Wintour 2000). The main motivating factors for visiting Greenwich included the Dome (12 per cent) but only 3 per cent of respondents had actually visited the Dome (ATLAS Cultural Tourism Survey 2000). Although visitor numbers to the centre of Greenwich technically doubled, many people had actually stayed away *because* of the Millennium Year (Smith 2000).

Local responses to the Dome were mainly negative too (Smith 2009):

> A waste of money and the most ugliest thing that was ever put on the earth.
> (Local woman in focus group 2002)

> For me regeneration's about both the physical renewal and human invigoration of a specific area. Both go together. It's no good renewing an area without the people bit too. The Dome is a perfect dead example.
> (Local artist 2001)

> Packed with really bright ideas but there was a lack of planning.
> (Local woman in focus group 2002)

It seems that only a few local residents had actually visited, and those who did perceived it as too big, impersonal, noisy and crowded, as well as being too expensive. There were problems of access for women with pushchairs, elderly people and the disabled. Finally, some local people were trained by Welcome Host but were then not employed.

This means that the Millennium Dome is usually cited as being a 'failure' despite being the most popular visitor attraction in Europe during the year that it remained open. The notoriously negative press was mainly due to excessive political intervention, as well as its dramatic cost (£800 million or so). It also remained empty for five years or more before it became the O2 Arena.

However, it is hoped that the London Olympic Games in 2012 will use the Dome as a venue, and that the impacts for Greenwich may be largely positive. The leader of Greenwich Council stated that lessons had been learned from the Dome and that the choreography of such events was now familiar. As a result, he believed that 'legacy is always more than you imagined it would be' (Roberts 2008), and that the local area, its people and tourism would all benefit significantly.

The Millennium Dome is not the only example of an expensive 'white elephant' (numerous Olympic Games and Expos have suffered the same fate), though lessons are at least being learnt from previous mistakes. For example, the importance of long-term legacy has been recognised and is now being built into the bidding process for large-scale projects. Smith (2007) suggests that event regeneration should involve a series of diverse tourism initiatives, which coincide with major flagship projects. In addition, local social progammes must accompany the main event or, better still, events should be used to accelerate and assist *pre-existing* plans and objectives. This can help to enhance everyday life and improve lived experiences.

Cultural, ethnic and mixed-use quarters

Many cities create integrated 'cultural districts' or 'cultural quarters' as part of regeneration strategies. Wynne (1992: 19) describes a 'cultural quarter' as being 'that geographical area which contains the highest concentration of cultural and entertainment facilities in a city or town'. This may include entertainment facilities, retail outlets and eating and drinking establishments, as well as cultural venues or attractions (e.g. museums, galleries, theatres). Increasingly, its meaning can also include clusters of creative industries (e.g. media, design, technology) and creative individuals and groups. Cultural and creative developments are sometimes integrated into mixed-use districts designated also for office space, residential, hotel, catering, retail and recreational use.

Some theorists advocate the production of mixed-use spaces in regeneration. For example, Murayama and Parker (2007) suggest that sustainable regeneration is dependent on the ability of planners to improve quality of life by balancing the 'play', 'work' and 'live' elements of urban life. This is closer to the concept of culturally integrated regeneration; however, it is currently more common for cities to develop successful business or financial districts or tourist areas where few people live. Aiesha and Evans (2007) say that '[a]n imbalance or neglect of an area's liveability risks the commodification all too familiar in tourism and other mono-cultural usage of urban sites (e.g. major retail, leisure developments)', which suggests that everyday life should be a priority when developing cultural quarters.

Some cultural quarters develop more 'organically', for example so-called 'ethnic quarters' or 'ethnoscapes' like 'China Towns', 'Arab Quarters' or 'Little Italies'. This can sometimes lead to a form of 'ghettoisation', which is particularly common in large cities in the US. The other side of the coin might be an enhanced sense of community on the part of diasporic groups in search of a common identity in a new or foreign environment.

Ethnic quarters can also become so popular with residents and visitors alike, that they regularly feature in tourist brochures as cultural attractions, with gastronomy, shopping and festivals topping the list of activities. As noted by Shaw (2007: 49), 'Places whose very names once signified the poverty of marginalised urban communities are now being promoted to appeal to visitors with sophisticated and cosmopolitan tastes.' He suggests that expressions of multiculturalism are increasingly being exploited as picturesque backdrops in order to animate urban areas.

There have been fears that such developments are leading to an appropriation or invasion of social or lived space. Culture is no longer being articulated by those who are indigenous or original inhabitants. There may even be security risks or fears or displacement. For example, in London, Asian women may fear going out unaccompanied in Brick Lane as there are now so many (white) men frequenting curry houses there. Residents of Notting Hill have faced displacement from their homes as gentrification of the area increases and the Carnival becomes more of a 'white' spectacle (Smith 2003). It has also been noted that some Asian mela festivals are being globalised and hybridised to suit white tastes (Smith and Carnegie 2006).

Although this may appear to be a challenge to the authenticity of an area in the short term, in the long term it can bring economic advantages such as increases in house prices, business investment and tourist spending. The extent to which local residents will benefit depends partly on the degree of political control. In some cases, the concentration or clustering of certain groups can be highly beneficial to an area in terms of regeneration, for example, gay quarters. It is interesting to note that many gay areas of cities are becoming more gentrified, no doubt to capitalise on the strength of the 'pink pound'. This is certainly true of London's Compton Street (Soho), Manchester's 'Gay Village' and Brighton's Kemptown in the UK. Florida (2002) emphasises the strong links between a high 'gay index' and clusters of creative and technoglogical activities. The Gay Pride event or Mardi Gras is increasingly being used as a means of asserting gay identity, but also of attracting visitors. Manchester and Brighton Gay Pride events are becoming almost as popular as London's, and cities like Birmingham, Leicester and Sheffield in the UK are following suit. Although this event has sometimes been criticised for becoming depoliticised, mainly due to the growing number of heterosexual revellers 'crashing' the party, the publicity and tourist interest they generate can be significant. Shaw (2007) emphasises how, with careful planning and management, the development of the cultural industries and visitor economies can help to foster the role of ethnic and minority entrepreneurs as active agents of regeneration (see Box 8.3).

> **Box 8.3**
>
> ### Case study of an ethnoscape in Brick Lane, London
>
> Brick Lane is the heart of London's Bangladeshi community (the largest in the UK) and is sometimes known as Banglatown. The name Brick Lane comes from the middle ages when this part of the east end was the centre for bricks and manufacturing. In recent decades it has become the home of Bangladeshi curry houses, and there are now over 60 restaurants, cafés and sweet shops. It has sometimes been called the 'Indian equivalent of Chinatown'. As a result, it has become a popular visitor destination. Shaw and MacLeod (2000: 1) describe it as: 'a rambling alley – of the kind guidebooks call "Dickensian" – lined with unforgettably spiced Bangladeshi restaurants, with Indian sweet shops and sari emporia'.
>
> In the 1990s, the area was a focus of regeneration initiatives, as the Bangladeshi community had suffered from considerable poverty and deprivation, and the area was somewhat rundown. As part of the regeneration project, the Brick Lane Festival was created. This includes music, food, crafts, fashion shows and a funfair. 65,000 people attended the 2006 Festival, and although only a small number of visitors come from overseas and the rest of the UK, the Festival attracts large numbers of Londoners (Brick Lane Festival 2006: Evaluation Report).
>
> In addition to the Brick Lane Festival, there is the Banglatown International Curry Festival. The Curry Festival is a two-week event, which coincides with the first day of the Brick Lane Festival. As a result of the large numbers of restaurants in Brick Lane, the competition for customers is intense. Many visitors find the levels of harassment to enter restaurants intolerable, and the quality of the food has frequently been criticised (e.g. Muir 2004; Cohen 2006). It was therefore hoped that the Curry Festival competition would help to counter these criticisms and prove that the food in Brick Lane really was of a high and authentic standard.
>
> Shortly before the 2006 Festivals, Brick Lane hit the headlines, as a vociferous minority of local residents and business people protested against the planned filming of a version of Monica Ali's novel *Brick Lane* in the street because of its unflattering images of Sylheti women and the area generally. Although the novel *Brick Lane* has brought the area even more publicity, it arguably did little to improve the image which regeneration projects had been trying to address for years.

The arts, festivals and community development

In Britain, the USA and most other Western countries, there has been an emergence of 'arts-led' urban regeneration strategies in recent decades. As advocated by Lefèbvre (1974), the arts and festivals can help to animate the city and enhance lived space. It was hoped that such strategies would serve to reconstruct cities' external image, making them attractive to potential investors and visitors, as well as triggering a process of physical and environmental revitalisation. Inspiration was drawn from the American experience of the 1970s in cities like Pittsburgh, Boston and Baltimore. Mayors in these cities were keen to relaunch the image of downtown areas, develop cultural districts and mixed-use areas, and to boost the local economy through art-related activities (Bianchini 1993). Contemporary examples in the US also exist.

For example, Spirou (2007) analyses the local impacts of large-scale cultural regeneration projects undertaken in Chicago; Bounds (2007) evaluates the 'Avenue of the Arts' initiative in Philadelphia; and Breitbart and Stanton (2007) discuss cultural and creative industries-led regeneration in New England towns.

Jacobs (1961: 386) emphasises the importance of a thriving cultural life for American cities. Arts activities can make a positive contribution to community life, attracting people to an area, creating a lively ambience and improving safety on the streets. As noted by Fisher and Owen (1991), the arts are just as essential for a city's identity as any other civic services. Sharp *et al.* (2005) suggest that public art can contribute to local distinctiveness, attract investment, boost cultural tourism, enhance land values, create employment, increase use of urban space, and reduce vandalism. Clearly, large, cosmopolitan cities have become more culturally diverse over the past few decades. The consequence has been a proliferation of exciting and colourful festivals, events and spectacles, many of which have global appeal. As stated by Sandercock (1998: 213), 'Our deepest feelings about city and community are expressed on special occasions such as carnivals and festivals.' Tourism has helped to raise the profile of ethnic festivals, and tourists are clearly motivated by an interest in the cultural origins of festivals.

The arts typically suffer from problems of under-funding and under-valorisation. Governments frequently take a rather tokenistic approach to the arts, exploiting their economic and social potential, but without adequate reinvestment and support (Belfiore 2002). More research and evaluation is therefore needed to prove the true worth of the arts to the process of regeneration (unfortunately, often a time-consuming, difficult and expensive process). Research by Evans and Shaw (2004) has started to provide a good indication of the significance of culture to regeneration in the UK, but such studies are still few and far between.

It is important too that the arts are not seen as some kind of panacea for urban decline. Breitbart and Stanton (2007) note that the arts are somewhat elusive and cannot easily compensate for high unemployment, anachronistic economies and notoriously negative images. Florida (2002) and others suggest that there is an inextricable link between culture, creativity, economics, business and technology. Whilst the creation of new public museums, galleries, events and festivals can serve a useful social and educational function, they will arguably succeed only if they can become profitable businesses too. This means that more than one articulation of culture is required for integrated regeneration (i.e. cultural attractions need to promote themselves as not only artistic venues, but also as economically viable enterprises, educational institutions and enjoyable attractions).

The 'heritagisation' of urban space

Many theorists have been somewhat cynical about the way in which heritage has been used in the production of regeneration spaces. Sudjic (1993: 166) states: 'When there is nothing else left to sustain their economies, cities start to rediscover their own history, or at least the history that they would like to have had. They use it as a catalyst for their attempts at regeneration.' Soja (2000: 246) suggests that this is linked to a sense of urban nostalgia, 'a longing for what is called the "historical city", a once more clearly definable urbanism that is believed to have been civilized, urbane, and richly creative'. This may be true, but it is difficult for many cities (especially former industrial cities) to sell themselves otherwise, given that the urban landscape has often been blighted by heavy industry. The growth of industrial heritage tourism is now well documented, but it is not always easy to develop or promote.

There is also a temptation to aestheticise reproduced spaces. Walsh (1992) complains of a phenomenon, which he calls 'heritagisation', whereby the past is transformed by a process of 'ahistoric aestheticisation' creating fantasy spaces, which are home to no one and have few local associations or affiliations. Similarly, Hughes (1998) suggests that care must be taken not to 'overwrite' the original significance of heritage spaces when developing tourism, and Middleton (1987) comments on the problems of towns becoming too sanitised in insidious attempts to clean up and prettify. Regeneration initiatives arguably need not only to conserve as much local heritage as possible, but also to encourage the articulation of hidden or alternative histories, especially those of local or diasporic communities. The re-use of heritage buildings (e.g. former factories, railway stations) for modern purposes is a common regeneration strategy, but this can be problematic as the original workers may feel no affiliation with the new structure (and not all ex-factory workers can or want to be retrained as curators or retail managers).

Harvey (2007) makes the important distinction between regeneration that focuses on tourism development, and regeneration that prioritises local heritage. In the context of Black heritage in New Jersey, he demonstrates that so-called 'successful' tourism projects have failed to critically examine the dissonant past, thus excluding aspects of culture that are particularly pertinent to ethnic minorities (e.g. abolition of slavery, emancipation). Of course, interpretation within all heritage contexts is limited by space and resources, but there has been a noticeable shift in the rhetoric of US, European and Australasian governments towards supporting ethnic and indigenous cultures.

Waterfront and dockland development schemes

Sieber (1993) describes how the revitalisation of urban waterfronts is a seemingly ubiquitous process in North America, Europe and Australasia, and one which inevitably seems to involve gentrification. Despite the intentions of developers and planners to create integrated mixed-use development, combining residential, recreational and cultural developments, the result is the production of an often gentrified space largely occupied by strangers to the city (e.g. urban professionals, suburban communities, tourists). The failure to provide access for locals or, worse still, the displacement and exclusion of local communities is an issue that needs to be addressed by governments in their regulation of private-sector development and planning.

Cooper (1993) suggests that waterfronts have been likened to 'urban frontiers' by geographers. They have largely become isolated 'landscapes of consumption' awash with gentrified cultural and recreational activities, which often fail to reflect the diverse cultural traditions of local people. Cooper claims that this is true of Toronto. It is also starkly in evidence in Cape Town, where the commercialised, internationalised, 'could-be-anywhere' sense of space experienced at the waterfront stands in sharp contrast to the troubled heritage of the Black and Coloured townships. Given the city's history of spatial and racial segregation, it is surprising to encounter a contemporary version of a similar process. Cooper suggests that whatever diversity exists at the waterfront, it is certainly not local heritage. Nevertheless, the waterfront is immensely popular with international tourists arguably *because* of its cosmopolitan environment and its rather safe and sanitised atmosphere. It also imports wealth which would not otherwise come to the locality and which can, given the right circumstances, be distributed to locals.

Edwards (1996: 93) states that many waterfront developments have been criticised because of their 'poor design, lack of character and generally unimpressive environments'. Hoyle (2002) discusses different models of waterfront regeneration, some of which create bland standardisation, globalisation and gentrification, and others which focus more on heritage renaissance, community development or contemporary culture. Such conflicts are not easily resolved within the context of urban (re)development. Similarly, the resolution of global/local tensions is a key dilemma as discussed earlier in the context of 'flagship' projects.

Jones (2007) notes that some of the most successful waterfront regeneration projects have tended to be small scale, less prestigious and more public spirited, combining public and private sector partnership. He advocates a blend of the more commercially orientated American approach and the more community orientated approaches of continental Europe with projects being better integrated into existing developments. Avery (2007) describes how port towns have traditionally attracted artists, tourists and developers due to their cosmopolitan charms. Therefore culture-led regeneration is by no means incompatible with local history and traditions. She describes, for example, how cities in the UK, like Liverpool and Cardiff, have successfully transformed themselves into cultural destinations, for which the waterfront developments have acted as a catalyst (see Box 8.4).

Box 8.4

Case study of Liverpool

Despite its greatness in the eighteenth century, and key role in the Atlantic economy and Industrial Revolution, Liverpool declined significantly in the twentieth century. The fall of empire followed by the bombings during the Second World War left the city in a state of decline.

However, in the early 1980s Liverpool's startling renaissance began with the 1984 Liverpool Garden Festival. In 1987, Liverpool City Council produced its innovative *Arts and Cultural Industries Strategy* document, linking cultural policy with local tourism, city centre and economic development strategies. By 1988 the city had transformed the Albert Docks into a spectacular arts, leisure and retail complex, including the Tate Gallery, a Maritime Museum and Granada TV's regional news centre and offices. The legacy of the Beatles and the success of the Liverpool-based British soap opera *Brookside* helped to further enhance the city's image, as did Liverpool Football Club.

In 2004 Liverpool Maritime Mercantile City became a World Heritage Site. The World Heritage Site stretches along the waterfront from Albert Dock, through The Pier Head and up to Stanley Dock, and up through the historic commercial districts and the Rope Walks area to the cultural quarter which is dominated by the magnificent St George's Hall.

However, Walsh (1992: 143) cites Liverpool as an example of a city that has allowed the 'heritagisation' of its public spaces to erode any sense of local heritage and identity. He describes the Albert Dock as 'a de-historicised place', 'a contrived place' and a form of 'ersatz-tourism' (1992: 143–4), where visitors do not encounter the real Liverpool or real people because they have all been displaced. The local sense of place has been eroded in order to provide a sanitised leisure experience that fails to capture the significance of Liverpool's industrial heritage and community life. Nevertheless, he concedes that although Merseyside has not attracted as much inward investment as it would have liked, there is no denying that the economic benefits of tourism have been significant.

Walsh's (1992) concerns were later addressed (at least partly) in Liverpool's bid to become European Capital of Culture in 2008 beating strong opposition from Birmingham, Bristol, Cardiff, Newcastle–Gateshead and Oxford. Its focus on regeneration was seen as a major deciding factor, as was its emphasis on supporting disadvantaged communities and improving everyday life for residents.

Overall, Liverpool is an excellent example of an incremental approach to regeneration, which builds on a series of successful developments and initiatives to change radically the cultural offer and image of a city.

Tourism and the globalisation of urban space

Hughes (1998) describes how tourism is a spatially differentiating activity, which can lead to the homogenisation of culture, but which can also help to 're-vision' or 're-imagine' space:

> Tourism . . . differentiates space in a ceaseless attempt to attract and keep its market
> share. In the face of growing global cultural homogenisation, local tourist agencies
> strive to assert their spatial distinctiveness and cultural particularities in a bid to
> market each place as an attractive tourist destination.
>
> (Hughes 1998: 30)

Something similar could be said of the regeneration process. Various destinations are
actively engaging in the reconfiguration of their identity in an attempt to reposition
themselves or to put themselves on the tourist map. However, Walsh's (1992) fears
about bland standardisation and the heritagisation of public space are not unfounded.
It is evident that numerous town centres, particularly in Britain, are starting to rely on
inward investment from global businesses, which render them at best homogenous
and at worst soulless. The same is true of some rural areas, which are becoming more
standardised and losing their character (see CPRE 2003). Although it is clear that
former industrial cities often have little option but to court such investment, it can
quite feasibly be channelled into the development of innovative new projects,
initiatives and attractions, rather than bland retail developments. Tourism development
is likely to be threatened if all places start to look the same (Ritzer 2004).

The entertainment spaces of tourists are only temporary and often require a
heightened experience that is different to or better than that which could be gained
back home. On the other hand, local people need their lived experiences to be more
stable, consistent and functional, and therefore the production of tourist spaces may
not be compatible with the real needs of local residents. However, Maitland (2007)
suggests that many tourists, especially repeat visitors to destinations, are seeking
alternative experiences that are based on the 'authenticity' of local areas. Some of
these are surprisingly ordinary, but the fact that they are based in 'fringe' areas of
cities inhabited by local residents and characterised by more organic developments
means that they are appealing to visitors. This implies that sometimes the 'true'
cultures of cities are more desirable than purpose-built attractions. They offer
elements of surprise whilst helping to maintain a sense of place. In this case, the
production of 'real' local spaces is very much what the tourist is seeking.

Creativity and regeneration

Many authors have recently been advocating a more creative approach to regeneration
in order to combat standardisation and serial reproduction, and to support cultural and
community diversity. For example, Richards and Wilson (2007) examine the
increasing importance of creative strategies for cities wishing to avoid the pitfalls of
homogenisation and serial monotony. Areas become attractive to creative practitioners
because of their unique atmosphere or character (and, of course, affordable rents and
property). Florida's (2002) seminal work shows clearly that the most attractive and
economically successful cities tend to be those with the highest concentration of

creative and bohemian people. Nevertheless, care must be taken not to gentrify regeneration areas to the extent that original residents and artists are priced out.

Sandercock (1998) suggests that spaces for fantasy are essential to a city, and Rojek (1993) emphasises the importance of 'playfulness' in tourism and leisure. Many tourists enjoy fantastical spaces with high levels of technological interaction (the enduring popularity of theme parks is testimony to that). New global destinations which might be described as 'hyper-real' (e.g. Dubai) are currently some of the most appealing, due to their innovative and creative approaches to architectural and attractions development, and their clear understanding of the 'experience economy' (Pine and Gilmore 1999). Local people can also enjoy such playful spaces if urban development is planned ethically, rather than being victims of manipulation and exploitation (a common problem in Dubai which relies on cheap foreign labour to build a dream for an elite).

Csikszentmihalyi (1996: 28) notes the potential of creativity for cities: 'Creativity is any act, idea, or product that changes an existing domain or that transforms an existing domain into a new one.' Many destinations can no longer compete simply on the strength of their heritage attractions, especially where repeat visitation is desirable. Many cities (e.g. industrial or global) have relatively few heritage attractions to develop and promote, thus the emphasis on contemporary, experiential and creative tourism becomes of pivotal importance. Creative cities arguably need creative governments and creative leadership (Florida 2002). They also need creative communities, who depend on that leadership for encouragement and support (see Box 8.5).

Box 8.5

Case study of a creative city: Barcelona

Barcelona has successfully been regenerated in the past two decades, changing its image from that of an industrial and commercial city into that of a cosmopolitan Mediterranean metropolis (Richards and Wilson 2007). Barcelona has placed culture at the centre of urban development through cultural policies that are committed to innovation and creativity. As with many successful regeneration schemes Barcelona has built on a number of initiatives, including the Olympics in 1992 and the Universal Forum of Cultures in 2004. This provided a catalyst for the improvement of infrastructure and the creation of public space. Many post-Forum events provided arenas for local creative events, such as street theatre, outdoor concerts and cinema.

There is also the emergence of creative clusters such as the Poble Nou district of the city, a former manufacturing district. 200 hectares of industrial land in Poble Nou were converted into an innovative productive district for new-generation activities within the scope of education, creativity and innovation.

Barcelona houses a number of cultural facilities and creative industries, such as publishing, audiovisuals, design and fashion. The Cultural Centre for Design has new facilities measuring

20,000 square metres that will become a platform for the promotion of design developed in Barcelona and Catalonia. Museums are also seen as generators of international capital, therefore a basic network of museums of capital calibre was established. This included the Museu National d'Art Catalunya, Montjuïc Barcelona Museum of Contemporary Art, Museu Picasso, Fundació Miró and Fundació Tàpies.

Theme years have also been created, for example, Gaudí Year (2002), to contribute to the revaluation of heritage and collective memory; the Year of Design (2003), to promote design, one of Barcelona's most powerful creative industries; the Year of the Book and Reading (2005), to support the publishing industry and foster the habit of reading; and the Year of Science (2007), an instrument to endorse the integration of the scientific culture in the city's overall cultural construction. In addition, there is Barcelona's Grec Festival, a festival of creation with a firm commitment to creative people; and the BAM Urban Music Festival.

(after Mascarell 2008)

Richards and Wilson (2007) emphasise the need to create visible, tangible examples of creative development in order to attract consumers and to convince planners and investors of their importance. Importing a creative class as advocated by Florida (2002) can serve to exclude local residents, and many critics have seen the use of the word 'class' as divisive (e.g. Evans 2005b). He describes the 'creative class' as 'new wine in old bottles' and argues that there is little evidence to suggest a definite causality between 'creative index' and productivity or innovation. In other words, creativity can become an elusive buzzword if its management is not considered carefully.

Cultural planning for regeneration

The concept of cultural planning has started to take into consideration multiple articulations, especially those of local residents. The origins of cultural planning go back several decades; however, the concept has only existed in its current form since the mid-1990s. Its implementation has not therefore been extensively researched, especially in the context of regeneration. Cultural planning aims to transform physical space and is technically about the way in which governments or planners integrate cultural resources into the everyday lives of people. Cultural planning considers the diverse benefits that cultural resources can bring to a community if planned for strategically.

Cultural planning has the following characteristics:

- People-orientated approach to development
- Consultative and inclusive
- Pluralistic and diverse
- Promotes importance of access and tolerance

- Aims to improve quality of life
- Recognises the importance of place and character of environment
- Includes intangible and symbolic aspects of culture
- Advocates creative approaches to development
  (Mercer 1991; Bianchini and Ghilardi 1997; Ghilardi 2001; Evans 2005a)

Evans (2001) provides an interesting analysis of the development of arts and cultural planning within the context of urban renaissance. He suggests that geographers and urban planners have often failed to appreciate the significance of culture and arts practice and participation in urban planning. He describes it as a means of integrating cultural resources into strategic urban development. It is not sustainable to construct cultural 'flagships' in isolation from the rest of urban development (as seen in the previous chapter). If local residents fail to engage with such developments, there is little chance of them surviving. Equally, if a sense of place is to be maintained or enhanced, a balance must be struck between the emphasis that is placed on heritage and the celebration of contemporary culture and the arts. Although care must be taken not to 'over-write' the significance of heritage with new developments, the diversity of both indigenous and non-indigenous local community cultures should be adequately represented. All urban planning needs to take into consideration people's lifestyles, cultural associations and identity if it is to have any resonance with local communities.

Sandercock (1998) describes how the 'voices from the borderlands' – i.e. those of the marginalised, displaced, oppressed or dominated – are increasingly being listened to. Cultural differences should not simply be tolerated, they must be valorised, which requires a new kind of 'multicultural literacy'. This includes the histories of 'imagined communities' such as gays and lesbians, and women, as well as ethnic and diasporic communities. A more 'discursive' form of planning may help to ensure that the true meaning and significance of city space is not overlooked. Ploger (2001: 64) suggests that the aestheticisation of the built environment must also aim to improve living conditions and shape social networks. He looks at planning as a 'discursive practice', which 'produces a sense of place, place-identity and common cultural schemes'. This includes a combination of aesthetic regeneration (e.g. environmental and architectural enhancement), social engineering (e.g. inviting higher socio-economic groups to become actively involved in community activities) and economic development (e.g. attracting inward investment and tourism).

Planning for the regeneration of tourist destinations and spaces is a complex process. As demonstrated by failed 'flagship' projects, it is not simply enough to 'beam in' an attraction of supposed international significance and acclaim. It must have some local resonance and connections with a sense of place and identity, otherwise, dissent becomes inevitable. The same is true of World Heritage Sites, which promote themselves as panaceas for the regeneration of industrial or rural areas. Local people should be involved in their interpretation and representation as national or global icons. As stated by Evans:

The focus on world and symbolic heritage sites in the cities of both developed and developing countries requires that a balance be struck between local and national imperatives – qualities of life, economic and physical access, minimising gentrification effects.

Evans (2001: 226)

Table 8.3 is compiled from extensive reading of academic and practitioner sources relating to cultural planning.

The fourth category in Table 8.3 adds an important dimension once the first three categories have been addressed, which is to provide unique and exciting experiences, which help people to transcend the 'ordinariness' or mundanity of everyday life (e.g. through the arts, architecture, festivals, creative industries). These have the benefit of attracting tourists to a location and developing an external place identity

Table 8.3 Main elements of a cultural planning approach to regeneration

Consideration of local, multiple culture(s)	Local cultures at the centre of and integral to planning
	Aesthetics discourse'
	Takes account of cultural diversity
	Recognition of multiple histories/heritages
	Multiple representations
	Recognition of hybrid and multiple identities
	Negotiation of the local versus the national and the global
Involvement and empowerment of local stakeholders	Democratic and community-orientated
	'Bottom-up' approach
	Pluralist, multi-stakeholder approach
	Predominantly 'anthropological' in approach
	Local participation in the arts and cultural activities
	Fostering civic pride, a sense of local identity and ownership
Emphasis on everyday life practices	Emphasis on 'quality of life'
	Awareness of intangible aspects of culture
	Access to public spaces (physical and psychological)
	New, more 'tolerant' spaces for social interaction
	Spiritual and 'sacred' spaces
	Place and culture inextricably intertwined
	Emphasis on place identity and place marketing
	Retention of local 'authenticity'
Creative and experiential approaches	Creative approaches to development
	High 'Creative' and 'Bohemian' Indices
	Animation of cities through culture and creativity
	Space for fantasy
	Aesthetics discourse

which is attractive and competitive. The emphasis is on locally inspired playfulness. Rojek (1993) suggests that postmodern societies tend to be playful in their approach to leisure and tourism, and Sheller and Urry (2004) refer to the playfulness of places, which are always on the move, consisting of different mobilisations of memories, emotions, performances, bodies, etc. Playfulness embraces contradictions, crossovers and hybrids, and, as stated by Junemo (2004), in playful locations, globalisation is not seen as a threat, but is embraced wholeheartedly in urban planning. The aesthetic here would not be a universalising notion of 'beauty' or 'heritage', but a celebration of the contemporary uniqueness of the locality, for example, people and buildings in 'performance'.

Many theorists and practitioners advocate an anthropological or community-based approach to cultural planning, and it is true that an area's people are often its most unique asset. A sense of place and animation is arguably created through and by the people resident in an area, coupled with the social and cultural programmes that are provided for and supported by them. Public spaces need animation, perhaps through the development of cultural festivals or the presence of public art. Increasingly, areas of ethnic and cultural diversity are becoming popular areas of cities (e.g. Shaw *et al.* 2004), and the most attractive cities seem to be those with a high concentration of creative and bohemian people (Florida 2002).

Conclusion

In terms of cultural development, politicians and strategists often favour high-profile, expensive flagship projects or tourism-generating initiatives, but their impacts are usually short-lived and legacy is limited. Conversely, the small, community events that can truly enhance local lives are generally underfunded and their continuity becomes threatened as a result. Many large cultural projects succeed on one level (e.g. they become popular tourist attractions like the Greenwich World Heritage Site), but can fail on another (i.e. they fail to engage local residents). Even as tourist attractions, their appeal can be short-lived resulting in inadequate legacies for a destination. Conversely, projects can be developed with considerable local community involvement only to lack the commercial support to be viable in the long-term. This is the result of overly narrow approaches to spatial thinking and planning which can be addressed more positively through a cultural planning framework. This needs to be holistic or integrated (Bianchini 2000); ethical (Sandercock 1998); personal and sensitive to local needs and empowering (Miles 1997); enhancing quality of life (Fenster 2004); and creative (Florida 2002). However, although culture can help to attract investment and sponsorship, this should not become a substitute for true social and welfare support. Indeed, however important the arts and creativity may be to the regeneration of an area, they are often very elusive and intangible, and cannot therefore replace or entirely compensate for industrial development.

9 The growth of experiential cultural tourism

> Today's travellers want to learn, discover and undergo unique experiences. They are looking for something interactive. They want to know how other people live, go behind the scenes and visit places that tourists do not usually see. An experience can be triggered by anything from one small detail to an overall concept.
>
> (Laliberté 2005)

Introduction

In Chapter 7 I discussed the growth in more contemporary forms of cultural tourism which are based on the development of the creative industries. However, even in more traditional areas of cultural tourism (e.g. heritage, museums, arts and indigenous tourism), there is an increasing desire on the part of tourists for more interactive and experiential activities. There is also something of a contradictory phenomenon whereby many cultural tourists crave greater authenticity as the world becomes more globalised and technologically advanced, whereas others embrace wholeheartedly the inauthenticity which accompanies more experiential forms of tourism. Although it could be argued that cultural tourists are more drawn to authentic environments than other types of tourist, further analysis is required as cultural tourism diversifies and cultural tourists become more complex and demanding.

The importance of the experience economy in cultural tourism

Cultural tourism is as much based on experiencing as it is on seeing. Therefore Williams's (1958) definitions of culture as a whole way of life as well as the arts and learning are particularly relevant here. Past definitions of cultural tourism have placed too much emphasis on cultural tourism as a form of arts or heritage tourism in its narrowest sense; for example, visiting museums, monuments, galleries and theatres. Cultural tourists are also interested in the more experiential aspects of culture. In an international context, particularly in the context of indigenous or ethnic tourism, the way of life of a people can be a central focus, where the traveller is motivated primarily by first-hand, authentic or intimate contact with people whose ethnic or cultural background is different from their own.

The tourism industry has always been in the business of providing experiences for visitors; however, the staging of experiences has become a more important element in recent years following the growth of the so-called 'experience economy'. The experience economy was hailed as the new economic era by Pine and Gilmore in the late 1990s (1998). They suggest that the experience economy is the fourth economic stage in human progress: first, in the agrarian era, we extracted commodities from the earth, then during the industrial era, we manufactured goods. The industrial economy then gave way to the third economic era, the service economy, where services were delivered. Finally, the experience economy evolved, where the main economic offering is the staging of experience. Pine and Gilmore differentiate experiences from services as follows:

> Experiences are a distinct economic offering, as different from services as services are from goods. Today we can identify and describe this fourth economic offering because consumers unquestionably desire experiences and more and more businesses are responding by explicitly designing and promoting them.
>
> (Pine and Gilmore 1998: 97)

Here, we are not entirely sure which came first – the creation of experiences by businesses, or the desire for experiences on the part of consumers. What is certain, however, is that consumers are responding positively to experience creation and are clamouring for more. Most capitalist societies go through stages in which materialism is viewed as the highest good, and the accumulation of possessions is paramount. One possibility is that the majority of people who are wealthy enough to travel have already accumulated all the material possessions they need to be happy and now wish to focus on experiences. Another is that many people are disillusioned with material goods as they wish to 'downsize' or become more spiritual. The Trends Research Institute estimates that by the end of the decade, 15 per cent of American adults will be living 'the simple life' or downsizing (Humphreys 2007). However, this may not exclude travel possibilities.

Two of the main principles of experience creation are based on customer participation, which can range from passive to active, and connection between the customer and the experience, ranging from absorption to immersion. Clearly, the most memorable experiences are those that engage the customer in active participation in an activity in which they are fully immersed. This might require the engagement of all five senses or the provision of memorabilia. It is only in recent decades, however, that the true significance of the experience economy is being embraced by the tourism sectors.

Pine and Gilmore (1998) suggest that an experience is only truly valued if it is paid for. This is a somewhat narrow view, especially with regards to tourism, and Richards (2001d) states that if only bought experiences are valued, this misses out on the importance of spontaneous happenings that characterise any tourist trip. These chance encounters cost nothing and yet can be the most memorable aspects of a visit. Even tour operators recognise this, and are providing more flexible packages where tourists play a greater role in the construction of their own experiences. Tour operators, especially those which promote special interest tourism, focus on providing the visitor with unique encounters in previously under-visited destinations. This might include remote wildlife or tribal destinations, adventure tours or extreme sports. Even the marketing of tourism destinations tends to promote the more intangible and experiential aspects of the destination, such as the atmosphere, animation or sense of place. Tourists tend to become co-producers of the experience, as they view destinations and events through their own personal lens, and are influenced by their social and cultural values. These can vary considerably, and expectations may be very different according to whether a tourist is seeking 'authentic' culture or merely seeking 'experience'.

Munsters and Freund de Klumbis (2005: 28) discuss the growing importance of 'lifestyle' and 'design' hotels, which are an important part of the whole experience economy. They describe how hotel guests are searching for unique experiences, multi-entertainment and (aesthetic) adventure. Lifestyle hotels can often be autonomous cultural tourism products because of their architecture, special features and attractions. Design hotels are appealing because of their combination of exterior and interior design, fashion, arts, technology, luxury and quality. They also refer to 'eatertainment', which can include feasts and banquets livened up by entertainers.

In 2007, Forbes Traveler released a ranking of the world's 50 most visited tourist attractions. The top ten are listed in Table 9.1.

It is fascinating to note how many of these attractions are theme parks. This implies that many tourists are enjoying simulated worlds even more than the real world! Of

Table 9.1 Forbes top ten most visited tourist attractions in the world

1	Times Square, New York City, United States
2	National Mall and Memorial Parks, Washington, DC, United States
3	Walt Disney World Resort's Magic Kingdom, Lake Buena Vista, Orlando, United States
4	Trafalgar Square, London, United Kingdom
5	Disneyland, Anaheim, California, United States
6	Niagara Falls, Ontario, Canada, and New York, United States
7	Fisherman's Wharf and Golden Gate, United States, San Francisco, California
8	Tokyo Disneyland and Tokyo DisneySea, Tokyo, Japan
9	Notre Dame de Paris, Paris,
10	Disneyland Paris, Paris, France

course, the statistics do not refer to what we might describe as 'cultural tourists', but this is still an interesting trend. The appeal of theme parks should therefore be discussed further, as there is no attraction more experiential than a theme park. Walt Disney is considered by Pine and Gilmore to be an 'experience-economy pioneer' and has been in the experience business since the 1950s. The Disney concept arguably epitomises all that a successful theme park should be. Warren (1999: 109) describes Disney theme parks as 'the tourist meccas of the late twentieth century', and Zukin (1995: 50) states that 'Disneyland and Disney World are the most important tourist sites of the late 20th century'. Although Disney is most commonly depicted as epitomising American culture, the brand is truly global, and the Disney Company is one of the most successful multimedia corporations of all time. The name is synonymous with global enterprise and initiative. Although there was initial concern that such a phenomenon could not be transported easily from its American home, Disneyland Paris has proved to be an unprecedented success in Europe. For example, more people now visit Disneyland Paris each year than the Eiffel Tower.

Theme parks – the ultimate tourism experience?

Ritzer and Liska (1997) describe how McDonald's and Disney have become as much symbols of the postmodern (or experiential) tourist landscape as any other cultural icons. They are also symbols of increasing globalisation. As stated by Warren (1999: 123) in her discussion of Disney theme parks, 'Disneyland Paris speaks to a fear lurking deep in social theory: that the nation-state is obsolete, about to be eclipsed by the multinational corporation.' Ritzer and Liska (1997) suggest that the homogenising omnipresence – the 'McDonaldisation' and McDisneyisation' of the world – has undermined somewhat the fundamental reason for tourism, which is to experience something new and different.

However, as theme parks continue to top the charts of world attractions, we must consider that they are doing something right in the eyes of consumers. Commercial theme parks are perhaps the ideal visitor attraction. Craik (1997) suggests that artificial theme parks are much more appealing than many themed heritage attractions or museums because they can offer the visitor a more exciting, entertaining and integrated experience. Philips (1999: 93) describes how 'the theme park is a space unequivocally devoted to pleasure'. This differentiates it from heritage sites which generally purport to being educational in some way. This is not to say that visitors will learn nothing of value in the theme park, but this is not its primary aim. Craik (1997: 115) describes theme parks as the ultimate 'tourist bubble' (a safe, controlled environment) out of which tourists can selectively step to 'sample predictable forms of experiences'. Theme parks, especially Disney parks, are viewed as safe, secure and dependable: 'Disney World is highly predictable. . . . Indeed, Disney theme parks work hard to be sure that the visitor experiences no surprises at all' (Ritzer and Liska 1997: 97).

Philips (1999) describes how theme parks tend to be constructed around a number of specific themes which often correspond to popular literary genres, such as science fiction, fairy or folk-tales, and explorers and treasure islands. Again, this blend of fiction and fantasy is what gives the theme park its main appeal. Rojek (1993) describes all theme parks as being based around the 'meta-themes' of velocity and time–space compression. By this he is referring to the 'thrill factor' provided by fast rides, and the way in which time and space are dissolved in a diversity of experiences and spectacles. Visitors may have the experience of moving through time or travelling across continents, all within the space of a few hours. Philips describes a theme park as a space without clocks, as well as being a bounded space which is located outside the familiar environs of everyday life:

> The theme park explicitly offers a 'phantasmagoria': it celebrates the fact that it can bring together 'absent others', and revels in the exoticism of its attractions. The theme park is a space which is unapologetically penetrated by influences quite distant from their geographical location, and which distances itself from the actual locale.
>
> (Philips 1999: 106)

Zukin (1995) suggests that Disney World represents a privatised, sanitised, aestheticised, idealised world in which people can take refuge from the harsh realities of the outside world. However, she also suggests that there is much to be admired about the way in which Disney has managed effectively to create an environment that is in some ways more real than hyper-real:

> Like all the world's fairs that preceded it, this is a visual narrative for a compact tourism of exotic places. And it is a world's fair brought to you by a world-class corporation, whose references to its own cultural products are so entangled with references to those of real places that Disney World is indistinguishable from the real world.
>
> (Zukin 1995: 58)

For many visitors, especially children, it is the perfect visitor experience. It is a world of fantasy and escapism, combining dreamscapes with simulations of real places, a curious blend of fiction and reality.

Many companies try to recreate the success of Disney, with some of the Asian theme parks becoming the most spectacular. For example, Lotte World opened in Korea in July 1989 and is regarded as a world-class theme park. About 8 million visitors go to Lotte World each year, and the total number of visitors is well over 100 million. About 10 per cent of the visitors are foreigners, and the number shows the status of Lotte World as a world-renowned tourist spot as well as the most visited theme park domestically. It is ranked seventh in the world (Lotte World 2009).

Box 9.1

Case study of Branson, USA

Branson, Missouri in the USA is not very well known to foreign visitors, but it is a huge entertainment destination for domestic tourists, and especially families. It is less than a day's drive from one-third of the US population. It has a seven-mile stretch of live music and comedy shows, numerous restaurants, theme parks, shopping outlets and myriad hotels. With over 50 theatres and 100 different shows, Branson has more live shows than anywhere else in the country, and it attracts more than 7 million visitors per year. Branson is home to some of America's top theme parks such as Silver Dollar City and Celebration City. Silver Dollar City is a late 1800s theme park which has over 20 rides, including several seasonal festivals, multiple shows daily and 60 unique shops. It shows 1880s Ozarks culture with over 100 craftworkers demonstrating glass blowing, basket weaving, blacksmithing, pottery, candy making, candle making and many other disciplines. Leeking (2001) describes why he and his family visit year after year:

> We enjoy Silver Dollar City because it provides the complete package. We aren't going to the park just to ride a roller coaster or eat kettle corn. We're paying to participate in a version of 1880s southern Missouri and to have some memorable family-oriented fun in the process. We are there for the *experience*.

Celebration City has over 30 rides and attractions, including themed restaurants. Branson has more than 350 restaurants. There are three lakes, a water park and a beach, as well as numerous outdoor activities such as golf (over 12 championship courses), sailing, bungee jumping and parasailing. Branson has some interesting museums, including the Titanic Museum which opened in 2006 and includes artefacts from the wreck. The two-storey museum is shaped like the *Titanic* herself, at half-scale. Another museum in Branson is the American Presidents Museum, which showcases the lives and presidencies of those who have led the United States.

(after Branson Tourism 2009)

The kind of tourists who visit theme parks and other attractions of an experiential nature have sometime been described as 'post-tourists'. The following section describes this phenomenon and its relationship to cultural tourism.

Post-tourism and the experience economy

Urry (1990: 87) describes tourism as being the quintessential postmodern industry: 'because of its particular combination of the visual, the aesthetic and the popular'. Rojek and Urry (1997: 3) write about the development of a 'post-modern cultural paradigm [which] involves the breaking down of conventional distinctions, such as high/low culture, art/life, culture/street life, home/abroad'. Lofgren (2003) states that the new experience economy is highly integrated and illlustrates how tourism is combined with retail trade, architecture, event management, the entertainment and heritage industries as well as the media world under a common umbrella.

Kirschenblatt-Gimblett (1998: 9) describes how the world has become a kind of museum of itself: 'Tourists travel to actual destinations to experience virtual places.' Theme parks, shopping malls and fast food have all become part and parcel of the same postmodern consumption experience. Barber summarises the concept of 'McWorld' as:

> an entertainment shopping experience that brings together malls, multiplex movie theatres, theme parks, spectator sports arenas, fast-food chains (with their endless movie tie-ins), and television (with its burgeoning shopping networks) into a single vast enterprise that, on the way to maximising its profits, transforms human beings.
>
> (Barber 1995: 97)

These are the ultimate integrated, 'inauthentic' experiences, and this would all suggest that there is increasingly very little differentiation between the leisure, recreation and tourism experiences of our lives (see Urry 1990). Zukin (1995: 188) describes how late twentieth-century shopping malls have become viewed by many social theorists as being 'primary public spaces of postmodernity'. The public culture of mass consumption has found its home in the multiplex shopping mall which aims to combine retail therapy with other leisure and recreational pursuits, such as cinema, roller-skating or ten-pin bowling. It is clear that the shopping centre, like the theme park, is becoming a symbol of global consumerism, embodying Barber's (1995) concept of 'McWorld'. Under one roof, visitors have the chance to experience a wide range of global fashion and international cuisine. Sarup (1996) refers to the shopping mall as an alternative life-world in which one can create alternative selves or identities.

The combination of shopping with other recreational pursuits suggests that the boundaries between retail and leisure are becoming more blurred, as are the boundaries between leisure and tourism. For example, many leisure complexes are now being developed as self-contained holiday destinations. The Center Parcs concept is a good example of this, and it is interesting to note that many of these complexes have been built in the colder climates of northern Europe (e.g. the Netherlands, Belgium, Britain and France). Once again, it is a form of simulated attraction – the creation of a kind of displaced tropical paradise in which those deprived of sunshine and beaches can indulge their fantasies. The world's geography can be experienced vicariously as simulacrum through themed environments such as Expos, which contain national displays of cultural activities (Urry 2002). One country can even be recreated in another, as the case study in Box 9.2 shows. Here, the replica country is the Netherlands, but several others have been created or are in progress. Hendry (2000) suggests that 'theme park' is perhaps not the right expression for such attractions, arguing that they represent quite sophisticated forms of cultural display, and are more like museums or world fairs.

Box 9.2

Case study of Huis Ten Bosch

Huis Ten Bosch is a residential-style resort built after a mediaeval 17th century Dutch town. It was built with special permission from the Dutch royal family and is a reproduction of the residence of the Queen of the Netherlands. In English, Huis Ten Bosch means 'house in the forest'. And true to its name this residential-style resort has canals running throughout, is surrounded by greenery, forests, amusements, shops, restaurants, five distinct hotels, a marina and residential area. This spacious 152-hectare resort, roughly the same size as Monaco, is striving to become the top flower resort in the world and flowers in full bloom can be found all throughout the year. Each season transforms this European resort into something completely new.

Huis Ten Bosch was opened on March 25 1992 in Nagasaki Prefecture, Kyushu Island. During the Edo period when Japan was closed to the outside world, Nagasaki was the only port open for international trade. The arrival of a ship named De Liefde from Holland in 1600 at Kyushu Island was the start of exchange between Japan and Holland. As a result, Nagasaki was extremely prosperous during the Meiji Period (late 19th century), but modern advances eventually surpassed it and the advantage was lost. Historians, architects, oceanographers, and environmentalists all came together with an appreciation for the shared history and culture of Holland and Nagasaki, and with the backing of the government of Holland and many Japanese corporations the Huis Ten Bosch project was formed.

Although Huis Ten Bosch is suffused with the essence of Europe, the district also features numerous spots that convey the history and romance of Japan and are likely to arouse the interest of tourists. In particular, visitors can go to Arita and Imari. These sites were amongst the birthplaces of the ceramics craft and were the subject of fascination even in Europe.

(Huis Ten Bosch 2009)

The profile of the postmodern tourist is discussed by both Urry (1990) and Walsh (1992). They describe how many postmodern consumers receive much of their cultural capital through media representations, including travel. They cite Feifer (1985), describing the 'post-tourist' as one who does not necessarily have to leave the house in order to view the typical objects of the tourist gaze. The simulated tourist experience is brought into our living rooms through television travel shows, internet sites and software programs. As stated by Adair (1992: 24), 'Culture, in short, is something which "happens" to us increasingly at home.' Urry (2002: 83) refers to the concept of a 'three minute culture', which is characteristic of the media and its televisual influence. Bayles uses (albeit cynically) the metaphor of the television to describe contemporary cultural consumption:

> It is now academic orthodoxy that all of culture – indeed, reality itself – is a torrent of images cut off from one another and from time, space, and meaningful reference and without emotional impact. To put the matter in nontheoretical parlance: Life is channel zapping.
>
> (Bayles 1999: 166)

Baudrillard (1988) suggests that many individuals are trapped in a world of simulacra or 'hyper-reality' (perpetuated mainly by television and mass media) where the spectacle and the real are indistinguishable.

McCabe (2002) argues that tourism has become such an established part of everyday life, culture and consumption that it is hard to differentiate it from other domestic and leisure activities. The tourist experience becomes little more than an exaggeration, enhancement or enrichment of everyday activities: 'Tourism represents a microcosm of everyday life, a magnifying glass through which the entire miscellany of life is distilled into a fragmentary week or fortnight' (McCabe 2002: 70). However, Urry (2002) suggests that tourists are still essentially looking for difference when they travel. Craik explores the relationship between home and abroad in more depth, suggesting that:

> Tourists revel in the otherness of destinations, people and activities because they offer the illusion or fantasy of otherness, of difference and counterpoint to the everyday. At the same time the advantages, comforts and benefits of home are reinforced through the exposure to difference.
>
> (Craik 1997: 114)

As the world becomes more globalised, the homogenisation and standardisation of cultural experiences and activities are perhaps inevitable; hence people may need to travel further afield in order to experience differences. It can be seen that the changing and diversifying tastes of the modern-day consumer are being catered for *par excellence* by the travel market. Tourism fuses international travel with the desire for leisure and recreational activities of all kinds, and, increasingly, an interest in the multifarious cultures of the world. The average tourist today is likely to want to combine a visit to a beach with a weekend's shopping, a day or two of sightseeing, an evening at the theatre or a concert, followed by a couple of bars or nightclubs. Many tourists can no longer be as easily pigeon-holed into the 'mass tourist' (beach and clubbing) type, and the 'cultural' (sightseeing and arts event) type.

For the post-tourist, tourism has become a game: 'the post-tourist knows that they are a tourist and that tourism is a game or a series of games with multiple texts and no single, authentic tourist experience' (Urry 1990: 100). Rojek (1993) sees the consumption experience as being accompanied by a sense of irony. He suggests that the quest for authenticity and self-realisation is at an end, and we are now in a stage of post-leisure and post-tourism. He describes the post-tourist as having three main characteristics. These are:

- An awareness of the commodification of the tourist experience, which the post-tourist treats playfully.
- The attraction to experience as an end in itself, rather than the pursuit of self-improvement through travel.
- The acceptance that the representations of the tourist sight are as important as the sight itself.

Smith (2005b) refers to one form of post-tourist, and that is the 'new leisure tourist'. It is suggested that this is a relatively young breed of tourist, who is seeking escapism, entertainment and fun. Disposable income levels are relatively high but time is generally short. Although comfort and security are sought, the tourism experience should afford an element of excitement or thrill. This might be in the safe confines of a hotel, resort or themed attraction. Typical attractions might include visiting adventure lands, cyberworlds or simulated environments. New leisure tourists enjoy landscapes that correspond to Barber's (1995) concept of 'McWorld', where a number of familiar global brands are clustered under one roof. It is of no consequence that such attractions could be located anywhere, it is the experiences gained which count. The new leisure tourist differs significantly from traditional visitors like cultural tourists. There is no pretension of being interested in local societies and cultures; instead, simulated environments may be preferred. For example, many theme parks seem to simulate environments like Egypt's Valley of the Kings, an Arabic souk or the jungles of Africa, without the inconvenience of further travel, and offer 'safer' experiences there.

However, although there are now overlaps between the profiles and motivations of tourists, it should be noted that cultural tourists generally have quite different interests from the so-called 'post' or 'new leisure' tourist (see Table 9.2).

The quest for authenticity seems to be one of the main differences between cultural tourists and the others. Although it could be argued that authenticity is constructed, perceptual or simply does not exist, the complexity of this phenomenon requires further discussion. This is particularly significant to the experience economy, as explored by Pine and Gilmore (2007) in their book *Authenticity*.

Authenticity and the cultural experience

The concept of authenticity is arguably a subjective attribution. Pine and Gilmore (2007) even go so far as to suggest that there is no such thing as an authentic or inauthentic experience, as experiences happen inside us and are our internal reaction to the events unfolding around us. Cohen (1988) proposes that authenticity is a 'socially constructed concept' whose meaning is negotiable. It is also a relative concept, as stated by Moore (2002: 55): 'One person's absolute fake is another's meaningful experience.' Getz (1994: 425) describes authenticity as 'a difficult concept open to many interpretations, but [is] of great importance in the context of cultural tourism'.

Jamal and Hill (2002) provide an excellent analysis of different typologies of authenticity. They differentiate between 'objective authenticity', which usually refers to traditional or historical sites or artefacts, and 'constructed authenticity', which may refer to staged events, moderated art objects or artificially created cultural attractions. The category of 'personal authenticity' is perhaps the most

Table 9.2 Comparing cultural tourists, post-tourists and new leisure tourists

The cultural tourist	The post-tourist	The new leisure tourist
Keen on personal displacement and the notion of 'travelling'	Enjoys simulated experiences, often in the home	Keen to escape from home and overwork culture
Actively seeking difference	Little differentiation between tourism, leisure and lifestyle	Seeking experiences more fantastical than at home
Seeking objective authenticity in cultural experiences	Acceptance that there is no true authentic experience	Looking for 'extra' or fake authenticity
Concerned with existential authenticity and enhancement of self	Treats the commodification of the tourist experience playfully	Wants to forget about self, be entertained and have fun
Earnest interaction with destinations and inhabitants	Ironic detachment from experiences and situations	Likes interactive experiences of a technological nature
May have idealised expectations of places and people	Little interest in differentiating between reality and fantasy	Aware that what they experience is not 'real' and little interest in local people
Interested in 'real' experiences	Interested in 'hyper-real' experiences	Actively travelling in 'hyper-reality'
Disdain for representations and simulacra	Acceptance of representations and simulacra	Loves representations and simulations

Source: Smith 2005

complex and the least researched, but may refer to the emotional and psychological experience of travel, subjective responses to and interpretation of sites and events experienced, or deeper existential aspects relating to personal meaning and identity.

Turner and Ash (1975) describe how tourists are placed in a circumscribed world devoid of responsibility and protected from reality, which includes any sense of authenticity. McKercher and Du Cros (2002) suggest that tourists actually want 'authenticity' but not the reality that goes with it. This means that they may not wish to experience any kind of personal hardship which may need to be endured in an 'authentic' setting (e.g. staying in a tribal village with no running water, strange food, poisonous insects, etc.). However, Goffmann (1959) suggests that it may be impossible for tourists to go beyond 'staged authenticity' and to penetrate the 'backstage' of people's lives, however much they want to. Crick (1988) even contends that all cultures are staged and are therefore inauthentic to an extent. However, this is difficult to accept for many cultural tourists who go to great lengths to *avoid* the inauthentic. They conform to MacCannell's (1976) description of tourists as being like contemporary pilgrims who are in search of authentic experiences in other places and other times.

Plate 9.1 Searching in vain for authentic local food in Bodrum, Turkey

(Source: László Puczkó)

Boorstin (1964) argues that many tourists deliberately go in search of inauthentic experiences or 'pseudo-events', and that tourism has become responsible for rendering most events superficial or 'pseudo'. This is certainly true of the so-called 'post-tourist' who is aware that the tourist experience is largely commodified, and that the quest for authenticity is somewhat futile. Boniface and Fowler state:

> We want extra-authenticity, that which is better than reality. We want a souped-up, fantastic experience. We want simulation of life ways as we would wish them to be, or to have been in the past. As is clear, the travel industry knows it is dealing in dreams.
>
> (Boniface and Fowler 1993: 7)

Myth and fantasy have always been central to the tourist experience. As stated by Rojek (1997: 52), 'Mention of the mythical is unavoidable in discussions of travel and tourism'; and Tresidder (1999: 147), 'tourism at its most simplistic level is concerned with the production and consumption of dreams'. Kirschenblatt-Gimblett (1998: 144) describes how representation has become almost more important than the destination: 'The industry prefers the world as a picture of itself.'

Tourism packages now offer the tourist a whole range of facilities to accompany their visit to major sights and destinations. Tourism has become a much more integrated experience, no longer simply a focused quest for knowledge, self-improvement and authenticity of experience on a whistle-stop tour of 'must see' sights. Shopping, eating, drinking and evening entertainment are becoming as much a part of the tourism product as visiting the world's major monuments. Ironically, many of these activities can serve as a form of compensation for the disappointed tourist whose experience of the world's major sights fails to live up to the glossy media images and other forms of representation with which the tourist has been presented. Deception or disappointment appear to be an accepted part of the tourist experience (Rojek 1997; Tresidder 1999). De Botton (2002) suggests that travel rarely lives up to our expectations, partly because images are idealised and romanticised in art, literature and media, and reality is often a far cry from the idyll. Who, for example, would have imagined from the postcards and tourist brochures that the Mona Lisa would be so small, or that the Pyramids would be surrounded by urban sprawl, or that the Taj Mahal would be discoloured and viewed through a haze of smog?

Many sights are now really viewed as only second-hand images which bear little resemblance to reality. For example, Urry (2002: 55) describes how the Niagara Falls 'now stand for kitsch, sex and commercial spectacle. It is as though the Falls are no longer there as such and can only be seen through their images.' However, many tourists appear to be content to gaze upon what is familiar to them. Urry (2002) describes tourists as semioticians who are searching for signifiers that are familiar to them through other media (e.g. a typical English village, French chateau, German beer garden, American skyscraper); see Box 9.3.

Box 9.3

Case study of Las Vegas: experiencing (in)authenticity at its best

Las Vegas is the most important spot for gambling, tourism and recreation in the USA, but it started out as a desert full of dunes. It attracts around 40 million visitors per year and is one of the top ten places to visit in the world, offering amazing shows, mega-resorts and five-star restaurants featuring every and any cuisine. Pine and Gilmore (2007) discuss how many tourists claimed to love Las Vegas because it is so 'real'! They suggest that although Vegas and 'authenticity' might in theory seem to be polar opposites, it seems that people enjoy the life-like simulations of places and experiences, for example:

- Bellagio (Lake Como, Italy)
- Luxor (ancient Egyptian city with pyramid)
- New York in the 1930s
- Mirage (a volcano)

Other examples include Paris and Monte Carlo. 'All these themed venues are inspired by sources many tourists are unlikely *ever* to encounter personally. In visiting the next best thing, they find that these places authentically recreate what they could not otherwise experience' (Pine and Gilmore 2007: 68).

Klingmann (2007: 195) suggests that:

> As visitors travel from the ancient Egyptian world into the dream world of Monte Carlo and through today's New York back to a romanticized Italian lakeside village in a matter of minutes, the strip functions like a channel-flipping device in real time what links a selection of tourist attractions within the confines of a few city blocks.

Klingmann describes how the architects and designers in Las Vegas try to stimulate the five senses and create a variety of sensory reactions by using 'mood design' in its buildings. Visitors become completely immersed in their experiences as a fictional narrative and a real space engage them simultaneously.

For instance, tourists know that sitting at the Bellagio Hotel and Casino in Las Vegas in the middle of an Italian setting with a view upon an artificial 'Lago di Como' does not mean being in Italy. The point is that they do not have any problems with this 'cultural discrepancy' (Beeck 2003). They do not seek 'authenticity', but enjoy the staged experiences like playing a game (Urry 2002; Xie 2004).

It can be seen therefore, that although authenticity may still be important to many cultural tourists, the 'real thing' can be disappointing in some way. It is also hard to recognise what is authentic and what is not. In some cases, the inauthentic may actually be less tedious, for example, in the case of cultural performances which are extremely long and ritualistic, or cultural experiences which are uncomfortable and inconvenient (e.g. staying in very basic conditions in local people's homes).

Within the experience economy, Pine and Gilmore (2007: 49) identify five genres of perceived authenticity:

Plate 9.2 Even better than the real thing? The Venetian, Las Vegas

(Source: Károly Novák)

- Commodities – natural authenticity
  People tend to perceive as authentic that which exists in its natural state in or of the earth, remaining untouched by human hands; not artificial or synthetic.
- Goods – original authenticity
  People tend to perceive as authentic that which possesses originality in design, being the first of its kind, never before seen by human eyes; not a copy of imitation.
- Services – exceptional authenticity
  People tend to perceive as authentic that which is done exceptionally well, executed individually and extraordinary by someone demonstrating human care; not unfeelingly or disingenuously performed.
- Experiences – referential authenticity
  People tend to perceive as authentic that which refers to some other context, drawing inspiration from human history, and tapping into our shared memories and longings; not derivative or trivial.
- Transformations – influential authenticity
  People tend to perceive as authentic that which exerts influence on other entities, calling human beings to a higher goal and providing a foretaste of better ways; not inconsequential or without meaning.

Originality is becoming increasingly important in tourism as competition increases. Offerings should also be shaped around the unique tastes or unusual preferences of customers (see Box 9.4).

Box 9.4

Case study of the Cirque du Soleil

Pine and Gilmore (2007: 73) describe Cirque du Soleil as an example of 'influential authenticity', as 'performances show the possibilities of what the human body can do physically, aesthetically and lyrically'. Cirque du Soleil was a new art form, therefore also providing an example of 'original authenticity'.

Cirque du Soleil began when a group of street performers in Quebec (Canada) decided to create a new venue for their passion. Under the guidance of Guy Laliberté, Cirque du Soleil has used its passion for creativity and innovation to redefine the entertainment landscape, and thrill audiences all around the world. A global showbiz empire that includes 3000 employees, about 700–750 performers. 'Our approach was very simple. It was about creating a universal language,' says Laliberté. 'A show that will be attractive toward every people coming from all over the world. And that was a big thing.'

Twenty full-time talent scouts scour the planet for the best benders, flyers, bouncers and spinners, and then bring them all to Montreal to teach them the 'Cirque way'. Nearly all the artists undergo artistic and acrobatic training at the Creation Studio. The performers come from nearly 40 different countries. Cirque du Soleil employs around 20 trainers from around the world to supervise performer-training programmes. Cirque's tent shows, each one completely different from the next, tour all around the world. But the most elaborate, over-the-top productions are in Las Vegas. Every night, roughly 10,000 people pay between $60 and $150 apiece to see their shows.

(after Cirque du Soleil 2009; Stahl 2005)

The 'experientialisation' of traditional cultural tourism

There has been considerable resistance to the 'experientialisation' of the traditional cultural sector. It is one thing to build a contemporary fantasy destination in a desert (e.g. Las Vegas or Dubai), but it is quite another to attempt to change the nature of what has existed and been lovingly preserved for centuries. Although the post-tourist is perhaps less concerned about authenticity than his or her predecessor, for cultural tourists the commodification of history can be a cause for concern. For example, a number of authors have criticised the way in which many heritage sites and landscapes have become more and more like theme parks (e.g. Hewison 1987; Walsh 1992; Kirschenblatt-Gimblett 1998). This is due largely to the postmodern pastiche of reality and fiction, and history and media, which can result in a kind of simulacra or 'time capsule'. However, Walsh (1992: 103) does differentiate between types of attraction, distinguishing between those that offer pure entertainment and those that offer a combination of education and entertainment, or the 'edu-tainment' phenomenon (Urry 1990).

Richards (2001d: 62) describes museums as 'experience factories', and Prentice (2001) suggests that museums are now forming part of what could be termed '*experiential cultural tourism*'. He describes this as the accumulation of experiences whereby visitors want to gain insight rather than engage in formal learning. However, the so-called 'new museology' which began in the early 1990s has not always been viewed favourably. For example, Evans (1995) describes the growing conflict between the education and tourism function of museums, especially given the growing pressures on museums to raise their own income. Many of the funding and income-generation mechanisms are based increasingly on commercial activities such as catering, publishing and retail. The 1988 marketing slogan of London's Victoria and Albert Museum – 'An ace caff with quite a nice museum attached' – is a good example of this phenomenon. Swarbrooke (2000: 421) takes this discussion further, arguing that whereas in the past museum professionals and the tourism industry 'viewed each other suspiciously across a sea of mutual distrust and ignorance', they are increasingly realising the benefits of collaboration. Tourism has become an invaluable means of generating income. However, he also argues that museums are likely to become the new theme parks for the third millennium if they continue to focus predominantly on entertainment, income generation and marketing at the expense of their traditional core function of being informative and educational. West (1988: 61) makes this point rather cynically in relation to the Ironbridge Gorge Museum in Shropshire, which, he argues, has become increasingly commodified and profit-orientated: 'if pressed to choose I would say that the Pleasure Beach at Blackpool or the amusements at Alton Towers are my idea of a good day out. At least on the big dipper, having paid your money, everyone agrees that the pleasure is in being taken for a ride!'

It is certainly becoming difficult to distinguish between museums and other kinds of visitor or tourist attractions, especially given the advent of interactive technology and multimedia. In addition, much modern art consists of video or media installations, and computer-generated images. It is evident that the experience of visiting a museum is becoming more of an integrated and interactive experience, but how far it is educational and informative as opposed to just another 'theme park' experience is another matter. Craik (1997: 115) suggests that artificial theme parks are becoming more successful than most preserved 'themed sites', mainly because they can offer the visitor a more exciting product and integrated experience:

> Compare the product on offer at theme parks with that offered by local history museums: certainly the former recreates impressions of the real while the latter preserves the authentic, but often the latter are immensely disappointing – under-resourced, lacking appeal or diversity, having poor facilities, staffed by enthusiastic but unprofessional volunteers, and so on. As a general rule, such museums are disappointing – and often meaningless – to the tourist.

Some of the newest museums are almost entirely interactive and are based on contemporary industries, e.g. the Washington Newseum (see Box 9.5).

Box 9.5

Case study of the Newseum, Washington: the world's most interactive museum?

The Newseum is an interactive museum of news and journalism in Washington, D.C. It opened at its first location in Rosslyn, Virginia, on 18 April 1997, where it admitted visitors without charge. Its stated mission is 'to help the public and the news media understand one another better'. The Newseum in Washington opened in April 2008 and large crowds queued to get in. The Newseum aims to tell the story of how journalism has changed over time through momentous events and the constantly changing means of communication. Museum curators say the idea is not to commemorate press barons, or individual journalists, but to pay homage to America's First Amendment – the right to free speech and a free press. The museum examines the traditions of American journalism, including reporters who risked everything to do their job.

One of the most expensive museums ever built, according to the *New York Times*, the Newseum contains 250,000 square feet of exhibit space, including 15 theatres, 14 galleries, two broadcast studios, a '4-D time-travel experience', interactive computer stations by the score, 50 tons of Tennessee marble, a three-level Wolfgang Puck restaurant, a food court and 6214 journalism artefacts together weighing more than 81,000 pounds.

Tours start with a '4-D' cinema experience in which visitors strap on goggles and watch a film about the founding days of American journalism, complete with shaking seats, water sprays, flying bullets and gusts of air which convince you that rats are running up your trouser legs.

There is a large chunk of the Berlin Wall, not to mention an East German watchtower; a vast room full of historic newspapers dating back to the eighteenth century and dramatic front pages from the twentieth century. Keep on moving down from the top of seven storeys and there are areas devoted to free speech around the world, the web and broadcasting. Kids can take part in interactive games involving journalism ethics, picture editing or reporting. There are banks of TV cameras ready for them to experiment with reading a simple script in front of a computer-generated White House. Among the artefacts are the radio tower from the north tower of the twin towers – against a backdrop of front pages from the day after 9/11 – and adjacent to a room with a loop tape of reporters describing how they covered the day itself. There is the bombed car in which Arizona Republic reporter Don Bolles was blown up. There is also the first web page ever, from 1992.

Despite the museum's apparent popularity with visitors, there have been some criticisms. For example, Shafer (2008) states: 'If you're genuinely curious about the story of the press, you can find a better representation in the works themselves, commonly available in books, on microfilm, on DVD, and on the Web, not in the simulacra.' *The Guardian* (2008) commentary also describes the attraction as 'two parts Disneyland to one part British Library'. This may or may not be considered a compliment for a museum!

(after The Guardian Online 2008)

Many heritage purists have objected to the creation of visitor experiences which fail to reflect the 'authenticity' of history. A good (or bad?) example of this is 'living history'. Fowler (1992: 113) is highly critical of this trend in the development of the heritage industry: 'One of the most dangerous varieties of history, much favoured in educational and entertainment circles, is that called "living history".' He goes on to argue that 'living history' is an impossible concept; therefore any attempt to reproduce it must be fraudulent. Sorenson (1989) is less damning, and writes with enthusiasm about the 'historic theme park'. He differentiates between sites that are based around surviving relics, and sites that are entirely artificial and do not depend on historic associations for their success. He refers to the concept of the 'time machine', 'time warp' or 'time capsule', which transports us to another time and another place for the purposes of education or entertainment. He appears to welcome this broadening of heritage interpretation and a new museology which is based on more than just collections: 'the study of living history and the recording of it should be based upon other criteria than the professional paralleling of the acquisitive preoccupations of the hobbyist' (Sorenson 1989: 72). Kirschenblatt-Gimblett is also fairly positive about the 'living history' phenomenon:

> Live displays, whether re-creations of daily activities or staged as formal performances, . . . create the illusion that the activities you watch are being done rather than represented, a practice that creates the effect of authenticity or realness. The impression is one of unmediated encounter.
>
> (Kirschenblatt-Gimblett 1998: 55)

If living history is done well, it can be both educational and informative. The case study in Box 9.6 gives an example of a site which even differentiates between the educational levels of visitors in order to provide the best information for them.

Box 9.6

Case study of Llancaiach Fawr Manor, Wales

Llancaiach Fawr Manor was the home of Colonel Edward Prichard during the Civil War years, and shows what life was like at the time of the English Civil War (1645). Guides are dressed in period costume and speak in the style of the 17th century. The house was built circa 1530 by Colonel Prichard's great grandfather and is a good example of a semi-fortified manor house of Tudor times. The parlour is panelled in oak. There are candlelight ghost tours in the winter months. Visitors can dress in period costumes and try out authentic crafts. There is an ongoing programme of events aimed at making this troubled time 'come alive' for visitors. The museum has been voted Best Family Attraction in Wales and is an excellent example of where living history is managed in an historically accurate, educational, but also entertaining way.

The learning programme is under continual development to maximise the learning potential of tours, activities, trails and workshops for all ages and abilities. There is a focus on active and sensory learning with an emphasis on learning through doing and education through enjoyment.

The museum offers what is calls a hands-on and 'minds-on' learning experience catering for various learning styles and intelligences, recognising that active learning takes place with interaction, involvement and participation. Different programmes and activities are offered for various levels of education (these reflect the British school system curriculum):

- For Foundation/Early Years and Key Stage 1 they offer a tour of the Manor with costumed staff and a simple introduction to life in the past.
- For Key Stage 2 History they routinely theme the tour to Tudors, Stuarts, Houses and Households or famous local people. Craft activities, workshops and other themes are available on request.
- For Key Stage 3 they cover the impact of the Civil War, often using the theme of 'Surgeons and Sweethearts' to emphasise the differences between life in the 17th century and the instant and constant communications young people enjoy today.
- They can also offer more in-depth workshops and direct participation by students by request.

Llancaiach Fawr organises practical and academic courses on various topics throughout the year. Previous themes have included Natural Dyeing Workshops, 17th Century Fashion and Clothing, Etiquette and the Chain of Being.

(Llancaiach Fawr Manor 2009)

Conclusion

This chapter has shown that the experience economy is becoming more and more important to all sectors, not only tourism. Tourism has always been about the creation of new and unique experiences, but it is even more challenging in an age when the sophisticated leisure industry competes for our time, attention and money. Destinations and attractions need to create something special to lure visitors away from their armchairs or laptops! Although cultural tourists may continue to travel purely to experience different cultures, the complexity of 'authenticity' and the disappointments which accompany many cultural experiences may mean that cultural tourists will carefully consider their options when choosing a holiday. They may be seeking something spectacular, and places like Las Vegas or Dubai, and attractions like Cirque du Soleil can offer them that, even if they seem to be almost entirely globalised. However, the new museology and experience creation at heritage sites demonstrates that even the smallest attraction can stage a wonderful, interesting, interactive exhibition. It is just a matter of being creative and using imagination, and considering how to engage the hearts and minds of today's experience-seeking visitors.

10 The future of cultural tourism

> There is no end to tourism other than limitless increase. There is no end for the tourist than to visit as many sites as possible.
>
> (Ritzer and Liska 2000: 155)

Introduction

The aim of this book has been to demonstrate the complexity and diversity of the phenomenon of cultural tourism. The broad definition of culture adopted from the outset has necessitated an in-depth discussion of a variety of issues, many of which are controversial, sensitive or highly politicised. However, the philosophy underpinning this book has been that culture is a contentious concept, but one which can be simultaneously inclusive or exclusive, advantageous or detrimental depending on the way in which it is managed. This final chapter discusses some of the key issues relating to the impacts of cultural tourism, as well as the management implications.

In the past, the assumption was made that cultural tourism was a niche form of tourism, attracting small numbers of well-educated and high-spending visitors, hence posing less of a threat to the destination and its indigenous population. However, the growth of international tourism and the diversification of the tourism product have led to an increase in demand for cultural activities, which are becoming an integral part of the visitor experience. The phenomenon of mass cultural tourism is increasingly becoming a cause for concern, whether it is the proliferation of short breaks in the historic cities of Europe, or hilltribe trekking in South-east Asia. Cultural tourism often appears to be an economically desirable prospect for the majority of governments, since it implies an interest in a country's people, its heritage and traditions, as well as the natural and built environment. This can lead to the enhancement of a country's image and the furthering of better international relations, always a priority for governments. However, there is a need for the wealth generated through tourism to be reinvested in the people themselves, rather than being channelled into other economic activities. Only then can the socio-economic and socio-cultural benefits of tourism be maximised and the development of community-based tourism encouraged.

Cultural tourism and paradise lost

During his visit to an island in the South Pacific, Frank, the protagonist of Jostein Gaarder's novel *Maya* (2000), comments on the apparently inherent human desire to be the first to experience a new place, especially a pristine wilderness. He considers that this is an experience that is possibly surpassed only by becoming the last to see a place before it becomes lost, ruined for all eternity. Smith (1997: 141) notes that some of the postmodern travel modes, such as ecotourism, adventure and wilderness tourism, 'posit a vague awareness of diminishing resources that individuals should *see while they still can*'. The same is true of cultural tourism, where tourists might be keen to be the last people to see a tribe in its natural habitat before modernisation forces displacement or permanent acculturation, for example. We are forever in search of the most idyllic, unspoilt and untouched destination. This quest is very well encapsulated in Alex Garland's best-selling novel *The Beach* (1996) (the irony of this being that one of the world's last remaining idyllic beaches in Thailand was partially destroyed while shooting the film of the same name). The eponymous beach is a jealously guarded secret, but his lead character is more than aware that its future fate is sealed:

> Set up in Bali, Ko Pha-Ngan, Ko Tao, Boracay, and the hordes are bound to follow. There's no way you can keep it out of the Lonely Planet, and once that happens it's countdown to doomsday.

The same could be said of most cultural tourism destinations if they are not managed carefully and sensitively. The pessimistic conclusion must be that in time, paradise found is almost invariably paradise lost, especially given that the world is a finite place with finite resources and no place on Earth is now inaccessible. It is surely only a matter of time before visits to a lunar paradise become commonplace; indeed, the first tourists have already made trips into space. One small step for space tourism perhaps, but how much of a giant leap for the future of mass tourism?

In 1995 television presenter Clive Anderson reported on a number of tourism destinations in a BBC series named *Our Man In . . . .* The programme examined some of the impacts of international tourism, and Anderson concludes:

> That 'each man kills the thing he loves' is certainly true of the tourist. We are all looking for the virgin country we can deflower, the unspoiled beach, so that we can be the people to spoil it. The best time to visit any tourist destination is always ten

years before you actually get there. Ten years ago the fishing village still had fishermen, and the local bar still had locals. Now, it's full of people like us.

(Anderson 1995: 53)

For example, Anderson describes how the people in Goa have often found tourism development to be at odds with existing industries and incompatible with local religions:

> The problems come from a clash between the rich, modern world of tourism and the uncomplicated lifestyle of the folk who have lived in idyllic simplicity for generations. My sympathy was with the Goans struggling to hang on to their paradise.
>
> (Anderson 1995: 53)

Interestingly in Goa, some tourists are themselves becoming the 'victims' of voyeur tourism, as groups of men from large Indian cities like Bombay spend much of their days watching Western women in bikinis or topless on the beach.

Burns (1999) provides an interesting analysis of the concept of paradise, which is so central to the 'imagineering' of tourist brochures. He cites the principal character of David Lodge's novel *Paradise News*, who ironically notes the way in which the constant repetition of the paradise motif in Hawaii serves to brainwash tourists into thinking that they must surely have arrived there! However, the reality is somewhat different. Native Hawaiians have been traditionally marginalised in society, and like many indigenous groups they tend to suffer from higher levels of economic deprivation and unemployment. Tourism has done little to remedy these socio-economic problems; on the contrary it has often exacerbated them, displacing local people who can no longer afford the cost of living in the resort areas. Nevertheless, they have little choice but to support tourism because their economic options are now so limited. Cultural activities such as traditional Hawaiian dancing have become a commodified spectacle, and tourists are usually greeted by 'Hula girls' at Honolulu Airport. This is ironic considering that when the Americans originally annexed Hawaii in 1898 they banned the Hula outright, along with the right of local people to speak their language (Trask 1998). Hula costumes now tend to feature mixed styles and motifs from different Polynesian cultures, and the dances and their performers are frequently eroticised. This of course undermines the spiritual and sacred nature of such indigenous traditions. Not surprisingly, local responses to tourism development have not been overwhelmingly positive in recent years. Trask (1998: 17) suggests: 'In principle and practice . . . the tourist industry in Hawaii violates the right of indigenous Hawaiian peoples to self-determination.' De Kadt (1994: 47) cites Pfafflin (1987: 577) who quoted a native Hawaiian as saying:

> We don't want tourism. We don't want you. We don't want to be degraded as servants and dancers. That is cultural prostitution. I don't want to see a single one of you in Hawaii. There are no innocent tourists.

Plate 10.1
Goan woman on the beach

(Source: Georgina Smith)

This is a clear example of a destination where tourism may feel like paradise for tourists, but it has become hell for locals. Hawaiians are, of course, not alone. Today, locals continue to protest in different locations, and not just in developing countries. Local people in Barcelona expressed concern that their town had become a party town where anything goes, and encouraged the police to crack down on tourists' anti-social or offensive behaviour (Tremlett 2005). Stag and hen parties are now rarely welcome anywhere, especially in some of the historic cities of Central and Eastern Europe, which have been exploited mainly for their cheap alcohol. Even British seaside destinations known for their 'fun' image such as Blackpool have started to crack down on stag and hen parties, which are said to be tarnishing the image of the town (Sims 2007). The Full Moon parties in Thailand on Kho Pha-ngan are legendary, and few would disagree that they are great fun for tourists, but largely inappropriate for the context and culture (see Box 10.1).

Box 10.1

Case study of Full Moon parties in Thailand

The Full Moon party started in the late 1980s (and grew in the early 1990s) when a group of tourists thought the moon was especially beautiful on the beach of Haad Rin on the island of Kho Pha-ngan in Thailand, therefore they started to celebrate on Full Moon night. Today, 10,000 to 30,000 people attend the Full Moon parties each month. The music is organised by DJs and there is everything from trance, to techno to bass to reggae. Fire eaters and jugglers also entertain the crowds (Full Moon Party 2009).

However, the Full Moon parties have started to gain a reputation of being too hedonistic, and many local people are offended by the nudity (Thais bathe fully clothed), drinking and drug-taking involved. Many tourists have also become victims of crime, and several each year end up in a Thai prison or hospital as a result of drug use.

Although the party has brought economic benefits to the island, and is no doubt its main attraction these days, there appear to be some negative aspects. These include cultural clashes, pressures on infrastructure and a rise in crime. Most resident islanders do not attend the parties, and some would like to get rid of them. However, others believe it is better to control the activities to encourage tourism and economic growth (it should be noted that Thailand is a particularly tolerant society on the whole). This is typical of many regions where tourism growth often divides a community. The segregation between tourists and local islanders is obvious, especially on Haad Rin beach where the Full Moon party is located.

In the future, it seems that the Thai government and tourism authorities need to encourage social responsibility by discouraging risky behaviour such as unlimited consumption of alcohol and caffeine or energy drinks during the Full Moon party. Regulations and punishment could be used to control both buyers and sellers, which would help to reduce the potential for offensive or even dangerous behaviour among the Full Moon party visitors.

(Wongkerd 2003)

The impacts of cultural tourism

Cultural tourism is by no means a homogeneous phenomenon; therefore its impacts are many and varied. Many of the forms of tourism discussed in this book were originally niche forms of tourism and their impacts were small compared to those of mass coastal tourism, for example. However, the growth of cultural tourism has meant that the impacts have increased in parallel. Although many of these are very positive,

Plate 10.2 Keralan fishermen

(Source: Melvyn Smith)

care must be taken to monitor the scale and nature of development before destinations become irrevocably damaged. It should not be assumed that the diversification of a tourism product into cultural tourism is necessarily the best development option. For example, in the case of fragile or remote locations where communities are traditional and close-knit, tourism can become intrusive and even divisive. It goes without saying that tourism development is not something that should be imposed on communities, but that communities should be allowed to decide for themselves how far tourism is a potentially positive development option. Even then, the size and nature of development should be strictly controlled.

Cultural tourism (like all forms of tourism) contains all the contradictory elements of the globalisation process, being something of a double-edged sword. While bestowing its much sought-after economic benefits on destinations and their host populations, it can despoil their habitat and rob them of their traditions. Like all global industries, tourism is dominated largely by major corporations and Western tourists from developed countries. Hence it is not surprising that it has often been described as a new form of imperialism. Like colonialism, it subjects others to its power, leaving them with little choice but to succumb to its influence. There are no easy solutions. Governments are frequently lured by the bait of tourism development simply because it appears to offer a 'quick-fix' solution to a country's economic difficulties, and potentially affords it the opportunity to enter the global arena. However, consideration is not always given to the long-term problems of such developments, nor is the revenue generated from tourism necessarily reinvested in the destinations and host populations.

Clearly, European imperialism left its mark on the world in a variety of contexts, not least in the field of culture. Indigenous peoples the world over were generally displaced from their lands and their homes, forced to adhere to colonial rule and all its concomitant customs and traditions. Not only were native traditions usually considered to be inferior, but they were even deemed unworthy of continuation; hence they were often suppressed, discarded or forbidden. The legacy for such peoples has inevitably been one of great loss and disinheritance. It has only been in recent years that a small number of sympathetic governments, charities and action groups have been dedicated specifically to their cause. There has subsequently been, in some cases, a revival of customs and traditions, and a renewal of cultural pride. The role that cultural tourism can play in this process is a subject of ongoing debate, but this book has attempted to demonstrate the positive benefits tourism can have on indigenous populations if it is managed properly. Many of the issues relate to the furthering of local ownership and empowerment, processes that are possible only if adequate political, financial and moral support is provided.

However, it is not only among tribal groups that cultural tourism needs special management. European villages have often struggled to retain their traditions and identity in the face of mass tourism. One example of this is Hollókő, a World Heritage Site in Hungary (see Box 10.2).

Box 10.2

Case study of Hollókő in Hungary

Hollókő is a small village in the north of Hungary, the central part of which was designated a World Heritage Site in 1987. It represents the Palóc ethnic group in Hungary, but it is also typical of many European rural areas where traditional country life has declined. The inner part is the protected old village with 55 houses, an old church and the ruins of a mediaeval castle. In the 1970s and 1980s, almost 40 per cent of the population (mainly the young) left the village to seek work and find better living conditions. This was before the development of tourism, which began in the 1980s, partly as a result of the protected village houses. By the 1990s, Hollókő had 100–120 thousand visitors a year, but visitors mostly spend only 2–3 hours in the village, and few stay longer (Kovács 2004). However, the local population was also in sharp decline, and many residents now lived in the new part of Hollókő. It should be noted that after the Second World War young people gradually built a new village 'above' the old one which is now the living part of the village.

> By 2000, the old village had lost many of its characteristics of a living village, and only about 20 old people were living there. The other 340 or so local residents live in the new village or new part of the village which is not protected.
>
> As this small local community is an integral part of the heritage, the WHS Management Plan (Kovács 2004) aimed to help to preserve community life as well as architecture. However, Kovács (2004: 42) notes that 'The young people of Hollókő do not consider tourism and cherishing traditions promising.' Entrepreneurs tend to come from outside the village instead.
>
> Kovács (2008) notes that the original problem with the management of Hollókő was that it focused on buildings rather than people. Although WHS status may have helped tourism development, it did not encourage local residents to stay or work in the village, which became something of a 'living museum'. On the other hand, visitors report very positive experiences: for example, Kovács (2008) cites tourists who say that 'It was a wonderful and uplifting experience to spend some days in the past', 'Hollókő is the heart of Hungary, and it cannot be forgotten', 'It is simply wonderful and beyond grasp to have a journey back in time' and 'What a wonderful tribute and rememberance of our heritage.'
>
> However, all of these comments imply that Hollókő is not a living village in the present, but a memorial to the past. Tourism has fossilised culture, rather than contributing to dynamic change. The conclusion is perhaps that what is good for tourists is not always good for residents. Nevertheless, without tourism and WHS status, the village may no longer have existed at all.

It is not uncommon for tourists to be confined to 'enclaves' where contact with local residents is minimal. Chapter 9 discussed the concept of the postmodern 'tourist bubble' in some detail, but there reference was made largely to themed attractions. In the case of all-inclusive resorts, there are few benefits for the local economy, but in some ways socio-cultural impacts can be managed more easily, as host–guest contacts are minimal and controlled. This relationship allows for little spontaneity, but it is worth questioning how far host–guest relations have ever been truly authentic given the contrived nature and typically short duration of the average holiday.

In some destinations, however, all-inclusive resort development has required some intervention. In the case of Gambia, the organisation Gambia Tourism Concern was set up to help establish a more ethical and sustainable form of tourism. One of Gambia Tourism Concern's (2002) major battles in recent years has been the campaign against all-inclusive holidays, asserting that 'The message is loud and clear, the Gambia has more to offer than the dull, uninspiring and secluded worlds that are all-inclusive hotels.' As most of the cost of an all-inclusive holiday is paid for in the tourist's own country, few economic benefits are derived from this form of tourism. Indeed, it is possible for the tourist to remain within the hotel complex for the duration of a holiday, spending nothing in the local economy and having no contact with local people. Even ancillary services will be booked through the hotel. Jeng (2002) states: 'General opinion is that with package holidays, countries like The Gambia get the crumbs from the cake. All-inclusive holidays will deny us even those crumbs.' It seems that the government can do little about the situation at present, as the free market economy allows tour operators and hotel groups total freedom.

Plate 10.3 Fishing boats on a Gambian beach

(Source: Georgina Smith)

A campaign has therefore been waged to rally public opinion against all-inclusives instead. It is not simply a question of boosting economic benefits for the destination and its people. The hotels also make very little profit as the price of all-inclusives is so cheap. In addition, it could be argued that many tourists are missing out on some of the Gambia's most memorable attractions and interactions by remaining within the hotel complexes.

In recent years, the regeneration or rejuvenation of destinations has become a more widespread phenomenon. Many destinations have upgraded their product, diversified into new forms of tourism, and are targeting higher spending visitors. In terms of the physical environment, it is perhaps not that difficult to regenerate a resort that has stagnated and declined. However, it is perhaps less easy to win back the goodwill of local residents, many of whom may have moved out of the tourist destination due to sheer frustration and unhappiness. It could be argued that the economic and environmental impacts of tourism are easier to measure and manage than the socio-cultural impacts, which are often intangible.

It is an inevitable fact of tourism that cultural changes occur primarily to the indigenous society's traditions, customs and values rather than to those of the tourist. In the majority of cases, local people are subjected to a steady stream of changing faces, while tourists frequently vary their destinations. Although tourism may be intermittent and seasonal in some destinations, the constant levels of visitation over time can have a considerable impact on the social and cultural fabric of the host society. In some countries where tourism is largely seasonal (e.g. Greece or Turkey), many local people lead a split life whereby they work in a tourist resort during the summer months, but return home during the winter. This means that the cultural changes that appear to take place within the society constitute a kind of cultural drift rather than acculturation. Anthropologists have been studying acculturation for decades, and it is recognised that tourism is only one of many factors that can lead to permanent cultural change. Mathieson and Wall (1992) differentiate between acculturation and cultural drift, stating that cultural drift is a phenotypic change to the hosts' behaviour which takes place only when they are in contact with tourists, but which may revert back to normal once the tourists leave. Genotypic behaviour is a more permanent phenomenon whereby cultural changes are handed down from one generation to another. This is most likely to occur where tourism is non-seasonal, its influence is strongly pervasive, and local people are favourably disposed towards its development.

There are fears that host culture and identity may be assimilated into the more dominant or pervasive culture of the tourist. The homogenisation of culture is often exacerbated by tourists whose behavioural patterns are sometimes copied by local residents (the 'demonstration effect'). This may simply mean that local people feel obliged to learn the language of the tourist in order to converse, but it may also mean the consumption of non-local food or drink, the wearing of non-traditional fashions, and the desire to indulge in the same forms of entertainment as tourists. In non-traditional societies this creates few problems, but in societies which are strictly religious, patriarchal or close-knit, this can impact adversely upon the social fabric. The creation of intra-generational conflicts can become problematic, especially in traditional societies where the younger generations might aspire to Western-style or global living, whereas older generations are keen to protect traditional lifestyles. The role of women can also change rapidly, which can be positive in that it leads to the further emancipation of females within a society. However, in traditional, patriarchal societies this may be the cause of conflict, for example, if women become the main breadwinners within a family.

At some stage, the majority of tourists, even long-term backpackers, tend to crave Western-style amenities. Hence destinations are usually forced to cater to tourists' tastes often supplying fast food, alcohol and brand cigarettes, for example. Not only does this create economic leakages in many cases, but it also threatens the production of local goods, especially if local people develop a preference for Western-style products as well. Conversely, excessive tourist demand for local products can lead to the mass production of traditional goods, which can have the effect of commercialising or commodifying culture. The same is true of traditional events or activities where tourists are keen to spectate or participate. Authenticity becomes a key issue, especially when rituals are performed in isolation from their traditional context. However, 'staged authenticity' in the form of displaced ceremonies, activities and events has become widespread. Although the authenticity of the tourist experience is of some importance (as discussed in Chapter 9), it is more crucial to ensure that local communities feel comfortable with their role as performers and entertainers. This includes the degree to which they are prepared to allow the commodification of their culture for touristic purposes. It should, of course, be understood that some religious or spiritual cultural practices might not be appropriate spectacles for the tourist gaze.

Maximising the benefits of cultural tourism

Cultural tourism often appears to be a more environmentally and culturally sensitive form of tourism. This can, of course, be true, but again, as cultural tourism becomes more mainstream and definitions broaden, so then does the profile of cultural tourists. It can no longer be assumed that cultural tourists will have access to better education or superior knowledge; therefore an educative approach perhaps needs to be taken with regard to the management of sites and their tourists. In some cases, local guides can act as 'culture brokers', or informative guides and leaflets can be distributed to tourists by tour operators prior to or on arrival at the destination. Although many destinations attempt to restrict entry or to price out undesirable tourists, it should not be assumed that those tourists with money are likely to be more culturally aware or sensitive.

Access to cultural facilities must be guaranteed for locals living within tourist destinations or resorts. This might involve the implementation of a dual pricing system or ensuring free entrance for locals. Where host–guest tensions are rife, there may be a case for adopting different entrance times, but clearly segregation of tourists and locals is not the ideal solution for enhancing host–guest interaction (although it seems to work quite well in the Maldives, where only certain islands are developed for tourism and 'local' islands restrict access for tourists). Access to certain cultural facilities or events may be denied to tourists if local people feel that this is appropriate. Equally, governments may wish to restrict access to certain areas or destinations at any one time, for example, by issuing a limited number of visas.

Clearly, many destinations practise selective marketing as a means of ensuring that tourism development remains small-scale and appropriate. For example, this has even become necessary for many historic cities in Europe. It could also be used to ensure that a certain profile of visitor is attracted. However, this is a delicate balance, since the tourists who are the highest spending and will hence benefit the local economy the most may not necessarily be the most culturally sensitive. For example, many backpackers display a greater degree of cultural interest and awareness, but they tend to be low-spending tourists. As discussed earlier in the chapter, access issues are difficult to manage, particularly as tourism is a growth industry and the diversification of the market means that tourists are increasingly keen to visit more remote locations.

However, certain forms of tourism, which are more environmentally friendly and culturally sensitive, are being developed in accordance with these changing trends. A good example of this is the ecotourism phenomenon.

It is important to note that in the field of cultural tourism management and planning there are very different philosophies governing the various sectors, which can lead to conflicts of interest between stakeholders (see Table 10.1).

One of the key management issues that is dealt with in some detail in this book is that of the interpretation and representation of culture through heritage and museum collections, both of which constitute an important element of the cultural tourism product. This is perhaps one of the most complex and sensitive areas of cultural tourism management. In the past there was very little recognition of minority, ethnic or indigenous cultures. As stated earlier, the history and culture of indigenous peoples were often suppressed or destroyed by colonial powers who considered them to be inferior, primitive or even barbaric. Ironically, however, when worthwhile objects or artefacts were discovered, they were often removed and placed in European museums. The subject of ownership of cultural property is consequently still a hotly debated issue within museum studies.

Although the situation is slowly changing, it has only been since postmodern debates about the rejection of so-called 'grand narratives' came along that there has been a growing interest in the history and culture of previously marginalised or oppressed peoples. This has altered not only approaches to the study of history (which has always been predominantly a white, Western, patriarchical account of the past), but it has also affected the nature of heritage interpretation, arguably for the better. Although many critics have argued that the heritage and museums 'industries' have been over-commercialised and trivialised as a consequence, some might contend that this is merely an elitist or Eurocentric stance. The representation of the history and heritage of the working classes, women, ethnic minorities and indigenous peoples is

Table 10.1 Differing priorities for cultural sectors

Heritage	Conservation, interpretation, access, visitor management, education, authenticity
Visual arts/museums	Collections management, interpretation, exhibition management, visitor flows, access, education
Performing arts	Audience development, programming, audience experience,
Festivals and events	Programming, sponsorship, audience development, crowd management
Cultural tourism	Visitor satisfaction, marketing, impact management
Indigenous/everyday culture	Ownership, consultation, intepretation, representation
Entertainment centres	Visitor experience, attractions management
Creative industries	Entertainment, entrepreneurship, distribution, networks

surely a welcome development in an age when there is such a definite need to move towards more inclusive, democratic and participatory approaches to cultural development. It is clear that there are still too few ethnic or indigenous curators in many museums and galleries (hence interpretation is often carried out by those with only second-hand knowledge), but the formal recognition of this problem indicates, with any luck, a willingness to change.

Significant changes are also taking place within the heritage field as attempts are being made to diversify the concept of worthwhile heritage. Emphasis is being placed on historical value or 'historicity' rather than the mere aesthetics of sites. For example, there has been a shift away from the dominance of royal palaces, castles and country houses on the World Heritage List to the inclusion of industrial heritage sites or more intangible forms of heritage belonging to indigenous peoples or the working classes. Again, this is a welcome development, although there are some concerns that the integrity of the World Heritage List will in some way be compromised by this development. It could of course be argued that World Heritage should not only be unique, it should also be awe-inspiring. How far therefore can a former mining landscape compete with the splendour of the Taj Mahal? Again, this is a subject of ongoing debate, but the fundamental principle of adopting a more inclusive and less Eurocentric approach is surely a positive one.

The concept of access is clearly an important one for UNESCO, and part of the organisation's remit is to make World Heritage Sites available to the widest possible public. However, this can bring significant problems in its wake, particularly as the inscribing of sites on the List generally raises their profile and puts them on the tourist map. Although tourism can help to provide useful funds for conservation, questions must be raised about the extent to which fragile sites can withstand the ravages of cultural tourism for all eternity. The concept of sustainability was developed partly in order to address the issue of perpetuity; that is, the consideration of heritage as being not only about the past, but also about the present and future. Clearly, there is little point in preserving the heritage for future generations if current generations cannot benefit from it in the meantime. However, the growth of international tourism is creating enormous problems, especially for some of the world's 'must-see' heritage sites, many of which are inscribed on the World Heritage List. Care must be taken to manage the sensitive balance between conservation, access and visitor management. There is also the question of the local community and their relationship to heritage sites, especially if they happen to live within it (i.e. in the case of historic towns or national parks). Issues of multiple interpretation also clearly need to be addressed.

In Hungary, World Heritage Site inscription has partially created significant problems for local inhabitants. Hodgson (2008) describes how several villages in the famous Tokaj wine region in north-eastern Hungary are considering renouncing their UNESCO World Heritage status. The status means that factories cannot be built even though there is high unemployment in the region, and some feel the status is causing more harm than good. A spokesperson for the Hungarian National World Heritage Commission said that no region had ever sought to reduce its protected area; however, in the long run no area will retain the status unless it actually wants to.

Many World Heritage Sites have become victims of their own success (see Box 10.3).

Box 10.3

Case study of Stonehenge, England

Stonehenge is a much-loved and over-visited monument in the county of Wiltshire in England, which was inscribed on the WHS List in 1986. It is the remains of a prehistoric monument, which is of special interest to archaeologists, but also to modern-day Druids and 'New Age' culture because of its supposed links to Celtic mysticism. It can receive more than 1 million visitors per year, and there are up to 2000 visitors per day in July and August (Mason and Kuo 2006). Despite its fame, Baxter and Chippindale (2006: 149) note:

> Stonehenge is relatively well understood in historical and environmental terms, but the multi-layered contexts within which the cultural tourist as stakeholder exists, at a World Heritage Site managed in a sustainable fashion, are only at the early stages of study.

In fact Baxter and Chippindale (2006) and Millar (2006) both quote the description of Stonehenge as 'a national disgrace' by English Heritage in 2005. The biggest problem with managing Stonehenge is the conflict of interests in terms of its physical management, such as who owns the site, but also its different public audiences. Heavy traffic runs close by causing pollution, vibration, noise and visual intrusion. Ideally, this would be resolved by a 'cut and cover' scheme, where cars sink into a tunnel. Car-parking and visitor facilities are inadequate for the large numbers of visitors. This could be solved by a visitor centre outside the WHS boundary; however, this would involve visitors walking for a distance of more than 2km. The local council rejected the idea of a proposed land train from the visitor centre to the site. The professionals dealing with the conservation and protection of the site are unhappy with the various impacts on the site. The stones became damaged as a result of visitors touching them and climbing on them, so now access is restricted. However, tourists (especially 'New Age' visitors) now feel they cannot engage with the site as access is restricted to a circumference path some 50m distant from the monument.

Millar (2006) suggests that one of the problems for Stonehenge is that it was inscribed as a prehistoric monument on the WHS List rather than a cultural landscape. The latter category would have afforded it extra protection rights, e.g. from the traffic and surrounding activities such as farming.

(Baxter and Chippindale 2006; Millar 2006; Mason and Kuo 2006)

The management of tourism in urban environments and historic cities clearly requires a more integrated approach than individual heritage sites. Policies and planning decisions need to be integrated into a broader urban development context, and conflicts of interest between urban planners, tourism developers, conservationists and the local resident population need to be addressed. Historic towns are inhabited by thriving, working communities, and should not be viewed simply as historic attractions to be 'fossilised' or turned into 'living museums' by the tourism or heritage industries for the benefit of visitors. It is often difficult to resolve many of the conflicts that arise in the context of historic town management. For example, the pedestrianisation of a town can serve the purpose of minimising congestion and pollution, helping to prevent the erosion of historic buildings, and enhancing the experience of local residents and visitor alike, However, the rerouting of traffic can often create bottlenecks outside the town centre. Access is reduced for taxis and buses, and residential areas often suffer from increased congestion and pollution. It can also create problems for local traders and small businesses in the town centre that traditionally rely on deliveries to their door. Organisations such as ICOMOS, the English Historic Towns Forum, the European Association of Historic Towns and Regions, and the Walled Towns Friendship are actively involved in the development of sustainable tourism in historic towns.

In terms of marketing, many historic towns have sometimes had to engage in *de*-marketing because their centres have become overly congested and the historic fabric is threatened. Historic towns that are also World Heritage Sites often attract even higher numbers of tourists because of their enhanced status and global profile. Many towns are keen to attract smaller numbers of high-spending, educated cultural or business tourists, rather than low-spending backpackers and language students (e.g. Cambridge in the UK). Where the tourist/local visitor ratio is especially high

Plate 10.4 Life goes on around the heritage in Rome

(Source: László Puczkó)

(e.g. Canterbury in the UK), local residents are likely to become less favourably disposed towards tourism. Cities such as Venice in Italy have become almost like 'living museums', yet visitor numbers show no sign of declining. Local residents often choose to move out of the city centre rather than become part of the tourist attraction themselves. Addressing the problems of seasonality can sometimes help to ease congestion during certain periods of the year. Special events, exhibitions or the development of business and conference tourism can help with this. However, developing non-seasonal tourism can mean that local residents never have a break from tourists, which is equally contentious.

Visitor management can be controlled through the creation of tourist 'gateways' and information centres that help to control visitor flows through the provision of selective information. Guiding services can also help to steer visitors in a certain direction so as to minimise congestion at major sites. Timed ticketing can also be appropriate in some cases as a way of limiting visitor numbers to an attraction at any one time. Self-directed or guided heritage trails or walks are also being used to encourage tourists to consider alternative routes and attractions. Puczkó and Rátz (2007: 131) discuss the advantages of using trails, itineraries or themed routes as tourism products, because they can:

- be developed with relatively small investment,
- diversify and spread demand for tourism in time, especially in space,
- contribute to the utilisation in tourism of unexploited resources, and,
- develop new segments of demand for certain types of tourism (e.g. cultural tourism, heritage tourism, or wine tourism).

Although cultural trails or routes can span several countries (e.g. in the case of European Cultural Routes), it is more practical for visitors to follow trails which are limited in time and space. Sometimes two or three different themed trails may be used in a city to try to distribute visitors to different parts of the city or to separate segments (e.g. schoolchildren from pensioners).

Tourism has been criticised for reducing the heritage and museum sectors to a mere entertainment forum. The (often severe) lack of funding for conservation and collections management has forced heritage sites and museums to diversify into other activities (e.g. tourism or retail development), often at the perceived cost of their core function. This is a serious issue, and questions should be raised about the extent to which it is acceptable for museums and heritage sites to resemble theme parks or entertainment zones. After all, there is still a place for education, particularly within the field of cultural tourism. Again, striking a balance between the education and entertainment functions of such attractions is the key challenge. It is particularly difficult in the case of 'dissonant' heritage sites to provide a form of interpretation that is sensitive to all parties. It may not be appropriate to develop tourism in these cases, and such sites should remain educational memorials.

Of course, it is not only in the heritage and museum sectors that issues relating to inclusion, access and democracy have become a major priority. They have perhaps become even more of a key issue within the arts. There has been growing concern that the arts have been traditionally elitist in their focus on so-called high culture and their dismissal of popular or mass culture. Although many mass forms of culture (e.g. pop music, fashion) can generate their own income much more easily than high arts which invariably need subsidies, it is more a question of prevailing attitudes that need to be changed. The post-colonial legacy has led to increasing multiculturalism and ethnic diversity in many societies; hence the culture and arts of such groups need to be given some recognition and support. Although many arts activities such as the Notting Hill Carnival (see Box 10.4) have grown organically from a strong community base, their future continuation is highly dependent on funding and political support. This book has considered in some detail the artistic events and festivals of ethnic and minority groups, many of which are community-based. Although large tourist audiences are not always welcome at such events, it can help to raise their international status and provide the communities with an enhanced profile, and ultimately, the possibility of increased political power. From the tourists' perspective, such events are an increasingly attractive part of the cultural tourism product. There are few barriers to access, many such events are free, they are participatory, and they afford the participant a glimpse of authentic, indigenous or ethnic culture. Of course, if the events become less spontaneous and 'staged' for the benefit of tourists, then they will inevitably lose their authenticity and ultimately their appeal. However, it appears to be the case with festivals and carnivals that such events are still largely spontaneous, mainly because they are usually a celebration of a particular phenomenon or moment in time.

Box 10.4

Case study of the Notting Hill Carnival

The Notting Hill Carnival is the second largest carnival in the world after Rio, attracting over 1 million visitors. It has its origins in the culture and heritage of the local African Caribbean communities, particularly those from Trinidad. Whereas during slavery in Trinidad slaves could not walk on the pavements, after their liberation in 1834 they appropriated the Carnival and took to the streets. The Notting Hill Carnival was traditionally developed as a means of expressing and celebrating the vibrancy and diversity of diasporic Caribbean culture in the mid-1960s.

However, it has not been without its problems, starting in the mid-1970s when objections to its growth were lodged by the resident white community. Race relations were fraught, especially as rioting and unrest had led to a need to increase security and police presence. It is now an example of a local event which has arguably outgrown its original location and cultural roots, making it difficult to manage. Burr (2006) lists the problems of crowd congestion, organisational and procession chaos, an increase in crime and violence including two murders in 2000, health and safety issues from litter and urination in the street, and deafening noise.

Suggestions to move the event to another location (e.g. Hyde Park in London) were met with protests from the local African Caribbean inhabitants of Notting Hill, who consider its origins in that area of London to be important for cultural continuity. Some of those inhabitants have also become frustrated by the increasing number of white revellers 'gatecrashing' their party and spoiling the atmosphere. Many carnivalists believe that the event should be 'bacchanal' and spontaneous, not constrained by regulations and rigid organisation. This could be seen as interference with the liberty of slaves to walk freely on the streets again (Burr 2006).

The Notting Hill Carnival has survived despite being traditionally underfunded like many other ethnic events, but its future survival has frequently been threatened until the last minute by the apparent unavailability of sponsorship. Although the ownership should be retained by the original community, if the Carnival continues to descend into chaos, external funding may be even harder to come by. Although the event has become increasingly popular with large numbers of tourists, they do not make any financial contribution to the staging of the event. However, if it were moved and commercialised further, it would almost undoubtedly lose its cultural roots.

The relationship between tourism and the arts has often been less than harmonious, mainly because there is some fear within arts circles that tourism will somehow compromise the artistic integrity or authenticity of performances or events. Like the heritage and museum sectors, the arts have often been forced to adapt their core product to attract more diverse audiences, partly because of access issues but also because of lack of funding. In many cases, programming is constrained by these factors, which is a great pity. In the case of creative tourism where creative industries have become a major attraction, the relationship between tourism and the arts is more comfortable. This is because creative tourism often includes more mediatised and digitalised arts forms which are mass produced (e.g. films and TV programmes).

There has also been much debate about the use of the arts for other functions; for example, as a tool for urban regeneration. Many cities have developed cultural quarters or 'flagship' projects based on the arts and related activities. It has even reached the stage where the content of a museum or gallery is somehow becoming less relevant than the building's potential as a catalyst for regeneration and the attraction of investment. Both the Guggenheim in Bilbao and Tate Modern in London have been criticised for being examples of this phenomenon (see Box 10.5). Certainly, the arts should not always be thought of as a tool for economic or business development. This is merely a legacy from governments which are basically unwilling to subsidise the arts, forcing them into a position where they have to rely on business sponsorship or tourism in order to survive. It is inevitable that artistic content will somehow be compromised along the way.

Box 10.5

Case study of Bilbao

Bilbao was originally a city of heavy industry and of little interest to tourists. However, it embarked on a highly successful process of economic and cultural renewal using architecture and art as a catalyst. Frank Gehry's Guggenheim Museum design was the centrepiece for this initiative and it is mainly the originality of the architecture which has propelled Bilbao onto the world stage.

Klingmann (2007) notes that in the first few years the museum attracted more visitors per year than the population of the city. In addition, 86 per cent of visitors said they were keen to return. She suggests that it was the psychological effect of the development on the city which helped it to regenerate, as it had suffered from a loss of self-esteem as its industry declined. Following the success of the Guggenheim, many other smaller economic and cultural developments took place which further enhanced the city's image and attractions portfolio.

However, the Guggenheim development is not without its critics. Some say that it was developed specifically to attract international tourists and to raise the city's profile, rather than attracting local people or promoting their heritage. It has been subject to the criticism that it represents typical postmodern examples of 'style over content'. It is also true that the museum could technically be anywhere and represents little of local culture. Sudjic (1999: 180) cynically suggests that this development is symptomatic of 'the neurotic difficulties of small nations attempting to be noticed on an international level'. He notes that an American architect was imported to design the building and a collection was franchised from the Guggenheim, and he highlights the tensions between 'metropolitan culture and a people's distinctive local sense of self and identity'.

Nevertheless, the 'Guggenheim effect' is one which many cities would like to emulate, but it should not be assumed that it is possible to reproduce such an effect elsewhere. It is the uniqueness of the structure, its location and cultural context that partly shaped its success. In addition, Klingmann (2007) notes that Bilbao's city authorities fought hard for the Guggenheim and it was part of a carefully designed plan.

The future of cultural tourism

Many tourists are now travelling to seek difference outside the home as their everyday lives have become an integral part of the standardised global process. Although the world of cyberspace has afforded people the capacity to escape virtually at any time, paradoxically this has led to a marked increase rather than a decrease in the demand for tourism. Tourism and cultural tourism are clearly still growth industries, despite the assumption that the home entertainment revolution would increase people's desire to stay at home. Cynics might argue that we are less than happy with the world that we have created for ourselves, and are only too keen to escape at the earliest opportunity and 'get away from it all'. It is no coincidence that stress levels are rising as working hours increase, and we are becoming more and more suffocated by technology and communications, the monsters of our own making. It is also ironic that many developing societies are hankering after the same economic 'progress' and lifestyle that many Westerners are now so keen to escape. However, other indigenous communities are keen to preserve their culture and traditions which involve being at one with nature and at peace with themselves. Sometimes this is even envied by tourists, who have a romanticised view of native living. It is therefore no surprise that increasing numbers of Western tourists are embarking on trips in which they 'get back to nature', or engage in some kind of spiritual quest.

However, many citizens in both developed and developing countries of the world are fully embracing the technological revolution. Some of the fastest-growing developments are taking place in India and China, for example. Technology can be seen as a way of facilitating tourism development (the internet revolution for bookings is a simple example of this), as well as helping to create more experiential forms of tourism. Without high-tech developments, there would be no theme parks and simulated attractions, which, as demonstrated in Chapter 9, are some of the most popular tourism products in the world. Although it is still debatable how far an artificial attraction is part of cultural tourism, the opportunities afforded by artificial 'country' or 'world' developments have great appeal for those who do not have the time or money to see the real world!

Sigala (2005) describes the various ways in which cultural tourism has been enhanced by new media and technologies, such as the 'webification' of cultural heritage attractions and the creation of virtual communities of cultural practitioners, visitors and educators. Multimedia information systems allow for the creation and promotion of new cultural experiences, for example, chat rooms, web forums and newsgroups, which can be real-time and interactive. Visitors can access large amounts of information pre- or post-visit. The emergence of numerous travel blogs on the internet has created a new source of 'real' information for tourists provided by other visitors to the same places. Although these are not official sources, they often provide a much more realistic and balanced picture for tourists than glossy tourism promotions which usually fail to mention any negative aspects of a destination or experience.

Despite this growth in new technology and the experience economy, it must be accepted that globalisation and 'progress' are still very unevenly distributed throughout the world. Even Western societies are still as polarised as they ever were, both economically and socially (especially in some of the post-socialist transition countries of Central and Eastern Europe), and arguably they have a long way to go before they become truly democratic and inclusive. In other parts of the world, many communities are barely subsistent. Abandoned or oppressed by their governments, tourism often appears like the elusive coffer of gold at the end of a rainbow. Of course, if managed well, cultural tourism can become something of a panacea – not just for the wealthy Westerner, keen to experience cultural difference, or in need of physical, mental or spiritual rejuvenation; but also for those societies that really need an alternative economic development option in order to survive. Thus although it has been argued by Williams (1958) that culture is ordinary, with the right conditions, cultural tourism has the potential to become truly extraordinary.

Bibliography

Adair, G. (1992) *The Postmodernist Always Rings Twice: Reflections on Culture in the 90s*, London: Fourth Estate.

Adams, R. (1986) *A Book of British Music Festivals*, London: Robert Royce.

Adorno, T. W. (2001) *The Culture Industry: Selected Essays on Mass Culture*, London: Routledge.

—— and Horkheimer, M. (1979) *Dialectic of Enlightenment*, London: Verso (first published in 1947).

Aiesha, R. and Evans, G. (2007) 'VivaCity: mixed-use and urban tourism', in Smith, M. K. (ed.) *Tourism, Culture and Regeneration*, Wallingford: CABI, pp. 35–48.

Alaska Wilderness Recreation and Tourism Association (AWRTA) (2009) http://www.awrta.org (accessed 3 February 2009).

Ali, Y. (1991) 'Echoes of empire: towards a politics of representation', in Corner, J. and Harvey, S. (eds) *Enterprise and Heritage: Crosscurrents of National Culture*, London: Routledge, pp. 194–211.

Alleyne-Dettmers, P. T. (1996) *Carnival: The Historical Legacy*, London: Arts Council of England.

Alon, S. (2008) 'Resurrecting ghosts: the revival of Jewish memory in Poland', *The Current: The Journal of Contemporary Culture, Politics and Jewish Affairs*, http://www.columbia.edu/cu/current/articles/fall2008/alon.html (accessed 6 February 2009).

Anderson, C. (1995) *Our Man In . . .* , London: BBC Books.

Appleton, J. (2006) 'UK museum policy and interpretation: implications for cultural tourism', in Smith, M. K. and Robinson, M. (eds) *Cultural Tourism in Changing World: Politics, Participation and (Re)presentation*, Clevedon: Channel View, pp. 257–70.

Arlidge, J. and Wintour, P. (2000) 'How the Dome dream collapsed', *The Guardian*, 6 February.

Arnold, M. (1875) *Culture and Anarchy*, London: Smith, Elder.

Arnold, N. (2001) 'Festival tourism: recognising the challenges, linking multiple pathways between global villages of the new century', in Faulkener *et al.* (eds), *Tourism in the 21st Century: Reflections on Experience*, London: Continuum, pp. 130–57.

ARTe Media (2009) 'European Museum of the Year Award 2008', http://weblogart.blogspot.com/2008/05/2008-european-museum-of-year-award.html (accessed 19 February 2009).

Arts and Humanities Research Council (AHRC) (1998) *Response to Consultations: Culture and Creativity: The Next Ten Years (DCMS)*, http://www.ahrc.ac.uk/about/policy/response/culture_creativity_in_next_10_years.asp (accessed 11 November 2006).

ATLAS (2007) *ATLAS Cultural Tourism Research Project*, Tram Research, http://www.tram-research.com/atlas/aboutproject.htm (accessed 10 March 2008).

Avery, P. (2007) 'Born again: from dock cities to cities of culture', in Smith, M. K. (ed.) *Tourism, Culture and Regeneration*, Wallingford: CABI, pp. 151–62.

Azara, I. and Crouch, D. (2006) 'La Cavalcata Sarda: performing identities in a contemporary Sardinian festival', in Picard, D. and Robinson, M. (eds) *Festivals, Tourism and Social Change: Remaking Worlds*, Clevedon: Channel View, pp. 32–45.

Bakhtin, M. (1965) *Rabelais and his World*, Cambridge: MIT Press.

Barber, B. (1992) *Jihad vs. McWorld*, March, http://www.theatlantic.com/doc/199203/barber (accessed 26 January 2009).

—— (1995) *Jihad vs McWorld*, New York: Times Books.

Barnett, S. (1997) 'Maori tourism', *Tourism Management*, 18 (7), pp. 471–3.

Baudrillard, J. (1988) *Selected Writings*, ed. M. Poster, Cambridge: Polity Press.

Bauman, Z. (1998) *Globalization: The Human Consequences*, Oxford: Blackwell.

Baxter, I. and Chippindale, C. (2006) 'Managing Stonehenge: the tourism impact and the impact on tourism', in Sigala, M. and Leslie, D. (eds) *International Cultural Tourism: Management, Implications and Cases*, Oxford: Butterworth Heinemann, pp. 137–50.

Baxter, J. (2001) 'Mali: What price tourism?', Monday 16 April, *BBC News*, http://news.bbc.co.uk/2/hi/africa/1280076.stm (accessed 8 February 2009).

Bayles, M. (1999) 'Tubular nonsense: how not to criticise television', in Melzer, A. M., Weinberger, J. and Zinman, M. R. (eds) *Democracy and the Arts*, Ithaca and London: Cornell University Press, pp. 159–71.

Beeck, S. (2003) 'Parallel worlds: theming – analysis of a method of visual communication for semantic programming, related to the context of architecture and city building in the 21st century', Doctoral dissertation, University of Karlsruhe.

Beeton, S. (2005) *Film-induced Tourism*, Clevedon: Channel View.

Belfiore, E. (2002) 'Art as a means of alleviating social exclusion: does it really work? A critique of instrumental cultural policies and social impact studies in the UK', *International Journal of Cultural Policy*, 8 (1), pp. 91–106.

Bianchini, F. (1993) 'Culture, conflict and cities: issues and prospects for the 1990s', in Bianchini, F. and Parkinson, M. (eds) *Cultural Policy and Regeneration: The West European Experience*, Manchester: Manchester University Press, pp. 199–213.

—— (2000) 'From "cultural policy" to "cultural planning"', *Artsbusiness*, 27 March, pp. 5–6.

—— and Ghilardi, L. (1997) *Culture and Neighbourhoods: A Comparative Report*, Strasbourg: Council of Europe.

Black, G. (2005) *The Engaging Museum: Developing Museums for Visitor Involvement*, London: Routledge.

Black History Month (2009) http://www.black-history-month.co.uk/index.html (accessed 16 February 2009).

Blakey, M. (1994) 'American nationality and ethnicity in the depicted past', in Gathercole, P. and Lowenthal, D. (eds) *The Politics of the Past*, London: Routledge, pp. 38–48.

Bohol Tourism (2009) 'Eco-cultural tourism', http://www.bohol-island.com/tourism-main.htm (accessed 12 February 2009).

Boissevain, J. (1997) 'Problems with cultural tourism in Malta', in Fsadni, C. and Selwyn, T. (eds) *Sustainable Tourism in Mediterranean Islands and Small Cities*, London: MED-CAMPUS, pp. 19–29.

Boniface, P. and Fowler, P. J. (1993) *Heritage and Tourism in 'the Global Village'*, London: Routledge.

Boorstin, D. (1964) *The Image: A Guide to Pseudo-Events in America*, New York: Harper & Row.

Botton de, A. (2002) *The Art of Travel*, London: Hamish Hamilton.

Bounds, A. (2007) 'Philadelphia's Avenue of the Arts: the challenges of a cultural district initiative', in Smith, M. K. (ed.) *Tourism, Culture and Regeneration*, Wallingford: CABI, pp. 132–42.

Bourdieu, P. (1984) *Distinction: A Critique of the Judgement of Taste*, London: Routledge.
—— (1996) *The Rules of Art*, Cambridge: Polity Press.

Brah, A. (1996) *Cartographies of Diasporas: Contesting Identities,* London: Routledge.

Branson Tourism (2009) http://www.bransontourisminformation.com (accessed 15 February 2009).

Breitbart, M. and Stanton, C. (2007) 'Touring templates: cultural workers and regeneration in small New England cities', in Smith, M. K. (ed.) *Tourism, Culture and Regeneration*, Wallingford: CABI, pp. 111–22.

Brick Lane Festival 2006 Evaluation Report (2006) http://www.equal-works.com/resources/contentfiles/3449.pdf (accessed 2 February 2009).

Briedenhann, J. and Ramchander, P. (2006) 'Township tourism – blessing or blight? The case of Soweto in South Africa', in Smith, M. K. and Robinson, M. (eds) *Cultural Tourism in a Changing World: Politics, Participation and (Re)presentation*, Clevedon: Channel View, pp. 124–42.

British Tourist Authority (BTA) (1999) 'Millennium News', *British Tourist Authority Millennium Campaign*, 1 (2), July.

Brown, M. F. (2003) 'Safeguarding the intangible', *Cultural Commons*, November, http://www.culturalpolicy.org/commons/comment-print.cfm?ID=12 (accessed 3 February 2009).

Burns, P. M. (1999) *An Introduction to Tourism and Anthropology*, London: Routledge.

Burr, A. (2006) 'The "Freedom of the Slaves to Walk the Streets": celebration, spontaneity and revelry versus logistics at the Notting Hill Carnival', in Picard, D. and Robinson, M. (eds) *Festivals, Tourism and Social Change: Remaking Worlds*, Clevedon: Channel View, pp. 84–98.

Busby, G. and Klug, J. (2001) 'Movie-induced tourism: the challenge of measurement and other issues', *Journal of Vacation Marketing*, 7 (4), pp. 316–32.

Butcher, J. (2001) 'Cultural baggage and cultural tourism', in *Innovations in Cultural Tourism*, Proceedings of the 5th ATLAS International Conference, Rethymnon, Crete, 1998, Tilburg: ATLAS, pp. 11–18.

Butler, R. and Hinch, T. (eds) (1996) *Tourism and Indigenous Peoples*, London: International Thomson Business Press.
—— and —— (eds) (2007) *Tourism and Indigenous Peoples: Issues and Implications*, Oxford: Butterworth-Heinemann.

Cabot, V. (2009) 'Jews everywhere – and nowhere: remembrance, remorse stimulate Polish Jewish revival', Jewish News of Greater Phoenix, http://www.jewishaz.com/jewishnews/980417/jews.shtml (accessed 6 February 2009).

Campaign for the Protection of Rural England (CPRE) (2003) *Lie of the Land*, London: CPRE.

Candida-Smith, R. (2002) (ed.) *Art and the Performance of Memory: Sounds and Gestures of Recollection*, London: Routledge.

Carlson, M. (1996) *Performance: A Critical Introduction*, London: Routledge.

Carnegie, E. (1996) 'Trying to be an honest woman: making women's histories', in Kavanagh, G. (ed.) *Making Histories in Museums*, London: Leicester University Press, pp. 54–65.

Carnegie, E. and Smith, M. K. (2006) 'Mobility, diaspora and the hybridisation of festivity: the case of the Edinburgh Mela', in Picard, D. and Robinson, M. (eds) *Festivals, Tourism and Social Change: Remaking Worlds*, Clevedon: Channel View, pp. 255–68.

Castro-Gomez, S. (2001) 'Traditional vs. critical cultural theory', *Cultural Critique*, 49 (autumn), pp. 139–54.

Chacko, H. E. and Schaffer, J. D. (1993) 'The evolution of a festival – Creole Christmas in New Orleans', *Tourism Management*, 14, pp. 475–82.

Chappel, S. and Loades, G. (2006) 'The Camp Oven Festival and Australian identity', in Picard, D. and Robinson, M. (eds) *Festivals, Tourism and Social Change: Remaking Worlds*, Clevedon: Channel View, pp. 191–208.

Chen, Y. (2007) 'Regeneration and sustainable development in China's transformation', ENHR *Sustainable Urban Areas International Conference*, Rotterdam, 25–8 June.

Cirque du Soleil (2009) http://www.cirquedusoleil.com/ (accessed 27 January 2009).

Cohen, D. (2006) 'The battle of Brick Lane', *Evening Standard*, 25 July.

Cohen, E. (1972) 'Towards a sociology of international tourism', *Social Research*, 39 (1), pp. 64–82.

—— (1988) 'Authenticity and commoditization in tourism', *Annals of Tourism Research*, 15, pp. 371–86.

Connections (2009) http://www.connectionsworldwide.co.uk/holiday.asp?pc=COMA (accessed 26 January 2009).

Convict Creations (2009) 'Does Australia need a national identity?', http://www.convict creations.com/research/identity.htm (accessed 26 January 2009).

Cooper, M. (1993) 'Access to the waterfront: transformations of meaning on the Toronto lakeshore', in Rotenburg, R. and McDonogh, G. (eds) *The Cultural Meaning of Urban Space*, Westport: Bergin & Garvey, pp. 157–71.

Cortijo Romero (2009) http://www.cortijo-romero.co.uk (accessed 1 February 2009).

Craik, J. (1994) 'Peripheral pleasures: the peculiarities of post-colonial tourism', *Culture and Policy*, 6 (1), pp. 21–31.

—— (1997) 'The culture of tourism', in Rojek, C. and Urry, J. (eds) *Touring Cultures*, London: Routledge.

Creamer, H. (1990) 'Cultural resource management in Australia', in Gathercole, P. and Lowenthal, D. (eds) *The Politics of the Past*, London: Unwin Hyman, pp. 130–9.

Creative Cultures (2004) *Leading the Good Life: Guidance on Integrating Cultural and Community Strategies*, London: DCMS.

Creative Tourism New Zealand (2009) http://www.creativetourism.co.nz (accessed 7 February 2009).

Crick, M. (1988) 'Sun, sex, sights, savings and servility', *Criticism, Heresy and Interpretation*, 1, pp. 37–76.

Cummins, A. (1996) 'Making histories of African Caribbeans', in Kavanagh, G. (ed.) *Making Histories in Museums*, London: Leicester University Press, pp. 92–104.

Csikszentmihalyi, M. (1996) *Creativity Flow and the Psychology of Discovery and Invention*, London: HarperCollins.

—— (1997) *Creativity: Flow and the Psychology of Discovery and Invention*, London: Harper Perennial.

Cyprus Agrotourism Company (2004) http://www.agrotourism.com.cy (accessed 13 February 2009).

Dance Holidays (2009) http://www.danceholidays.com (accessed 15 February 2009).

Dann, G. (1996) 'Images of destination people in travelogues', in Butler, R. and Hinch, T. (eds) *Tourism and Indigenous Peoples*, London: International Thomson Business Press, pp. 349–75.

Dapkus, L. (2006) 'Lithuanians jeer symbols of communist past at "Stalin's World" theme park', *Associated Press*, 5 May, http://www.usatoday.com/travel/destinations/2006-05-05-stalins-world_x.htm (accessed 28 January 2009).

Deacon, H. (2004) 'Intangible heritage in conservation planning: the case of Robben Island', *International Journal of Heritage Studies*, 10 (3), pp. 309–19.

De Brito, S. (2008) 'This is our story', *The Guardian*, Saturday 20 December (accessed 11 February 2009).

De Kadt, E. (1994) 'Making the alternative sustainable: lessons from development for tourism', in Smith, V. L. and Eadington, W. R. (eds) *Tourism Alternatives: Potentials and Problems in the Development of Tourism*, Chichester: John Wiley & Sons, pp. 47–75.

Department for Culture, Media and Sport (DCMS) (1998) *Creative Industries Mapping Document*, London: DCMS.

—— (1999a) *A Report to the Social Exclusion Unit: Arts and Sports*, Policy Action Team 10, London: DCMS.

—— (1999b) *Research Report: Arts and Neighbourhood Renewal*, Policy Action Team 10, London: DCMS.

—— (2001)*The Creative Industries Mapping Document 2001*, London: DCMS.

—— (2004) *Culture at the Heart of Regeneration*, London: DCMS.

De Vidas, A. A. (1995) 'Textiles, memory and the souvenir industry in the Andes', in Lanfant, M., Allcock, J. B. and Bruner, E. M. (eds) *International Tourism: Identity and Change*, London: Sage, pp. 67–83.

Dimaggio, P. and Useem, M. (1978) 'Social class and arts consumption: the origin and consequences of class differences in exposure to the arts in America', *Theory and Society*, 5, pp. 141–61.

Dimon, J. (2008) Stalin World in Lithuania, March 26, http://www.wordtravels.tv/articles.php?articleid=48 (accessed 26 January 2009).

Dirlik, A. (1999) 'Is there history after Eurocentrism? Globalism, postcolonialism, and the disavowal of history', *Cultural Critique*, 42 (spring), pp. 1–34.

Dobszay, J. (2008) 'A sebek helye', 23 August, *HVG*, Hungary.

Dubailand (2009) www.dubailand.ae (accessed 14 February 2009).

Durrans, B. (1988) 'The future of the other: changing cultures on display in ethnographic museums', in Lumley, R. (ed.) *The Museum Time Machine*, London: Routledge, pp. 144–69.

Eagleton, T. (2000) *The Idea of Culture*, Oxford: Blackwell.

Edensor, T. (2001) 'Performing tourism, staging tourism: (re)producing tourist space and practice', *Tourist Studies*, 1 (1), pp. 59–81.

Edinburgh Mela Artistic Policy Document (2003) www.edinburghfestivals.co.uk (accessed 19 January 2008).

Edwards, J. A. (1996) 'Waterfronts, tourism and economic sustainability: the United Kingdom experience', in Priestley, G. K., Edwards, J. A. and Coccossis, H. (eds) *Sustainable Tourism? European Experiences*, Wallingford: CABI, pp. 86–98.

—— and Llurdes, J. C. (1996) 'Mines and quarries: industrial heritage tourism', *Annals of Tourism Research*, 23 (2), pp. 341–63.

Eirne, R. (2007) 'Papua New Guinea's untouched paradise', July, http://www.news.com.au/travel/story/0,23483,22002505–5006180,00.html (accessed 20 January 2009).

Errol, J. (1986) 'Mama look a Mas', in *Masquerading: The Art of the Notting Hill Carnival*, London: Arts Council of Great Britain, pp. 7–19.

Evans, G. (1995) 'Tourism versus education – core functions of museums?', in Leslie, D. (ed.) *Tourism and Leisure: Culture, Heritage and Participation*, Brighton: LSA.

—— (1996) 'The Millennium Festival and urban regeneration – planning, politics and the party', in Robinson, M. *et al.* (eds) *Managing Cultural Resources for the Tourist*, Sunderland: Business Education Publishers, pp. 79–98.

—— (2001) *Cultural Planning: An Urban Renaissance?*, London: Routledge.

—— (2005a) 'Measure for measure: evaluating the evidence of culture's contribution to regeneration', *Urban Studies*, 42 (5/6), pp. 959–84.

—— (2005b) 'Creativity, tourism and the city', Keynote Address at *Tourism, Creativity and Development Conference*, ATLAS, Barcelona, 2–4 November.

—— and Shaw, P. (2004) *The Contribution of Culture to Regeneration in the UK: A Review of Evidence: A Report to the DCMS*, London: DCMS.

Falconer, C. (1999) '"The Dome does good" says Lord Falconer', Cabinet Office Press Release, CAB 301/99.

Feifer, M. (1985) *Going Places: The Ways of the Tourist from Imperial Rome to the Present Day*, London: Macmillan.

Fenster, T. (2004) *The Global City and the Holy City: Narratives on Knowledge, Planning and Diversity*, Harlow: Pearson.

Ferguson, R. (1998) *Representing 'Race': Ideology, Identity and the Media*, London: Arnold.

Fernandes, C. and Sousa, L. (1999) 'Initiatives for developing textile crafts in the Alto Minho, Portugal', in Richards, G. (ed.) *Developing and Marketing Crafts Tourism*, Tilburg: ATLAS, pp. 55–72.

Fisher, D. (2004) 'A colonial town for neocolonial tourism', in Hall, C. M. and Tucker, H. (eds) *Tourism and Postcolonialism*, pp. 126–39.

Fisher, M. and Owen, U. (eds) (1991) *Whose Cities?*, London: Penguin.

Florida, R. (2002) *The Rise of the Creative Class*, New York: Basic Books.

—— (2005) *Cities and the Creative Class*, London: Routledge.

Forbes Traveler (2007) 'Forbes Traveler 50 Most Visited Tourist Attractions', http://www.forbestraveler.com/ftdc (accessed 4 February 2009).

Fourmile, H. (1994) 'Aboriginal arts in relation to multiculturalism', in Gunew, S. and Rizvi, F. (eds) *Culture, Difference and the Arts*, St Leonards: Allen & Unwin, pp. 69–85.

Fowler, P. J. (1992) *The Past in Contemporary Society: Then, Now*, London: Routledge.

Free Library (2005) 'How homophobic is the Caribbean? Find out where you can be gay and "feel irie" on your next island hop', http://www.thefreelibrary.com/How+homophobic+ is+the+Caribbean%3F+Find+out+where+you+can+be+gay+and . . . -a0133014823 (accessed 26 January 2009).

Frideres, J. S. (1988) *Native Peoples in Canada: Contemporary Conflicts*, Scarborough, Ontario: Prentice Hall Canada.

Friedman, T. (1999) *The Lexus and the Olive Tree: Understanding Globalization*, Anchor Books, New York.

Full Moon Party (2009) http://fullmoonparty-thailand.com/ (accessed 20 February 2009).

Gaarder, J. (2000) *Maya*, London: Phoenix.

Gambia Tourism Concern (2002) http://www.gambiatourismconcern.com/ and http://www. subuk.net/tourism/ (accessed 15 September 2002).

Garland, A. (1996) *The Beach*, London: Penguin.

Garnham, N. (1990) *Capitalism and Communication*, London: Sage.

Gathercole, P. and Lowenthal, D. (eds) (1994) *The Politics of the Past*, London: Routledge.

Geertz, C. (1973) 'From the native's point of view: on the nature of anthropological understanding', in Rabinow, P. and Sullivan, W. M. (eds) *Interpretive Social Science: A Reader*, Berkley: University of California Press, pp. 225–41.

Getz, D. (1994) 'Event tourism and the authenticity dilemma', in Theobald, W. F. (ed.) *Global Tourism*, Oxford: Butterworth Heinemann, pp. 409–27.

Ghilardi, L. (2001) *Cultural Planning and Cultural Diversity,* London: Noema Research and Planning Ltd.

Giddens, A. (2000) *The Third Way and its Critics*, Cambridge: Polity Press.

Gilmore, F. (2004) 'Brand Shanghai: harnessing the inner force of people and place', in Morgan, N., Pritchard, A. and Pride, R. (eds) *Destination Branding: Creating the Unique Destination Proposition*, Oxford: Butterworth Heinemann, pp. 169–84.

Goffman, E. (1959) *The Presentation of Self in Everyday Life*, New York: Doubleday.

GNWT (Government of the Northwest Territories) (1983) *Community Based Tourism: A Strategy for the Northwest Territories Tourism Industry*, Yellowknife: Department of Economic Development and Tourism.

Graburn, N. H. (ed.) (1976) *Ethnic and Tourist Arts: Cultural Expressions from the Fourth World*, Berkeley: University of California Press.

Graham, B., Ashworth, G. J. and Tunbridge, J. E. (2000) *A Geography of Heritage: Power, Culture and Economy*, London: Arnold.

Gruffudd, P. (1995) 'Heritage as national identity: histories and prospects of the national pasts', in Herbert, D. T. (ed.) *Heritage, Tourism and Society*, London: Mansell Publishing, pp. 49–67.

Gruner, S. (2007) 'Making the case for tourists in Georgia', *Wall Street Journal* 24 August, http://embassy.mfa.gov.ge/index.php?lang_id=ENGandsec_id=45andinfo_id=3379 (accessed 10 February 2009).

Grunwell, J. N. (1998) 'Ayahuasca tourism in South America', *Newsletter of the Multidisciplinary Association for Psychedelic Studies*, 8, 3 (autumn), pp. 59–62.

The Guardian Online (2008) http://www.guardian.co.uk/media/organgrinder/2008/apr/02/ withasenseoftiming (accessed 21 January 2009).

Haakanson, S. (2009) *Balancing Cultural Tourism*, Kodiak, USA, http://old.nrf.is/ Publications/The%20Resilient%20North/Plenary%203/3rd%20NRF_Plenary%203_PP_ Haakanson.pdf (accessed 21 January 2009).

Hall, C. M. (1992) *Hallmark Tourist Events: Impacts, Management, Planning*, London: Belhaven Press.

—— (1994) *Tourism and Politics: Policy, Power and Place*, Chichester: John Wiley & Sons.

—— and Tucker, H. (2004) (eds) *Tourism and Postcolonialism,* London: Routledge.

Hannerz, U. (1990) 'Cosmopolitans and locals in world culture', in Featherstone, M. (ed.) *Global Culture: Nationalism, Globalisation and Modernity*, London: Sage, pp. 237–52.

Harrison, E. (2006) 'Divine trash: the psychology of celebrity obsession', *Cosmos*, February, http://www.cosmosmagazine.com/node/414 (accessed 3 October 2007).

Hartley, J. (2005) (ed.) *Creative Industries*, Oxford: Blackwell.

Harvey, D. C. (2007) '(Re)creating culture through tourism: Black heritage sites in New Jersey', in Smith, M. K. (ed.) *Tourism, Culture and Regeneration*, Wallingford: CABI, pp. 59–68.

Hatzeira, O. A. (2007) 'Queens of the desert', *Israel Travel*, 16 August, http://www.ynet.co.il/ english/articles/0,7340,L-3437947,00.html (accessed 8 February 2009).

Hauksson, K. M. (2008) 'Finland Saami protect their cultural symbols', *Ice News*, 18 November, http://www.icenews.is/index.php/2008/11/18/finland%e2%80%99s- saami-protect-their-cultural-symbols (accessed 4 March 2009).

Hazlett, A. and Carter, S. (2007) 'Slow recovery for tourism and Bedouin', Cairo Calling, 9 March, http://regulus2.azstarnet.com/blogs/cairocalling/5452/ArticleSlowRecovery forTourismandBedouin (accessed 8 February 2009).

Hems, A. (2006) 'Introduction: beyond the graveyard – extending audiences, enhancing understanding', in Hems, A. and Blockley, M. (eds) *Heritage Interpretation*, London: Routledge, pp. 1–8.

—— and Blockley, M. (2006) (eds) *Heritage Interpretation*, London: Routledge.

Henderson, J. C. (2004) 'Tourism and British colonial heritage in Malaysia and Singapore', in Hall, C. M. and Tucker, H. (eds) *Tourism and Postcolonialism*, London: Routledge, pp. 113–25.

Hendry, J. (2000) 'Foreign country theme parks: a new theme or an old Japanese pattern?' *Social Science Japan Journal*, 3, pp. 207–20.

Herbert, D. T. (ed.) (1995a) *Heritage, Tourism and Society*, London: Mansell Publishing.

Hesmondhalgh, D. (2007) *The Cultural Industries*, 2nd edn, London: Sage.

Hewison, R. (1987) *The Heritage Industry – Britain in a Climate of Decline*, London: Methuen.

Heying, C. H., Burbank, M. J. and Andranovich, G. (2007) 'World class: using the Olympics to shape and brand the American metropolis' in Smith, M. K. (ed.) *Tourism, Culture and Regeneration*, Wallingford: CABI, pp. 101–10.

Hitters, E. (2007) 'Porto and Rotterdam as European Capitals of Culture', in Richards, G. (ed.) *Cultural Tourism: Global and Local Perspectives*, New York: Haworth Press, pp. 281–301.

Hobbs, J. J. and Tsunemi, F. (2007) 'Soft sedentarization: Bedouin tourist stations as a response to drought in Egypt's Eastern Desert', Human Ecology, 35, 2 (April), pp. 209–22.

Hölzl, K. (2007) 'Creative Industries in Europe and Austria: definition and potential', http://www.kmuforschung.ac.at/de/Forschungsberichte/Vortr%C3%A4ge/Creative%20Industries_Oulu%202006.pdf (accessed 20 September 2008).

Hooper-Greenhill, E. (2000) *Museums and the Interpretation of Visual Culture*, London: Routledge.

Horne, D. (1984) *The Great Museum*, London: Pluto Press.

Hoyau, P. (1988) 'Heritage and "the conserver society": the French case', in Lumley, R. (ed.) *The Museum Time Machine*, London: Routledge, pp. 27–35.

Hoyle, B. (2002) 'Waterfront revitalization in East African port cities', University of Greenwich Seminar, 27 November.

Huet, A. *et al.* (1978) *Capitalisme et industries culturelles*, Grenoble: Presses Universitaires de Grenoble.

Hughes, G. (1998) 'Tourism and the semiological realization of space', in Ringer, G. (ed.) *Destinations: Cultural Landscapes of Tourism*, London: Routledge, pp. 17–33.

Hughes, H. L. (1996) 'Redefining cultural tourism', *Annals of Tourism Research*, 23(3), pp. 707–9.

—— (2000) *Arts, Entertainment and Tourism*, Oxford: Butterworth Heinemann.

—— (2006) 'Gay and lesbian festivals: tourism in the change from politics to party', in Picard, D. and Robinson, M. (eds) *Festivals, Tourism and Social Change: Remaking Worlds*, Clevedon: Channel View, pp. 238–54.

Huis Ten Bosch (2009) http://english.huistenbosch.co.jp/about_htb/index.html (accessed 4 February 2009).

Humphreys, C. (2007) *Escaping the Rat Race,* ABC News.com, 30 June, http://www.geocities.com/RainForest/6783/DalyNewsSimplicity980630top.html (accessed 24 October 2007).

HVG (2008) 'Isteni bizniz', 9 February, *HVG*, Hungary.

Inter-Commission Task Force on Indigenous Peoples (IUCN) (1993) *Indigenous Peoples and Sustainability: A Guide for Action*, IUCN Inter-Commission Task Force on Indigenous

Peoples and the Secretariat of IUCN in Collaboration with the International Institute for Sustainable Development.

International Federation of Arts Councils and Culture Agencies (IFACCA) (2006) *Arts and Culture in Regeneration*, http://www.ifacca.org/files/25regeneration.pdf (accessed 12 January 2007).

International Museum of Women (2009) http://www.imow.org/home/index (accessed 15 February 2009).

Introducing Africa (2009) *Cultural Tourism in Tanzania,* http://www.introducingafricatz.com/culturaltourism.htm (accessed 2 February 2009).

Irvine, A. (1999) *The Battle for the Millennium Dome*, London: Irvine News Agency.

Iszák, N. (2008) 'Békétlen show', 29 November, *HVG*, Hungary.

Jacobs, J. M. (1961) *The Death and Life of Great American Cities*, New York: Penguin.

—— (1996) *Edge of Empire: Postcolonialism and the City*, London: Routledge.

Jamal, T. B. and Hill, S. (2002) 'The home and the world: (post)touristic spaces of (in)authenticity', in Dann, G. M. S. (ed.) *The Tourist as a Metaphor of the Social World*, Wallingford: CABI, pp. 77–108.

Javrova, Z. (2005) 'European integration is hard work', Presentation at *Europe: Challenges, Examples and Opportunities: The European Union Approach to Culture*, Euclid Seminar Series, London, 7 March.

Jeng, M. (2002) *All-inclusive Holidays Will Deny us Even the Crumbs*, Gambia Tourism Concern, http://www.subuk.net/tourism/ (accessed 17 February 2002).

Jermyn, H. and Desai, P. (2000) *Arts – What's in a Word?: Ethnic Minorities and the Arts*, London: Arts Council of England.

Jones, A. L. (1993) 'Contemporary issues in waterfront regeneration: a case study of the Swansea waterfront', M. Phil. thesis, University of Wales, Swansea.

—— (2007) 'On the water's edge: developing cultural regeneration paradigms for urban waterfronts', in Smith, M. K. (ed.) *Tourism, Culture and Regeneration*, Wallingford: CABI, pp. 143–50.

Jones, J. (2000) 'The regeneration game', *Guardian Unlimited*, 16 October, http://society.guardian.co.uk/regeneration/story/0,7940,395020,00.html (accessed 7 December 2005).

Joppe, M. (1996) 'Current issues: sustainable community tourism development revisited, *Tourism Management*, 17 (7), pp. 475–9.

Jordan, G. and Weedon, C. (1995) *Cultural Politics: Class, Gender, Race and the Postmodern World*, Oxford: Blackwell.

Jowell, T. (2004) 'Forward' in Department for Culture, Media and Sport, *Culture at the Heart of Regeneration*, London: DCMS, p. 5.

Junemo, M. (2004) '"Let's build a Palm Island!" Playfulness in complex times', in Sheller, M. and Urry, J.(eds) *Tourism Mobilities: Places to Play, Places in Play*, London: Routledge, pp. 181–91.

Kaur, R. and Hutnyk, J. (1999) *Travel Worlds: Journeys in Contemporary Cultural Politics*, London: Zed Books.

Kavanagh, G. (ed.) (1996) *Making Histories in Museums*, London: Leicester University Press.

Khan, N. (1976) *The Arts Britain Ignores: The Arts of Ethnic Minorities in Britain*, London: Commission for Racial Equality.

Kirschenblatt-Gimblett, B. (1998) *Destination Culture: Tourism, Museums and Heritage*, Berkeley: University of California Press.

Klingmann, A. (2007) *Brandscapes: Architecture in the Experience Economy*, Cambridge, MA: MIT Press.

Kolb, J. (2007) 'Grab bag: follow that gay!', *3 Quarks Daily*,18 June, http://3quarksdaily. blogs.com/3quarksdaily/2007/06/grab_bag_follow.html (accessed 19 February 2009).

Kovács D. (2004) *Hollókő World Heritage Site Management Plan*, Hungary: UNESCO.

—— (2008) 'Quality of life of local people in Hollókő, a World Heritage Village in Hungary', *Tourism and Quality of Life Workshop*, 13–14 November, Budapest, Hungary.

Laliberté, M. (2005) 'Defining a tourist experience', *Tourism Online*, 2 (6), http://www.corporate.canada.travel/corp/media/app/en/ca/magazine/article.do?issuePath= templatedata%5Cctx%5CmagIssue%5Cdata%5C2005%5Cissue06%5Cissue2005_06and path=templatedata%5Cctx%5CmagArticle%5Cdata%5Cen%5C2005%5Cissue06%5C industry%5Creseau_de_veille (accessed 18 January 2009).

Lanfant, M. (1995) 'Introduction', in Lanfant, M., Allcock, J. B. and Bruner, E. M. (eds) *International Tourism: Identity and Change*, London: Sage.

Lechner, F. J. and Boli, J. (2005) *World Culture – Origins and Consequences*, Oxford: Blackwell.

Leeking, D. (2001) 'Welcome to the experience economy', http://www.davidleeking.com/ pdf/Chap%2001.pdf (accessed 10 February 2009).

Lefèbvre, H. (1974) *The Production of Space*, Oxford: Blackwell.

Lewis, J. (1990) *Art, Culture and Enterprise*, London: Routledge.

Li, Fung Mei S. and Sofield, T. H. B. (2006) 'World Heritage Listing: the case of Huangshan (Yellow Mountain), China', in Leask, A. and Fyall, A. (eds) *Managing World Heritage Sites*, Oxford: Butterworth-Heinemann, pp. 250–62.

Li, V. (2000) 'What's in a name? Questioning "globalisation"', *Cultural Critique*, 45 (spring), pp. 1–39.

Light, D. (1995) 'Heritage as informal education', in Herbert, D. (ed.) *Heritage, Tourism and Society*, London: Mansell Publishing, pp. 117–45.

Lippard, L. (1990) *Mixed Blessings: New Art in a Multicultural America*, New York: Pantheon Books.

Llancaiach Fawr Manor (2009) http://www.caerphilly.gov.uk/llancaiachfawr/llan_english/ education.html (accessed 20 January 2009).

Lodge, D. (1991) *Paradise News*, Harmondsworth: Penguin.

Lofgren, O. (2003) 'The new economy: a cultural history', *Global Networks*, 3 (3), pp. 239–54.

London 2012 (2009) 'What is the Cultural Olympiad?', http://www.london2012.com/ get-involved/cultural-olympiad/what-is-the-cultural-olympiad.php (accessed 20 February 2009).

London Tourist Board (LTB) (1997) *Survey Amongst Overseas Visitors*, London: LTB.

Lowenthal, D. (1985) *The Past is a Foreign Country*, Cambridge: Cambridge University Press.

—— (1998) *The Heritage Crusade and the Spoils of History*, Cambridge: Cambridge University Press.

Lumley, R. (1994) 'The debate on heritage reviewed', in Miles, R. and Zavala, L. (eds) *Towards the Museum of the Future: New European Perspectives*, London: Routledge, pp. 57–69.

MacCannell, D. (1976) *The Tourist: A New Theory of the Leisure Class*, New York: Schocken.

MacDonald, D. (1994) 'A theory of mass culture', in Storey, J. (ed.) *Cultural Theory and Popular Culture – A Reader*, London: Harvester Wheatsheaf, pp. 28–43.

MacLeod, N. E. (2006) 'The placeless festival: identity and place in the post-modern festival', in Picard, D. and Robinson, M. (eds) *Festivals, Tourism and Social Change: Remaking Worlds*, Clevedon: Channel View, pp. 222–37.

Makhurane, J. P. (2003) 'Robben Island – developing an integrated environmental and heritage management system', Proceedings of the International Scientific Symposium of ICOMOS, *Place, Memory, Meaning: Preserving Intangible Values in Monuments and Sites*, Victoria Falls, Zimbabwe, 27–31 October, http://www.international.icomos.org/victoriafalls2003/papers.htm (accessed 18 February 2009).

Mail and Guardian Online (2006) 'Buenos Aires booms as gay tourist destination' 29 May, http://www.mg.co.za/article/2006-05-29-buenos-aires-booms-as-gay-tourist-destination (accessed 14 February 2009).

Maitland, R. (2007) 'Cultural tourism and the development of new tourism areas in London', in Richards, G. (ed.) *Cultural Tourism: Global and Local Perspectives*, New York: Haworth Press, pp. 113–28.

Maiztegui-Onate, C. and Areito Bertolin, M. T. (1996) 'Cultural tourism in Spain', in Richards, G. (ed.) *Cultural Tourism in Europe*, Wallingford: CABI, pp. 267–81.

Marschall, S. (2006) 'Creating the "Rainbow Nation": the National Women's Art Festival in Durban, South Africa', in Picard, D. and Robinson, M. (eds) *Festivals, Tourism and Social Change: Remaking Worlds*, Clevedon: Channel View, pp. 152–71.

Mascarell, F. (2008) *Creative Policies in Barcelona*, Barcelona: Institut de Cultura.

Mason, P. and Kuo, I-Ling (2006) 'Visitor management at Stonehenge, UK', in Leask, A. and Fyall, A. (eds) *Managing World Heritage Sites*, Oxford: Butterworth-Heinemann, pp.181–94.

Mathieson, A. and Wall, G. (1992) *Tourism: Economic, Physical and Social Impacts*, Harlow: Longman.

May, S. (1999) *The Pocket Philosopher: A Handbook of Aphorisms*, London: Metro.

Mazza, K. (2004) 'In defense of U.S. culture', 13 February, *The Dickinsonian*, http://dickinson.edu/dickinsonian/detail.cfm?226 (accessed 26 January 2009).

McCabe, S. (2002) 'The tourist experience and everyday life', in Dann, G. M. S. (ed.) *The Tourist as a Metaphor of the Social World*, Wallingford: CABI, pp. 61–76.

McKercher, B. and Du Cros, H. (2002) *Cultural Tourism: The Partnership between Tourism and Cultural Heritage Management,* New York: Haworth.

Meethan, K. (2001) *Tourism in Global Society: Place, Culture, Consumption*, London: Palgrave.

Mercer, C. (1991) 'What is cultural planning?', Paper presented to the *Community Arts Network National Conference*, Sydney, Australia, 10 October.

Merriman, N. (1991) *Beyond the Glass Case: The Past, the Heritage and the Public in Britain*, Leicester: Leicester University Press.

Middleton, M. (1987) *Man Made the Town*, London: The Bodley Head.

Miège. B. (1979) 'The cultural commodity', *Media, Culture and Society*, 1, pp. 297–311.

Miettinen, S. (1999) 'Crafts tourism in Lapland', in Richards, G. (ed.) *Developing and Marketing Crafts Tourism*, Tilburg: ATLAS, pp. 89–103.

Miles, M. (1997) *Arts, Space and the City: Public Arts and Urban Futures*, London: Routledge.

Millar, S. (2006) 'Stakeholders and community participation', in Leask, A. and Fyall, A. (eds) *Managing World Heritage Sites*, Oxford: Butterworth-Heinemann, pp. 37–54.

Milner, A. (1994) *Contemporary Cultural Theory: An Introduction*, London: UCL Press.

Minerbi, L. (1996) 'Hawaii', in Hall, C. M. and Page, S. J. (eds) *Tourism in the Pacific: Issues and Cases*, London: International Thomson Business Press, pp. 190–204.

Mongululs.net (2009) http://www.mongoluls.net/nadaam.shtml (accessed 17 February 2009).

Moore, K. (2002) 'The discursive tourist', in Dann, G. M. S. (ed.) *The Tourist as a Metaphor of the Social World*, Wallingford: CABI, pp. 41–60.

Morin, E. (1962) *L'Esprit du temps*, Paris: Bernard Grasset.

Morley, D. (2000) *Home Territories: Media, Mobility and Identity*, London: Routledge.

Mowforth, M. and Munt, I. (1998) *Tourism and Sustainability: New Tourism in the Third World*, London: Routledge.

Mowitt, J. (2001) 'In the wake of Eurocentrism: an introduction', *Cultural Critique*, 47 (winter), pp. 3–15.

Muir, H. (2004) 'Curry touts leave a bad taste in Brick Lane', *Guardian*, 20 May.

Munjeri, D. (2003) 'Intangible heritage in Africa: could be a case of much ado about nothing', ICOMOS 14th General Assembly and Scientific Symposium, *Place-Memory-Meaning: Preserving Intangible Values in Monuments and Sites*, Victoria Falls, Zimbabwe, 27–31 October.

Munsters, W. and Freund de Klumbis, D. (2005) 'Culture as a component of the hospitality product', in Sigala, M. and Leslie, D. (eds) *International Cultural Tourism: Management, Implications and Cases*, Oxford: Butterworth Heinemann, pp. 26–39.

Murayama, M. and Parker, G. (2007) 'Sustainable and responsible leisure and tourism space development in post-industrial cities? The case of Odaiba Waterfront City, Tokyo, Japan', in Smith, M. K. (ed.) *Tourism, Culture and Regeneration*, Wallingford: CABI, pp. 69–84.

Myerscough, J. (1988) *The Economic Contribution of the Arts and Tourism*, London: Policy Studies Institute.

Nagy, G. (2009) 'Hogy volt, mikor volt?', 24 January, *HVG*, Hungary.

Nash, D. (1977) 'Tourism as a form of imperialism', in Smith, V. (ed.) *Hosts and Guests: The Anthropology of Tourism*, Oxford: Blackwell, pp. 33–47.

—— (1989) 'Tourism as a form of imperialism', in Smith, V. (ed.) *Hosts and Guests: The Anthropology of Tourism*, Philadelphia: University of Pennsylvania Press, pp. 37–52.

Negus, K. (1997) 'The production of culture', in Du Gay, P. (ed.) *Production of Culture/Cultures of Production*, London: Sage, pp. 67–118.

Németh, A. (2008a) 'Mindennek ellenállók', 15 November, *HVG*, Hungary.

—— (2008b) 'Mint a moziban', 18 October, *HVG*, Hungary.

NOIE (2002) *Creative Industries Cluster Study Stage 1 Report*, NOIE/DCITA, http://www.noie.gov.au/publications/media_releases/2002/May/Cluster.htm (accessed 17 April 2008).

Official Tourism Site of the City of New Orleans (2009) http://www.neworleansonline.com (accessed 15 February 2009).

Owusu, K. (1986) *The Struggles for the Black Arts in Britain*, London: Comedia.

Pacific Island Travel (2007) 'Hawaiian Culture', http://www.pacificislandtravel.com/hawaii/about_destin/culture.html (accessed 10 February 2009).

The Parekh Report (2000) *The Future of Multi-ethnic Britain*, London: Profile Books.

Pfafflin, G. F. (1987) 'Concern for tourism: European perspective and response', *Annals of Tourism Research*, 14 (4), pp. 576–9.

Philips, D. (1999) 'Narrativised spaces: the functions of story in the theme park', in Crouch, D. (ed.) *Leisure/tourism Geographies: Practices and Geographical Knowledge*, London: Routledge, pp. 91–108.

Picard, D. and Robinson, M. (2006) (eds) *Festivals, Tourism and Social Change: Remaking Worlds*, Clevedon: Channel View.

Pine, B. J. and Gilmore, J. H (1998) 'Welcome to the Experience Economy', *Harvard Business Review*, 76 (4), pp. 97–105.

—— and —— (1999) *The Experience Economy*: *Work is Theatre and Everyday Business a Stage*, Boston, MA: Harvard Business School Press.

—— and —— (2007) *Authenticity*, Boston: Harvard Business School Press.

Ploger, J. (2001) 'Millennium urbanism – discursive planning', *European Urban and Regional Studies*, 8 (1), pp. 63–72.

Pocock, D. C. D. (1997) 'Some reflections on world heritage', *Area*, 29 (3), pp. 260–68.

Porter, G. (1988) 'Putting your house in order: representations of women and domestic life', in Lumley, R. (ed.) *The Museum Time Machine*, London: Routledge, pp. 102–27.

Power, K. (1997) 'The material of change: Aboriginal cultures as a source of empowerment', in Landry, C. (ed.) *The Art of Regeneration*, London: Demos Comedia, pp. 52–6.

Prentice, R. (2001) 'Experiential cultural tourism: museums and the marketing of the new romanticism of evoked authenticity', *Museum Management and Curatorship* 19 (1), pp. 5–26.

Puczkó, L. (2006) 'Interpretation in cultural tourism', in Smith, M. K. and Robinson, M. (eds) *Cultural Tourism in a Changing World: Politics, Participation and (Re)presentation*, Clevedon: Channel View, pp. 227–43.

—— and Rátz, T. (2007) 'Trailing Goethe, Humbert, and Ulysses: cultural routes in tourism', in Richards, G. (ed.) *Cultural Tourism: Global and Local Perspectives*, New York: Haworth Press, pp. 131–43.

Quinn, B. (2005) 'Arts festivals and the city', *Urban Studies*, 42 (5–6), pp. 927–43.

Ramchander, P. (2007) 'Township tourism – blessing or blight? The case of Soweto in South Africa', in Richards, G. (ed.) *Cultural Tourism: Global and Local Perspectives*, New York: Haworth Press, pp. 39–67.

Rátz, T. (2006) 'Interpretation in the House of Terror', in Smith, M. K. and Robinson, M. (eds) *Cultural Tourism in a Changing World: Politics, Participation and (Re)presentation*, Clevedon: Channel View, pp. 244–56.

Religious Tolerance (2003) 'Religious Conflicts in Sri Lanka', http://www.religioustolerance. org/rt_srilanka.htm (accessed 10 February 2009).

Richards, G. (ed.) (1996) *Cultural Tourism in Europe*, Wallingford: CABI.

—— (1999) 'Culture, crafts and tourism: a vital partnership', in Richards, G. (ed.) *Developing and Marketing Crafts Tourism*, Tilburg: ATLAS, pp. 11–35.

—— (2001a) 'The development of cultural tourism in Europe', in Richards, G. (ed.) *Cultural Attractions and European Tourism,* Wallingford: CABI, pp. 3–29.

—— (2001b) 'Cultural tourists or a culture of tourism? The European cultural tourism market', in Butcher, J. (ed.) *Innovations in Cultural Tourism*, Proceedings of the 5th ATLAS International Conference, Rethymnon, Crete, 1998, Tilburg: ATLAS.

—— (2001c) *Creative Tourism as a Factor in Destination Development*, ATLAS 10th Anniversary International Conference papers, 4–6 October, Dublin.

—— (2001d) 'The experience industry and the creation of attractions,' in G. Richards (ed.), *Cultural Attractions and European Tourism*, Wallingford: CABI Publishing, pp. 55–69.

—— (2005) (ed.) *Cultural Tourism*: *Global and Local Perspectives*, Binghampton: Haworth.

—— (2007) 'The creative turn in regeneration: creative spaces, spectacles and tourism in cities', in Smith, M. K. (ed.) *Tourism, Culture and Regeneration,*Wallingford: CABI, pp. 12–24.

—— and Raymond, C. (2000) 'Creative tourism', *ATLAS News*, 23, pp. 16–20.

Richards, R. and Wilson, J. (2006) 'Developing creativity in tourist experiences: a solution to the serial reproduction of culture?' *Tourism Management*, 27 (6), pp. 1209–23.

—— and —— (2007) 'The creative turn in regeneration: creative spaces, spectacles and tourism in cities' in Smith, M. K. (ed.) *Tourism, Culture and Regeneration*. Wallingford: CABI, pp. 12–24.

Richez, G. (1996) 'Sustaining local cultural identity: social unrest and tourism in Corsica', in Priestley, G. K., Edwards, J. A. and Coccossis, H. (eds) *Sustainable Tourism? European Experiences*, Wallingford: CABI, pp. 176–88.

Riley, R., Baker, D. and Van Doren, C. S. (1998) 'Movie induced tourism', *Annals of Tourism Research*, 25 (4), pp. 919–35.

Rio Carnival (2009) http://www.rio-carnival.net (accessed 12 January 2009).

Ritzer, G. (1993) *The McDonaldization of Society*, Thousand Oaks, CA: Pine Oak Press.

—— (2004) *The Globalization of Nothing*, London: Sage.

—— and Liska, A. (1997) '"McDisneyization" and "post-tourism": contemporary perspectives on contemporary tourism', in Rojek, C. and Urry, J. (eds) *Touring Cultures: Transformations of Travel and Theory*, London: Routledge, pp. 96–109.

—— and —— (2000) 'Postmodernism and tourism', in Beynon, J. and Dunkerley, D. (eds) *Globalization: The Reader*, London: Athlone Press, pp. 152–5.

Roberts, C. (2008) 'The Olympic legacy for Greenwich', *The Olympic Legacy: People, Place, Enterpise Conference*, 9 May, University of Greenwich, London.

Robertson, R. (1992) *Globalization. Social Theory and Global Culture,* SAGE Publications, London.

—— (1994) 'Globalization or Glocalization?', *Journal of International Communication*, 1, pp. 33–52.

Rockwell, J. (1999) 'Serious music', in Melzer, A. M., Weinberger, J. and Zinman, M. R. (eds) *Democracy and the Arts*, Ithaca and London: Cornell University Press, pp. 92–102.

Rojek, C. (1993) *Ways of Escape: Modern Transformations in Leisure and Travel*, London: Macmillan.

—— (1997) 'Indexing, dragging and the social construction of tourist sights', in Rojek, C. and Urry, J. (eds) *Touring Cultures: Transformations of Travel and Theory*, London: Routledge, pp. 52–74.

—— and Urry, J. (eds) (1997) *Touring Cultures: Transformations of Travel and Theory*, London: Routledge.

Rolfe, H. (1992) *Arts Festivals in the UK*, London: Policy Studies Institute.

Rosenberg, M. (2008) 'New countries of the world: the 33 new countries created since 1990', 18 February, http://geography.about.com/cs/countries/a/newcountries.htm (accessed 26 January 2009).

Ross, M. (2004) 'Interpreting the new museology', *Museum and Society*, 2 (2), pp. 84–103.

Rotterdam City of Architecture (2007) http://www.rotterdam2007.nl/english/programma/sitesandstories/index.php (accessed 4 January 2009).

Rushby, K. (2008) 'The Nadaam festival', *The Guardian*, Saturday 2 August, http://www.guardian.co.uk/travel/2008/aug/02/mongolia.festivals (accessed 21 January 2009).

Sampson, M. (1986) 'The origins of the Trinidad Carnival', in Arts Council of Great Britain, *Masquerading: The Art of the Notting Hill Carnival*, London: ACGB, pp. 30–4.

Sandercock, L. (1998) *Towards Cosmopolis*, Chichester: John Wiley.

Sardar, Z. and Wynn Davies, M. (2002) *Why Do People Hate America?*, London: Icon Books.

Sarup, M. (1996) *Identity, Culture and the Postmodern World*, Edinburgh: Edinburgh University Press.

Schadler, F. (1979) 'African arts and crafts in a world of changing values', in De Kadt, E. (ed.) *Tourism – Passport to Development?*, New York: Oxford University Press, pp. 146–56.

Schouten, F. F. J. (1995) 'Heritage as historical reality', in Herbert, D. (ed.) *Heritage, Tourism and Society*, London: Mansell Publishing, pp. 21–31.

Seaton, A. V. (2002) 'Tourism as metempsychosis and metensomatosis: the personae of eternal recurrence', in Dann, G. M. S. (ed.) *The Tourist as a Metaphor of the Social World*, Wallingford: CABI, pp. 135–68.

Selwyn, T. (ed.) (1996) *The Tourist Image: Myths and Myth-making in Tourism*, Chichester: John Wiley & Sons.

Shafer, J. (2008) 'Down with the Newseum', http://www.slate.com/id/2183936 (accessed 21 January 2009).

Sharp, J., Pollock, V. and Paddison, R. (2005) 'Just art for a just city: public art and social inclusion in urban regeneration', *Urban Studies*, 42 (5/6), pp. 1001–23.

Sharpley, R. (1994) *Tourism, Tourists and Society*, Huntingdon: ELM Publications.

Shaw, S. (2007) 'Ethnoscapes as cultural attractions in Canadian "World Cities"', in Smith, M. K. (ed.) *Tourism, Culture and Regeneration*, Wallingford: CABI, pp. 49–58.

——, Bagwell, S. and Karmowska, J. (2004) 'Ethnoscapes as spectacle: reimaging multicultural districts as new destinations for leisure and tourism consumption', *Urban Studies*, 41 (10), pp. 1983–2000.

Shaw, S. J. and MacLeod, N. E. (2000) 'Creativity and conflict: cultural tourism in London's city fringe', University of North London: Centre for Leisure and Tourism Studies.

Sheller, M. and Urry, J. (2004) (eds) *Tourism Mobilities: Places to Play, Places in Play*, London: Routledge.

Sieber, R. T. (1993) 'Public access on the urban waterfront: a question of vision', in Rotenburg, R. and McDonogh, G. (eds) *The Cultural Meaning of Urban Space*, Westport: Bergin & Garvey, pp. 173–93.

Sigala, M. (2005) 'New media and technologies: trends and management issues for cultural tourism', in Sigala, M. and Leslie, D. (eds) *International Cultural Tourism: Management, Implications and Cases*, Oxford: Butterworth Heinemann, pp. 168–80.

Simpson, M. (1996) *Making Representations: Museums in the Post-colonial Era*, London: Routledge.

Sims, P. (2007) 'Blackpool launches crackdown on stag and hen parties', September, *Mail Online*, http://www.dailymail.co.uk/news/article-480361/Blackpool-launches-crackdown-stag-hen-parties.html (accessed 23 February 2009).

Singh, N. (2006) 'Experience – Colors of Malaysia Festival', *Ezine Articles*, 25 August, http://ezinearticles.com/?id=281332 (accessed 20 February 2009).

Slater, J. (2004) 'Brand Louisiana: capitalizing on music and cuisine', in Morgan, N., Pritchard, A. and Pride, R. (eds) *Destination Branding: Creating the Unique Destination Proposition*, Oxford: Butterworth Heinemann, pp. 226–41.

Smith, A. (2007) 'After the circus leaves town: the relationship between sports events, tourism and urban regeneration', in Smith, M. K. (ed.) *Tourism, Culture and Regeneration*, Wallingford: CAB, pp. 85–100.

Smith, K. A. (2000) 'The road to world heritage site designation: Derwent Valley Mills, a work in progress', in Robinson, M. *et al.* (eds) *Tourism and Heritage Relationships: Global, National and Local Perspectives*, Sunderland: Business Education Publishers, pp. 397–416.

Smith, M. K. (2003) *Issues in Cultural Tourism Studies*, London: Routledge.

—— (2005a) 'Glocalisation', in Ritzer, G. (ed.) *Encyclopaedia of Sociology*, Blackwell: Oxford.

—— (2005b) 'New leisure tourism: fantasy futures', in Buhalis, D. and Costa, C. (eds) *New Tourism Consumers, Products and Industry: Present and Future Issues*, Oxford: Butterworth-Heinemann, pp. 220–7.

—— (2009) 'Re-articulating culture in the context of urban regeneration: a thirdspace approach', Unpublished PhD thesis, Greenwich, London.

—— and Carnegie, E. (2006) 'Bollywood dreams? The rise of the Asian mela as a global cultural phenomenon', *Public History Review Journal*, 12, pp. 1–10.

——, Puczkó, T. and Rátz, T. (2007) 'Old city, new image: perception, positioning and promotion of Budapest', *Journal of Travel and Tourism Marketing*, 22, 3–4 (October), pp. 21–34.

—— and Robinson, M. (2006) (eds) *Cultural Tourism in a Changing World: Politics, Participation and (Re)presentation,* Clevedon: Channel View Publications.

Smith, V. L. (ed.) (1989) *Hosts and Guests: An Anthropology of Tourism*, Philadelphia: University of Pennsylvania Press.

—— (1997) 'The four *H*s of tribal tourism: Acoma – A Pueblo case study', in Cooper, C. and Wanhill, S. (eds) *Tourism Development: Environmental and Community Issues*, London: John Wiley & Sons, pp. 141–51.

Smithsonian Institution (2009) *National Museum of the American Indian*, http://www.nmai.si.edu (accessed 5 February 2009).

Soja, E. W. (2000) *Postmetropolis: Critical Studies of Cities and Regions*, Malden: Blackwell.

Sorenson, C. (1989) 'Theme parks and time machines', in Vergo, P. (ed.) *The New Museology*, London: Reaktion Books, pp. 60–73.

Spirou, C. (2007) 'Cultural policy and urban restructuring in Chicago', in Smith, M. K. (ed.) *Tourism, Culture and Regeneration*, Wallingford: CABI, pp. 123–31.

Stahl, L. (2005) 'Viva Cirque du Soleil', http://www.cbsnews.com/stories/2005/02/18/60minutes/main675104.shtml (accessed 21 January 2009).

Steele-Prohaska, S. (1996) 'The greatest story never told: Native American initiatives into cultural heritage tourism', in Robinson, M. *et al.* (eds) *Tourism and Cultural Change*, Sunderland: Business Education Publishers, pp. 171–82.

Stone, P. R. (2005) http://www.dark-tourism.org.uk (accessed 26 January 2009).

Stuart, R. (2002) 'Ayahuasca tourism: a cautionary tale', *Maps*, 12, 2 (summer), http://www.maps.org/news-letters/v12n2/12236stu.pdf (accessed 4 February 2009).

Sudjic, D. (1993) *The 100 Mile City*, London: Flamingo.

—— (1999) 'Between the metropolitan and the provincial', in Nystrom, L. (ed.) *City and Culture: Cultural Processes and Urban Sustainability*, Kalmar: Swedish Urban Environment Council, pp. 178–85.

Sumner, G. (1999) 'Dome's day draws near', *Guide Magazine*, December, pp. 24–5.

Swarbrooke, J. (2000) 'Museums: theme parks of the third millennium?', in Robinson, M. *et al.* (eds) *Tourism and Heritage Relationships: Global, National and Local Perspectives*, Sunderland: Business Education Publishers, pp. 417–31.

Tahana, N. and Oppermann, M. (1998) 'Maori cultural performances and tourism', *Tourism Recreation Research*, 23 (1), pp. 23–30.

Tighe, A. J. (1986) 'The arts/tourism partnership', *Journal of Travel Research*, 24 (3), pp. 2–9.

Tilden, F. (1977) *Interpreting Our Heritage*, Chapel Hill: University of North Carolina Press.

Timothy, D. J. and Boyd, S. W. (2006) 'World Heritage Sites in the Americas', in Leask, A. and Fyall, A. (eds) *Managing World Heritage Sites*, Oxford: Butterworth-Heinemann, pp. 239–49.

Tourism NT (2007) 'Special Aboriginal art tours set NT apart', *Media Release*, http://www.tourismnt.com.au/nt/nttc/news/media_releases/mr/2007/mr_May30_aboriginaltour.html (accessed 11 February 2009).

Trask, M. (1998) 'Culture vultures', in *Indigenous Peoples, Human Rights and Tourism*, Tourism Concern, *In Focus*, 29 (autumn), pp. 14–17.

Travelpod (2007) 'Genocide tourism – the memorials', *Travelpod*, 28 May, http://www.travel pod.com/travel-blog-entries/djchurch/rtw-2006andon/1180344240/tpod.html (accessed 2 February 2009).

Tremlett, G. (2005) 'Barcelona plans crackdown on tourist louts', *Guardian Online*, 20 October, http://www.guardian.co.uk/world/2005/oct/20/spain.travelnews (accessed 21 February 2009).

Trendhunter (2008) *Dubai Builds Fashion Island*, http://www.trendhunter.com/trends/isla-moda (accessed 15 January 2009).

Tresidder, R. (1999) 'Tourism and sacred landscapes', in Crouch, D. (ed.) *Leisure/Tourism Geographies: Practices and Geographical Knowledge*, London: Routledge, pp. 137–48.

Trevor-Roper, H. (1965) *The Rise of Christian Europe*, London: Thames & Hudson.

Tunbridge, J. E. and Ashworth, G. J. (1996) *Dissonant Heritage: The Management of the Past as a Resource in Conflict*, London: John Wiley & Sons.

Turner, G. (1992) 'Tourism and the arts: let's work together', *Insights*, 3 (3), pp. A109–16.

Turner, L. and Ash, J. (1975) *The Golden Hordes: International Tourism and the Pleasure Periphery*, London: Constable.

Tyrell, B. and Mai, R. (2001) *Leisure 2010 – Experience Tomorrow*, Henley: Jones Lang La Salle.

UNESCO (1982) *Culture Industries: A Challenge for the Future of Culture*, Paris: UNESCO.

—— (2001) *Baltic Cultural Tourism Policy Paper 2001–2003*, http://portal.unesco.org/culture/en/files/23640/11033006043bct_short1.pdf/bct_short1.pdf (accessed 7 February 2009).

—— (2003) 'Bamiyan Valley, Afghanistan', http://whc.unesco.org/en/list/208 (accessed 11 February 2009).

—— (2006) *Discussion Report of the Planning Meeting for 2008 International Conference on Creative Tourism*, Santa Fe, New Mexico, 25–27 October.

—— (2009) *Intangible Cultural Heritage*, http://www.unesco.org/culture/ich/index.php?pg=00002 (accessed 6 February 2009).

URBACT Culture Network (2006) *Culture Regeneration*, http://72.14.221.104/search?q=cache:WbN9VvyWGRAJ:urbact.eu/fileadmin/subsites/Cultural_Activities_Cr/pdf/ConclusionsUC-English.pdf+defining+culture+in+regenerationandhl=enandgl=ukandct=clnkandcd=2 (accessed 15 December 2006).

Urry, J. (1990) *The Tourist Gaze: Leisure and Travel in Contemporary Societies*, London: Sage.

—— (2002) *The Tourist Gaze*, London: Sage, 2nd edn.

Uzzell, D. L. (ed.) (1989) *Heritage Interpretation: Vol. 1: The Natural and Built Environment*, London: Belhaven Press.

Van der Borg, J. and Costa, P. (1996) 'Cultural tourism in Italy', in Richards, G. (ed.) *Cultural Tourism in Europe*, Wallingford: CABI, pp. 215–31.

Van der Duim, R., Peters, K. and Akama, J. (2006) 'Cultural tourism in African communities: a comparison between cultural manyattas in Kenya and the cultural tourism project in Tanzania', in Smith, M. K. and Robinson, M. (eds) *Cultural Tourism in a Changing World: Politics, Participation and (Re)presentation*, Clevedon: Channel View, pp. 104–23.

Varlow, S. (1995) 'Tourism and the arts: the relationship matures', *Insights*, 6 (4), pp. A93–8.

Wallerstein, I. (1997) 'Uncertainty and Creativity', Forum 2000: Concerns and Hopes on the Threshold of the New Millennium, Prague, 3–6 September.

Walsh, K. (1992) *The Representation of the Past: Museums and Heritage in the Post-modern World*, London: Routledge.

Wang, N. (2000) *Tourism and Modernity: A Sociological Analysis*, Oxford: Pergamon Press.

Warren, S. (1999) 'Cultural contestation at Disneyland Paris', in Crouch, D. (ed.) *Leisure/Tourism Geographies: Practices and Geographical Knowledge*, London: Routledge, pp. 109–36.

Wels, H. (2004) 'About romance and reality: popular European imagery in postcolonial tourism in southern Africa', in Hall, C. M. and Tucker, H. (eds) *Tourism and Postcolonialism,* pp. 76–94.

West, B. (1988) 'The making of the English working past: a critical view of the Ironbridge Gorge Museum', in Lumley, R. (ed.) *The Museum Time Machine*, London: Routledge, pp. 36–62.

Whittaker, E. (2000) 'A century of indigenous images: the world according to the tourist postcard', in Robinson, M. *et al.* (eds) *Expressions of Culture, Identity and Meaning in Tourism*, Sunderland: Business Education Publishers, pp. 423–37.

Williams, R. (1958) 'Culture is ordinary', in Gale, R. (ed.) (1989) *Resources of Hope – Raymond Williams*, London: Verso.

Wongkerd, N. (2003) 'Tourists' perceptions of the Full Moon party on Pha-Ngan Island, Thailand', Unpublished master's thesis, Texas Tech University.

World Heritage Committee (1994) *Convention Concerning the Protection of the World Cultural and Natural Heritage*, Paris: UNESCO.

World Heritage Site (2009) http://www.worldheritagesite.org/sites/wieliczka.html (accessed 17 February 2009).

WTTC (2004) *World Travel and Tourism Council Forecasts that Montenegro will Become the Fastest Growing Travel and Tourism Economy in the World*, 15 March, London: WTTC.

Wynne, D. (1992) (ed.) *The Culture Industry: The Arts in Urban Regeneration*, Aldershot: Avebury.

Xie, P. F. (2004). 'Visitors' perceptions of authenticity at a rural heritage festival: a case study', *Event Management*, 8, pp. 151–60.

Zeppel, H. (2006) *Indigenous Ecotourism: Sustainable Development and Management*, Wallingford: CABI.

—— and Hall, C. M. (1992) 'Arts and heritage tourism', in Weiler, B. and Hall, C. M. (eds) *Special Interest Tourism*, London: Belhaven Press, pp. 47–65.

Zukin, S. (1995) *The Cultures of Cities*, Oxford: Blackwell.

Index

Page numbers in *italics* refer to case studies, tables and plates.